D0776989

FPCC

JUL 26 1993

St. Louis Community College

Forest Park
Florissant Valley
Meramec

Instructional Resources
St. Louis, Missouri

INVENTORY 98

ON
DEATH'S
BLOODY
TRAIL

ON
DEATH'S
BLOODY
TRAIL

MURDER AND THE ART OF
FORENSIC SCIENCE

Brian Marriner

St. Martin's Press
New York

In memory of John Dunning

ON DEATH'S BLOODY TRAIL. Copyright © 1991 by Brian Marriner. All rights reserved.
Printed in the United States of America. No part of this book may be used
or reproduced in any manner whatsoever without written permission except in
the case of brief quotations embodied in critical articles or reviews. For
information, address St. Martin's Press, 175 Fifth Avenue, New York, N.Y. 10010.

Library of Congress Cataloging-in-Publication Data

Marriner, Brian.
    On death's bloody trail : murder and the art of forensic science /
Brian Marriner ; introduction by Colin Wilson.
        p.   cm.
    ISBN 0-312-08866-3
    1. Murder—Investigation.   2. Forensic sciences—History.
3. Forensic sciences—Case studies.   I. Title.
HV8079.H6M37   1993
363.2′59523—dc20   92-43019
                                                                CIP

First published in Great Britain as *Forensic Clues to Murder* by Random Century Group.

First U.S. Edition: March 1993
10 9 8 7 6 5 4 3 2 1

Contents

ON
DEATH'S
BLOODY
TRAIL

INTRODUCTION

In 1881, the German police were called in to investigate the death of a mother and her five children. All had been found dead in a room that was bolted from the inside. The window was also locked from the inside. The mother had apparently killed the children, then committed suicide by hanging herself from a hook in the wardrobe. The inspector in charge of the case took an instant dislike to the husband, a man named Fritz Conrad, but had to agree that there was no way he could have been involved in the deaths of his family. Then, glancing idly through a few books on the shelf, the inspector picked out a volume called *Nena Sahib* by John Ratcliffe. It fell open at a certain page, and the inspector found himself reading a description of how a man murdered someone in a room, then made it look like suicide. He drilled a hole in the door, inserted a horsehair, which he tied round the end of the bolt, then locked the room from outside by pulling the horsehair; afterwards, he sealed up the hole in the door with brown wax. The inspector went and slid back the bolt in the death room. Underneath it, he found a tiny hole. On the outside of the door, the hole had been sealed with brown sealing wax. . . . Fritz Conrad was charged with the murder of his wife and family – he was hoping to marry another woman – and executed.

This is the type of criminal drama that fascinates the modern public – the battle of wits between the policeman and the murderer. Yet when Fritz Conrad murdered his family, the public knew little of such matters. The very word 'detective' had been invented a mere twenty-five years earlier – by Charles Dickens, who introduces his Inspector Bucket (in *Bleak House*) as a 'detective officer'. It would be another five years before a young and unsuccessful doctor named Conan Doyle would invent the most famous of all detectives, Sherlock Holmes.

Indeed, the story of modern criminology had begun only two years earlier, in 1879, in the police headquarters in Paris. A thin, undistinguished young man named Alphonse Bertillon began working for the Sûreté in March of that year, copying and filing descriptions of criminals. It was dreary and boring work. But Bertillon came from a family of scientists, and his grandfather had often aired his theory that no two human beings have identical physical measurements – for example, length of forearm, circumference of skull, chest measurements. . . . Bertillon asked permission to take various measurements of convicts who passed through the headquarters. It was granted, and within a matter of weeks, Bertillon had become convinced that his grandfather was correct. A few people might have one, or even two, measurements in common; but never more than that. However, Bertillon's superiors thought he was a crank, and it took him three years – until 1882 – before he could even persuade them to allow him to try out his new methods on an experimental basis. He was given three months to prove his point. And when the time was almost up, Bertillon had his first small success – identifying a petty crook who had given a false name in an attempt to qualify for treatment as a first offender. He followed up this success by identifying a number of nameless corpses that had been fished out of the Seine. And within a few years, Bertillon's system of identification was being used in police forces all over the world.

Unfortunately for Bertillon, an even more efficient method had already been invented by an Indian civil servant named William Herschel – fingerprinting. One of Herschel's jobs was to pay pensions to Indian ex-soldiers, and to the English eye, they all looked very much alike – so some of them succeeded in collecting twice. Herschel made them sign for their pensions by making an inky fingerprint beside their name on the list. And even while Bertillon was becoming famous as the first scientific crimefighter in Paris, Sir Francis Galton was busy devising a simple method by which fingerprints could be classified and filed. His book *Fingerprints* appeared in the year Bertillon scored one of his most spectacular triumphs – 1892 – when his method of classification trapped an anarchist bomber named Ravachol, and revealed him to be a wanted murderer called Koenigstein. Bertillon, a suspicious and bad-tempered individual, fought grimly for his own system; but in a short time it had been replaced by fingerprinting.

The next great step occurred in 1900, when Paul Uhlenhuth discovered how to test blood to find out if it was human. Blood serum – the watery liquid in which the red cells float – will develop defensive properties against germs (which is how we build up 'resistance') and also against organic substances. If a rabbit is injected with human blood, its serum develops a defence against it. If the rabbit's blood is then sucked out with a hypodermic syringe, and left in a test tube, it 'clots', and the serum separates out from the brown blood cells. Now if a drop of human blood, no matter how tiny, is introduced into the serum, the serum turns a milky colour. Uhlenhuth found that it even worked on very old bloodstains; they only had to be dissolved in salty water, and they would still react to the rabbit serum.

Just after the turn of the century, a sadistic German sex killer named Tessnow was convicted through Uhlenhuth's test [see pp. 80–1].

The changes in scientific criminology that have taken place in the past eighty years have been immense, and Brian Marriner has written a book that would have filled Sherlock Holmes with ecstatic excitement, and that every writer of detective stories will keep on his small shelf of indispensable reference books. As I read it, I found myself wishing that it had been written fifteen years ago, when I started writing my own 'procedural detective story', *The Schoolgirl Murder Case*. It opens with the discovery of a girl's body in a Hampstead garden, in the typical position of a sex murder; she is dressed in school uniform. The following day, the detective in charge of the case learns that the girl is older than she looks – she is a young prostitute who offers her services to clients of peculiar tastes. How would a policeman set out to investigate such a case? I had written more than half the novel when I met a London policeman who is also a writer, Donald Rumbelow, and asked him to read it. His comments made it obvious that I had to scrap the book and start all over again. To begin with, I had not realised that the man who superintends the first examination of the site of the murder is a scene of crimes officer, usually an ordinary constable with specialised training. Until the body has been photographed, examined and removed to the site of the post mortem, he is in charge, and can overrule anyone – even the Commissioner of Police himself – who tries to interfere. If Brian Marriner's book had been on my shelf, I would not have made such an elementary mistake as allowing a chief superintendent to examine the body before the photographer has arrived.

But if this book were concerned only with police procedure, it would be of interest only to experts. In fact, its real value lies in the cases that he uses to illustrate his explanations. Some of these will be familiar to students of real-life crimes – for example, the classic Blackburn murder case, in which the police ended by fingerprinting everybody in the town. (It must have been a moment of tremendous drama when the policeman looking through the latest batch of fingerprints suddenly shouted: 'I've got it!') Others were unknown to me, and will be unknown to the majority of readers.

But the cases that excited me most were those in which a psychiatrist had been able to offer some kind of a 'profile' of the criminal, based on the crimes themselves – as in the 'mad bomber' explosions or the crimes of the Boston Strangler. Here, it seems to me, criminology is moving into a field that is potentially the most fruitful of all. After all, the real problem of modern crime is not how to detect it 'scientifically', but simply how to understand the terrifying increase in the crime figures from year to year. When I wrote my *Encyclopedia of Murder* in 1960, the American murder rate was about ten thousand a year; now, in 1989, it is more than double that figure. (Yet England, with a population nearly a third the size of America's, has a mere five hundred a year.) Checking the violence of the modern world will require a concerted effort of policemen, politicians and criminologists; and of these three, the contribution of the criminologist could well be the most important. Certain practical measures can certainly improve the situation – like the current experiment in New York of giving habitual violent offenders *very* long terms in prison, on the proven assumption that such offenders account for a large percentage of violent crimes. But deeper understanding remains the primary need. The policeman of the future will need to be trained in psychology as well as in more practical disciplines.

In a recent case in Daytona Beach, Florida, a suspect

named Gerald Stano was pulled in by the police on suspicion of killing a girl. The investigating officer, Detective-Sergeant Paul Crow, had taken the trouble to learn something about 'body language', the unconscious gestures that reveal what we are thinking or feeling. Crow noticed that Stano would sit straight upright when telling the truth, and lean back, crossing his legs, when about to lie. And by the time Stano himself had realised that these gestures were giving him away, Crow had found out enough to convince him that Stano was the man the police wanted for the killing of six prostitutes and many attacks on others. Stano was given three consecutive life sentences.

Reflect upon the fact that a mere two centuries ago, England was suffering from the greatest crime wave in its history – a crime wave that began around 1700 with the introduction of the new cheap drink called gin (twopence a gallon), yet that there was no official police force. Two brothers called Henry and John Fielding halted the crime wave for a time by forming their own force – the Bow Street Runners – and taking various other practical and sensible measures. Books like this one make us aware of how far we have advanced since then.

Brian Marriner, a skilled crime writer whose knowledge of crime and the criminal mind is encyclopedic, has written a definitive text on forensic medicine which is destined to become a modern classic.

Colin Wilson

AUTHOR'S PREFACE

This book is intended to be a short primer on forensic science, not a comprehensive encyclopedia on every single esoteric branch of the subject; that would take many volumes, and given the rapid advances in the sciences it would be out of date before it was completed. Ideally, the book should stimulate the reader to investigate further and read the more specialised books on forensic science.

I have tried above all to be honest. Sherlock Holmes does not exist and the brilliant detective is the product of fiction, not fact. Crimes are solved by dull, plodding routine; the asking of questions and the study of the answers. The detective is required to be competent and professional, not gifted with genius or sudden intuitive 'hunches'.

The investigation of practically every crime involves the scientific specialists who work in the Home Office forensic laboratories around the country. They are not geniuses either, but experts who take painstaking care in the routine analysis of samples forwarded to them by the police.

Occasionally – though fortunately rarely – they get it wrong. I shall be reporting the lapses as well as the successes. For example, in the summer of 1983 a young man was acquitted of a charge of murdering his girl friend when a Home Office pathologist's evidence was found to be faulty. Dr Albert Goonetilleke had examined the body of the victim and declared that she had been hit over the head with a blunt instrument. A defence pathologist objected to his conclusion, and exhumation proved that the girl had been *shot*. Dr Goonetilleke had also appeared at the inquest on nurse Helen Smith . . .

In 1956 Dr Alan Moritz published a paper, 'Classic Mistakes in Forensic Pathology', in which he listed fourteen common errors. They are still being made. Scientists are human beings, and therefore fallible.

There is a little larceny in the best of us, they say, and given the right circumstances perhaps some of us could kill. In a situation of extreme stress, fear, drunken rage or jealousy, who could say for sure that they would not strike a lethal blow and become a murderer almost by accident.

Modern science is pretty well agreed that far from being fallen angels, human beings are risen killers, owing their predominant position on this planet to the fact that of all the killers – the lion, alligator, the wildest beasts of the jungle – man is the most lethal species.

Even so, to say that we are *all* part-killer is a broad generalisation. The fact is that the proportion of people capable of planning and carrying out a cold-blooded murder is very small indeed. If anyone is tempted to dispose of someone who stands in their way, and believes that they may possibly get away with it, an examination of the risks involved leads to one inescapable conclusion. You had better forget it!

Waiting to outwit and capture the murderer are the police. Even in this age of high-tech artificial intelligence, human intelligence still remains the best detective of all. But behind the police stands the massive armoury of the laboratory, in the field of forensic science.

'Forensic' means applied to law, while the term 'forensic science' means the use of science to aid the law. It has awesome capabilities. It can trap a killer on a

14

single hair, a twist of fibre, a bite-mark. There is no escaping the all-seeing eye of the electron microscope or the deductive abilities of gas chromatography.

Forensic science is not new, however. It has a history stretching back to ancient times. In fact, the first recorded example of identification by voice is in the Bible (*Judges* 12:6) when Jephthah was anxious to distinguish his own followers from the Ephraimites as they passed through Jordan. He asked each man to pronounce the word 'shibboleth'. Since the Ephraimites pronounced the word without the 'h', it was easy to identify his own followers.

This, though, was quite a simple test. Modern speech identification involves the use of voiceprint machines. In 1963, Lawrence Kersta, of New Jersey, USA, first demonstrated the use of the speech spectograph. Every voice, like every fingerprint, is unique, and methods of analysing voices have obvious applications in criminology: taping a blackmailer's voice, for example, in order to trap a suspect. The Michigan state police have been using speech spectograms since 1968 – and they have even been admitted as evidence in court trials.

While the identification of who said what might seem trivial, it must be remembered that the hoax Yorkshire Ripper tape consumed hundreds of hours of police time, a massive publicity campaign, plus the use of linguistic experts who were able to narrow the accent on the tape down to one specific town – Castletown, near Sunderland. As yet the hoaxer is uncaught – but his voiceprint remains on file.

The patron saint of forensic science is St Thomas, the disciple known as 'doubting Thomas'. John 20:25 records that Thomas said of the Resurrection: 'Except I shall see in his hands the print of the nails, and put my finger into the print of the nails, and thrust my hand into his side, I will not believe.' With that simple

15

commonsense credo he virtually summed up the work and attitude of modern forensic scientists.

They have a vast array of techniques, including fingerprinting, blood-typing and genetic profiling, ballistics, analysis of hairs and fibres, graphology, toxicology, chemistry and forensic odontology – the study of teeth – and finally there is the human detective. We shall be looking at some great real-life sleuths.

Most of the book is devoted to the detection of murder simply because the ultimate crime shows forensic science at the sharp end of aiding the law.

We shall be tracing the history and development of forensic science through the ages. In previous centuries there was a certain *passive* attitude towards crime: unless the criminal was caught in the act, it was just too bad. We know that Egyptian tombs were robbed. If the robbers were caught, no doubt they were cruelly put to death. But in reality the authorities adopted a defensive attitude, building pyramids with cunningly concealed entrances.

But by the second half of the nineteenth century a new and positive approach to crime was being developed. Crime was to be attacked even after the act, and if no guilty party was immediately apparent or witnesses were lacking, then the police concentrated on the evidence itself. It had to be made to speak. Shakespeare was extremely prescient in this respect when he wrote: 'For murder, though it have no tongue, will speak with most miraculous organ.'

Finally, it should never be assumed that the role of forensic science is simply to convict people of crimes. Forensic scientists are trained to be impartial, and they exist to find the truth – nothing else. Forensic science is truly a double-edged weapon. Not only does it serve to secure the conviction of the guilty, it also helps to clear the innocent from blame.

Brian Marriner

1

CRIME AND PUNISHMENT

The Old Testament is the first written record of violent crimes, detailing as it does so many cases of murder, rape and robbery. Indeed, the very first murder is recorded there – that of Abel by Cain. We can take it as our starting point: an indication that from earliest times crime has existed within human societies.

The first part of the Bible was not to be matched in scope or horror as a catalogue of sin and folly until the publication of the *Newgate Calendar* in 1774. This grim record of the felons who met their end dangling on the end of a rope at Tyburn Tree was a steady best-seller, and serves as proof – if any were needed – that man is basically a criminal, born to break the rules when he can.

But the real significance of the *Newgate Calendar* is this: it demonstrates that not much had changed in the three thousand or more years since the first record in the Old Testament. Crime was widespread in any society, and a *laissez-faire* attitude was adopted towards the problem. Crime seemed as natural as the seasons, part of the human condition. The tendency was to ignore crime in the hope that it would go away.

The great men of every age did not use their talents either to investigate crime or to detect criminals. They studied the stars or painted, wrote poetry or composed music. Crime was deemed to be somehow beneath the dignity of the man of genius. It was like looking in the mud, when the proper purpose of genius was to look at the heavens.

This was a mistaken view, since there is a close affinity between the criminal and the artist. Both are dissatisfied with life as it is, and seek to create change. Both seek to create order out of chaos. They demand that life should adapt to their terms. One thinks of Dostoyevsky's Raskolnikov in the moment when he cries out through gritted teeth: 'I will not *live* like this anymore!'

There is a very real sense in which both art and crime can be viewed as acts of magic. Magic can be defined as an act or a series of acts of a ritualistic nature designed to bring about beneficial change to the practitioner. (The ritualistic aspect of magic is most closely seen in sex murders.) In this sense every act of premeditated murder can be viewed as an act of magic. The killer believes that if he removes the obstacle in his path – his wife, mistress, children, rival – he will somehow enhance his own life. And that is the great paradox of murder: it is an act intended to gain more life through death. This belief that the act of murder will bring good is a pathetic fallacy, of course, and Sartre would have viewed it as a prime example of what he termed 'magical thinking'.

Arthur Alfred Rouse is a typical example. The amorous commercial traveller came to the realisation that he had made such a mess of his life that the only way out was to appear to die. He had seduced over eighty women on his travels and had to pay so many paternity orders that he couldn't manage on his salary. He had to find a 'double' to kill. His victim was a tramp who was hitching a lift. Rouse chose, in his own words, 'a down-and-out, the sort of man no one would miss', and after killing him, cremated him in his car. He put his personal items on the corpse, hoping the police would take it to be his. He could then be 'reborn' under a new identity. His ruse was uncovered by the police with ridiculous ease, and he was duly hanged for the murder of the unknown tramp on 6 November 1930.

But Rouse had committed more than simply a murder; he had attempted to perform magic. He had imagined that an act of murder would change his life beneficially.

It may seem a far-fetched view of human evolution to link crime and magic in the development of the human race. As we evolve, one would imagine that magical practices would vanish. That isn't the fact. Superstition abounds, and many professional criminals are highly superstitious, even to the extent of carrying a rabbit's foot on a bank raid.

It was the Scottish lawyer and criminologist William Roughhead (1870–1952) who wrote: 'Murder has a magic of its own. . . .' But he didn't mean it in the original sense of the term. He was part of the new scientific age which dismissed magic as mere primitive superstition and those who believed in magic as being in need of psychiatric treatment. Yet the entire history of mankind is steeped in magical belief; the pages of history are soaked in human sacrificial blood.

From our earliest beginnings, mankind has felt the need to worship gods and to offer sacrifices. When the Aztec priest slashed with his obsidian knife and ripped out the heart of the victim on the altar, holding it up still-beating as an offering to the sun god, he was praying for a good harvest or an end to famine. When Neolithic man drew his hunting pictures on the cave walls – the beauty of which have the power to astonish us to this day – he was not performing as an artist but as a magician. He believed that drawing pictures of bison felled by arrows would lead to this actually taking place. It was wishful – or magical – thinking. The earliest remains of man yet found, over a million years old, show evidence of ritual sacrifice, and it seems to be a human trait that from our very beginnings mankind has

19

felt the need to perform rituals and shed blood to various gods. The Old Testament is full of stories of human sacrifice; and even today in our churches, when we pray to God, we are in a sense attempting to perform an act of magic. We are asking for our lives to be made better by some divine providence.

If ritual remains an important element in religious worship, it also plays a vital role in murder and magic. Think of the intense care with which Jack the Ripper placed those coins at the feet of one of his victims. The obsessive signature of the Boston Strangler – that stocking ligature around the neck with a butterfly knot – and the compulsive drinking of human blood by Peter Kürten – the 'Monster of Düsseldorf' – by Albert Fish, or John George Haigh, the so-called 'Vampire Killer'.

If so far I have painted a bleak view of previous ages, it must be admitted that in every age there existed one bright spark of intelligence which viewed crime as a problem, if not to be solved, at least worthy of study. The Bible contains quite a few references to the solving of crimes. For example, there is the story of Susanna and the Elders; Daniel traps the Elders into an admission of guilt by his cunning questions. Chaucer wrote uncritically of cheerful villains, and Shakespeare was the first great master to delve into the psychology of the murderer; *Macbeth* is a study of the effects of guilt.

There are other examples throughout history, but essentially only in the form of fiction, like the detective-monk in Eco's *The Name of The Rose* – a clever modern pastiche of much earlier works. In Voltaire's *Zadig*, published in 1747, we have an example of the detective genre *before detectives existed*. The story relates how Zadig, without ever having seen the Queen's pet dog or the King's horse, both of which had disappeared, was able to describe them accurately. The bitch had recently had puppies, limped in the left foreleg and had long ears. The horse was five feet high, with small hooves shod with silver shoes. Zadig was flogged for lying, while there was suspicion that he must have been involved in the theft.

Later, however, he was able to verify his descriptions of the animals with a brilliant piece of deduction. In the case of the dog, there were traces of hanging teats and earmarks in the soft sand, with one paw more deeply impressed than the others. The horse had brushed leaves from a tree at a height of five feet and left traces of silver from its hooves on rocks. Even then, Voltaire had borrowed the details from a story published thirty years earlier.

We are beginning to identify the problem; the detective had been invented in fiction, but he did not exist in fact. However, life imitates art. One early example of the use of forensic science to trap a killer occurred in Scotland in 1786. A young woman was found murdered near her parents'᾿ cottage in Kirkcudbrightshire. The obvious suspect was a man named Richardson, but proof of his guilt was lacking. Yet footprints were found in the soft soil near the scene of the crime and – for the first time in British criminal history – plaster casts were taken of them. The court which tried Richardson was shown that hobnails in his boots matched the plaster impressions perfectly. As a result he was found guilty and executed.

Unfortunately, this was one bright light in an otherwise dark age, although it was an encouraging early example of men beginning to *think* about solving crime, instead of simply accepting it as a random act of nature.

The only practical way of dealing with crime in the Middle Ages and in succeeding centuries was to hope to detect the criminal in the act and then punish him cruelly, whatever the nature of his crime. Every parish had its 'watch and ward' system, in which each member of the community had to take his turn at being constable. Each town built its own house of correction to incarcerate those criminals they did not hang. There was no official police force, no government-funded prisons. The result was an anarchic and capricious system of justice.

The government employed torture as a matter of policy, the Tower of London being the most blood-stained building in England. Its construction was begun by William the Conqueror after he invaded in 1066, and was intended to secure his kingdom and ensure that the defeated Saxon people could not combine to rebel against him. He ordered his barons to build castles around the country, and within thirty years hundreds of castles had been erected. These huge stone structures served three purposes; they were the homes of the lords and barons; they served as regional centres for tax-gathering; and they were both courts of justice and prisons. Even today, part of Lancaster Castle is a modern crown court.

William was crowned on 25 December 1066, and one of his first public announcements was: 'I forbid that any person be hanged for any cause . . .' and for almost forty years afterwards no criminal was hanged in England. Instead they were horribly mutilated, for William's next words were: 'Instead, let their eyes be torn out and their testicles cut off.'

Torture was the only practical means of extracting information from a prisoner, and was always carried out in secret. From Tudor times there have come down to us documents listing the instruments of torture in the Tower, and their uses, and there even exists a document signed by James I *ordering* torture to be used. The rack was a frame consisting of three rollers. The prisoner was fastened by his wrists to the top roller, and by his feet to the bottom one. The middle roller had iron teeth at its ends so that it acted like a ratchet, holding the tension as the prisoner was stretched. It could add four inches to a man's height . . .

The 'scavenger's daughter' was a very cruel device of iron. Instead of stretching the body and pulling the joints apart, it was designed to crush the body. In 1586 an Irishman, Thomas Myagh, was brought to the Tower. An existing document from the man who tortured him records his disappointment. 'He was subjected to the torture . . . with so mutche sharpness as was in our judgement convenient, yet we can gette from hym no further matter.' Myagh must have been a tough customer indeed.

Apart from these devices there existed the usual implements of torture: the hot iron to burn, knives to slit the nostrils, the manacles and gauntlets from which to suspend a prisoner for hours on end. The pilliwinks, which were used to crush a man's hands, were replaced by the thumbscrews in the seventeenth century. Some prisoners were forced to wear an iron collar lined with spikes, weighing over ten pounds. Many nobles – even kings and queens – were beheaded in public on Tower Hill, the last being Lord Lovat in 1747. But the Tower – and torture – were reserved for those accused of treason.

It was under King John that the practice of 'outlawing' murderers who fled justice began, with their lands being forfeit to the Crown. Henry III outlawed over seventy murderers in 1255, thus obtaining their property. It was a highly profitable form of justice.

In 1241 hanging, drawing and quartering occurred for the first time in England, a mark of the age of cruelty when justice operated a policy of terror to deter crime. In Henry VIII's reign some 72,000 people were executed in England alone, but still crime flourished.

Tyburn had been a place of execution since the twelfth century, when the trees standing at the corner of Edgware Road and Bayswater Road – now the site of Marble Arch – were utilised to hang felons. It was in the sixteenth century that Tyburn gained its notoriety, when the scaffold was redesigned into a triangular shape, capable of hanging eight people from each of its three beams, which stood eighteen feet high. By the eighteenth century so many people were being hanged in London that the city became known throughout Europe as 'the city of the gallows'.

The history of Newgate and Tyburn are inseparable, for Newgate Prison was where the condemned were held prior to their final two-mile trip to Tyburn. Of the seven main gates into London, the principal ones were Newgate and Ludgate, which were not far apart. The wall between them was known as the Bailey – the first written record of the name appeared in 1423. It became the site of the Old Bailey, or the Central Criminal Court.

The convicts of the sixteenth and seventeenth centuries had to actually pay 'garnish' for the privilege of being imprisoned. Those who could not afford to pay for services – a whore for the night was twelve-pence – were kept chained and starved. When Newgate caught fire during the Great Fire of London in 1666, the convicts were transferred to the Clink Prison on the south side of the river. 'Clink' is still used as a synonym for prison.

In the seventeenth century many prisoners refused to plead guilty because if they did so, their lands and possessions were forfeit to the Crown and their dependents were left penniless. To counter this, the court would order prisoners who were 'mute' to be 'pressed'. This torture was known as *peine forte et dure* – 'strong and hard pain', and consisted of piling weights on to the prone man until he was forced to plead, or died. Relatives would often stand on top of the weights on the pressed man to hasten his end.

The infamous Jonathan Wild established his headquarters opposite Newgate, appointing himself 'Thief-Taker General'. He was in fact a receiver of stolen goods, and his clients were those people who had been robbed. For a fee he would see to it that their goods were returned to them. Wild controlled all crime in London, dividing the city into districts and allotting a district to each gang. They had to sell him their loot – or be hanged. With a London house and a country mansion, Wild flourished.

There was another side to Wild; he was a professional informer and a hypocrite, a man who ruthlessly sent hundreds of his followers to the gallows. Once he had evidence that a thief had committed a certain crime, he entered an 'X' against his name in his ledger. When the thief displeased him – by refusing to deal with him, or by asking too high a price – Wild put a second cross against his name, indicating that it was time to impeach him to the authorities for the £40 reward money. We owe our expression 'double-cross' directly to Wild.

London in the 1720s was in the grip of the worst crime wave in its history, with highwaymen, footpads, burglars and pickpockets preying on the populace – even in broad daylight. The city was in an administrative mess. Roads were deep in mud and poorly lit. A rabbit warren of hastily erected buildings became instant slums. While outlying districts like Chelsea, Islington, Bow and Stepney were still villages, the City of London and Westminster had a population of 660,000, and it was estimated that within the city walls lived over ten thousand professional thieves.

With no police force, several highly organised gangs of criminals had established a grip on the underworld, and the few peace officers – the Watch – were demoralised and intimidated into turning a blind eye to crime. Magistrates and even judges of the Old Bailey were not averse to accepting bribes, hanging small-time criminals in order to allow bigger ones to go free. It was an age of corruption, with London resembling the Chicago of two centuries later.

Hogarth, in his series of engravings 'A Rake's Progress', the 'Harlot's Progress' and 'Gin Lane', has left us with a vision of his society which is so ugly that it seems distorted; but it was all too true. The inhabitants of the sprawling squalor of London's slums lived in a state of perpetual terror. Life was cheap; it was the attitude of the time. In Hobbes' phrase, life was 'nasty, brutish, and short'.

One of the contributing factors to the crime wave – perhaps the main one – was the availability of a new drink called gin. It was cheap and easy to make. By 1720 one house in every ten in London was a gin shop, over six thousand of them. An advertisement of the period promised: 'Drunk for a penny, dead drunk for tuppence.' The poor drank it to ease their misery, even serving it to babies to soothe them. No one in government had foreseen the evils of gin. Previously, spirits had been taxed too highly for the working class to afford them.

Another of the root causes of the corruption which flourished was that every official had to 'buy his place'. The city could not afford many salaries – indeed, London had been declared bankrupt in 1694. Even prisoners had to pay 'garnish' or rent for their cells. And attempting to stem the flood-tide of crime were just two city marshals in charge of six men. Law officers received sixpence a head for every prisoner committed to the city jails, and were allowed to levy a pound a head for every market stall-holder, many of whom dealt openly in stolen goods. The situation cried out for a man of genius to control it, and he appeared in the form of Jonathan Wild, the man destined to become London's 'Prince of Darkness'.

Wild was born in Wolverhampton in 1683, but left his native Midlands to make his fortune in London. Ironically, Wild soon found himself in prison for debt. He spent four years inside the Wood Street Compter, unable to buy himself out, since a prisoner had to pay for his accommodation and thus incurred even more debt. It had been known for a man to go to prison for a farthing and spend the rest of his life there. Wild was a shrewd convict, soon learning the rules and becoming master of the prison rackets. He became a trusty at the Gate House, and here he met Mary Milliner in 1712. She was a 'buttock and file' – or prostitute – and on his discharge Wild set her up in a brothel in Covent Garden. The Wood Street Compter has long since vanished, but its former site is now occupied by an office block called Compter House, behind which, in Mitre Square, are the remaining dungeons. Used as wine cellars today, they may still be viewed by the curious.

The government's response to the crime explosion was to introduce the infamous 'Black Act' which made over 350 offences liable to hanging. A law of 1693 – the Highwayman Act – offered a reward of £40 to anyone who captured a highwayman. In 1706 a new law allowed a criminal who turned informer against his accomplices in crime not only a free pardon, but also £40 reward. The result was that every thief captured sold out his partners for the reward – or even 'named' innocent people – and armed with a free pardon, continued his trade. He was in effect allowed to 'bargain' with justice, much like the modern supergrass.

To combat the ferocious villains of the day were a handful of constables, unpaid, who were elected to serve for a period of one year from the roll of citizens. This duty was naturally unpopular, and wealthy men paid substitutes to serve their period of service for them. And since each citizen was supposed to act as his own policeman – to physically arrest the villain who had stolen from him, with all the risks of injury – a breed of professional 'thief-takers' sprang up, making their living from the rewards on offer, and a fee from the restoration of the stolen property to the grateful owner.

Wild did not *invent* thief-taking, but he was to become its supreme exponent.

In the *Daily Courant* of 26 May 1714 appeared the first of Wild's many advertisements. 'Lost on Friday Evening . . . a Day Book . . . Whoever shall bring the same to Mr Jonathan Wild against Cripplegate Church shall have a Guinea Reward and no Questions asked.' He opened an 'Office For The Recovery of Lost and Stolen Property', but very cleverly did not actually take possession of stolen goods, instead noting who had stolen them. Clients who had lost something visited his office, paid a five-shilling deposit or 'search fee' and had the details of their loss entered into a ledger. They were told to return in a day or two. Wild then contacted the thief and arranged for the transfer of the stolen goods back to the owner – via an intermediary – for a 'reward'. When once attacked for this practice, Wild claimed: 'Where is the Harm in all this? I neither see the Thief nor receive the Goods. . . .'

Wild was now the 'regulator' of the underworld, organising all crime and allocating districts to gangs. Those gangs who refused to cooperate, he set about smashing. Within three months he had personally arrested a dozen dangerous criminals, claiming rewards totalling £200 (£4,000 in today's money). In 1719 he moved to the Old Bailey or Old Bailey Street, his newspaper ads now terming him 'Jonathan Wild of the Old Bailey'. Business thrived.

Physically small – only five feet six inches in height – Wild was a brave man. Often knocked down, shot at, stabbed and beaten, he always got his man, arresting many highwaymen and watching them hang. He further enhanced his reputation by smashing several gangs and arresting over fifty robbers. The Kray brothers called their gang 'The Firm'. Wild called his 'The Corporation'. And while the Krays' gang was reputed to have controlled north London, with the Richardson gang running south London, Wild controlled *all* London.

He had power undreamed of by modern gangsters; not only did he control the underworld, he was also the police force. He truly was a pioneer, his genius fully revealed in his dual role. Eugène François Vidocq (1775–1857) was a French criminal who became head of the Paris detective division and founded the Sûreté, but Wild had beaten him by a century. The first modern gangster and the first modern policeman combined in one person. . . . He did not found Scotland Yard, but he was its spiritual designer. Little wonder that Daniel Defoe wrote of him: 'The Life of Jonathan Wild is a perfectly new Scene.'

Wild was now at the height of his success. In 1718 he formally adopted the title of 'Thief-Taker General of Great Britain and Ireland', pointing out that he had already 'brought to justice many notorious Malefactors, above Sixty in Number. . . .' Carrying a silver baton as his badge of office, Wild attended race meetings and prize fights, surrounded by a retinue of thieves.

Almost unnoticed, an Act was passed in 1719 – the Transportation Act – which was later to be called the Jonathan Wild Act. Sections 5 and 6 of the Act made it an offence for any person to transfer stolen goods back to the owner for gain, without apprehending the felon who had stolen them. Wild, the Machiavelli of Crime, exploited all the loopholes in the new Act, going from strength to strength. In 1720 he opened a second 'lost property office' because business was so good. His 'Corporation' was a self-financing scheme of some brilliance. The lost property office depended on regular supplies from thieves to supply the clients. The client's 'rewards' financed yet further robberies. But every now and again Wild was forced to sacrifice some of his thieves to the gallows to show 'good faith' in his role as policeman. He was to send over two hundred men to the gallows in this fashion.

In 1720 so great was his fame that the Privy Council solicited his advice about curbing highway robberies. Wild's advice was self-serving: *increase the reward money!* A Royal Proclamation increased the reward to £100, and Wild's pockets bulged still further.

The downfall of Wild coincided with his involvement with Jack Sheppard – although the underworld had already begun to hate him, and magistrates were increasingly wary of his 'framing' tactics. Jack Sheppard was a small, thin burglar with fair hair and a cockney sparrow's wit. He was to become the most famous jail-breaker in history. The film *Where's Jack?* was based on his exploits.

Sheppard was part of a gang of thieves which included his elder brother Thomas. When Sheppard scornfully refused to trade with Wild, Wild set out to smash the gang in his usual fashion. Thomas was arrested and quickly informed on Jack. Jack was arrested and locked up in the St Giles Roundhouse, from which he promptly escaped. Recaptured, he was now locked up in the New Prison at Clerkenwell. Again he escaped, this time on 25 May 1724.

Recaptured again several burglaries later, Jack was sentenced to hang, but escaped from the condemned cell. Wild was furious. Sheppard was finally captured on Finchley Common on 10 September and returned to Newgate as a celebrity. He gave interviews to the nobility in his cell, and to reporters – one of them a certain Daniel Defoe. . . . His warders placed him 'on view' to visitors at 3s 6d a time. His sayings were eagerly printed in the press, and his sage reflection: 'One file is worth all the Bibles in the world' set all London chuckling.

Once again Sheppard managed to escape from the condemned cell at Newgate, while shackled with heavy chains and padlocks. But when free he made the rounds of the taverns in Drury Lane and the Strand, dressed in newly stolen finery, and was soon turned in by an informer. He was the hero of the hour, the darling of London society. V. S. Pritchett has written almost grudgingly that 'Sheppard displayed a flash of cold genius'.

When he was recaptured, the authorities made sure that this time there would be no escape. Back in the condemned cell, he sat for Hogarth, and even King George I sent Sir James Thornhill, the King's Painter, to sketch the celebrity. The Lord Chancellor was given a private audience. On 16 November 1724 a crowd of two hundred thousand people gathered to watch the twenty-three-year-old Sheppard hang at Tyburn. Books and plays were to be written about him, the most famous being *The Beggar's Opera* by John Gay.

By killing a public hero, Wild had signed his own death warrant. He was no longer seen as a protector of the public, but as a brutal policeman. On 15 February 1725, Wild was arrested on a charge of receiving a £10 reward for stolen lace. He was tried, found guilty and sentenced to be hanged. He attempted to commit suicide in the condemned cell, but survived to be hanged at Tyburn on 24 May 1725, with a hostile crowd jeering him and calling out: 'Judas Wild'. The body of the forty-three-year-old Wild was buried at St Pancras churchyard, but was secretly dug up four days later and anatomised. In the nineteenth century a Dr Frederick Fowler presented the skeleton of Wild to the Royal College of Surgeons, and it is displayed yet in the Hunterian Museum at the college.

The first six convict ships sailed to Australia in 1787, the last in 1867; transportation was said to be more feared by convicts than hanging itself. But the hangings continued. There were other execution sites and other forms of execution. There were gallows at Putney

Common, the Old Kent Road and Smithfield, as well as one outside Newgate itself. Pirates were hanged at Execution Dock, the bodies being left until three tides had passed over them. Captain Kidd was hanged there. Burning at the stake was reserved for women, as it was thought to be less of a punishment than hanging. The woman would be covered in tar and tied to the stake, a long cord around her neck being used by the executioner to strangle her before the flames actually reached her. There was a specific crime of 'husband murder', and when Phoebe Harris was burned for this in 1786 in front of Newgate, a crowd of twenty thousand gathered to watch.

An execution was a very public event and a form of public entertainment. The mob of spectators would get drunk, buy snacks from hawkers and generally have a good time. That hanging failed to deter is apparent from Hogarth's print showing pickpockets at work in the shadow of the gallows.

Execution by hanging was supposed to deter other criminals. When it failed, the authorities tried other extremes. What could be worse than being hanged? *Being tortured after death.* In 1752 an 'Act for the Better Preventing the Horrid Crime of Murder' was passed, which was designed to punish the criminal after death. After being hanged, his body was to be publicly dissected by surgeons.

The same Act gave judges the discretion to order a body to be hanged in chains. As a result, every town and village had a gibbet, on which a body encased in an iron cage swung, to serve as an object of terror to the local populace.

The sheer size of the mobs put an end to Tyburn. It was too far from the city. The vast crowds blocked traffic and were a threat to the King's Peace. The City sheriffs insisted that executions at Tyburn must cease 'in consequence of the mischiefs which arise from a long parade of criminals from Newgate to Tyburn'. In future, all executions would be carried out immediately in front of Newgate Prison. The last execution at Tyburn was in 1783. The radical change did not please everyone. Dr Johnson growled that: 'It is not an improvement; they object that the old method drew together a multitude of spectators. Sir, executions are intended to draw spectators. If they don't draw spectators, they don't serve their purpose.'

The first execution at Newgate was on 9 December 1783, with ten people being hanged on the new gallows. If the authorities had hoped for orderly executions, they were to be disappointed. The mob, pressed into the small square in front of the prison, simply carried on as before. When John Holloway and Owen Haggerty were hanged on 23 February 1807, a crowd of forty-five thousand crammed into the narrow space panicked. As a result over one hundred people in the crowd were crushed to death.

It was the execution of François Courvoisier, the Swiss butler who murdered his employer, Lord William Russell, which marked the beginning of the end of public executions. All London society came to view the fun, including the writers Thackeray and Dickens. The experience so depressed Thackeray that he was unable to work for many days, writing to a friend: 'It is most curious the effect his death has on me.' He wrote an article about the execution for *Frazer's Magazine* entitled 'Going To See A Man Hanged'. After describing the details of the hanging, Thackeray went on: 'I am not ashamed to say that I could look no more, but shut my eyes as the last dreadful act was going on. . . . It seems that I have been abetting an act of frightful wickedness and violence, performed by one set of men against one of their fellows.'

The execution of husband and wife Frederick and Maria Manning on 13 November 1849 at Horsemonger

Lane Gaol was a real crowd-drawer. A crowd of over thirty thousand gathered to watch the pair twitch on the rope. Charles Dickens paid ten guineas for the use of a house to watch this execution, the following day writing to *The Times* condemning the ugly spectacle of public executions. He also used Maria Manning as the model for the murderous Frenchwoman, Hortense, in *Bleak House*.

The pressure was growing for all executions to be carried out in private, within prison walls. But all that was in the future. Franz Müller, the first person ever to commit a murder in a railway train, was hanged on 14 November 1864 before a crowd of five thousand outside Newgate, with thousands more packed into adjacent streets. On Monday 22 February 1864 a huge mob gathered to watch the execution of the 'five pirates' – five blacks who had mutinied on board the ship *Flowery Land*, bound for Singapore, murdering the captain and five crew members. The City of London Police had 330 officers to help keep order, while the Metropolitan Police sent 800 officers and mounted police to help out. The dregs of London's slums watched the men hanged by Calcraft. The wealthy watched from nearby windows, which for weeks before the execution had carried banners advertising: 'Seats to Rent. Good View of the Execution'. All five men were duly hanged by Calcraft, who had bowed and smiled at the crowd like a concert pianist. As the last Negro went through the trap a costermonger was overheard saying to another: 'So help me, Bill, ain't it fine: five of them, and all darkies!'

The population of London had quadrupled between 1730 and 1811, with a corresponding rise in crime. There had been food riots, burnings, lootings and mob violence. Inner-city rioting is by no means a modern phenomenon. As mob violence increased, the authorities had tried ever more repressive measures, including whipping, mutilation, the pillory, hanging, the corpse being subjected to further mutilation after death, but none of it worked, not even when trivial crimes became punishable by hanging. In 1831 a boy aged nine was hanged at Chelmsford for arson, and in 1833 another nine-year-old boy was hanged for poking a stick through a broken shop window and stealing two-penny-worth of paint. The last woman to be publicly burned alive was Christian Murphy on 18 March 1789, for coining offences.

But the old legal brutality of the past was slowly dying away. Justice had been crude, applied with brute force, with no thought of the legal niceties. Bill after Bill was being introduced in Parliament to end public executions, although there was still reaction to change. When a Bill to abolish capital punishment for cutting down trees was being debated, Lord Eldon complained that while it was 'an undoubted hardship to be hanged for cutting down a single tree', if the law were changed 'a person might cut down a whole plantation without fear. . . .'

Human evolution is painfully slow. Pressure for social change usually takes a century or more to work its way into the system.

The first *written* records in existence of a legal system are the codes of criminal law promulgated by Hammurabi (2285–2242 BC). Those codes included capital punishment; the taking of life by judicial process has a long pedigree.

By 1179 BC murder was a capital offence among the Greeks and Egyptians. In 700 BC Draco tried to suppress crime in Greece by making *every* crime subject to capital punishment. It predictably failed in its purpose, leaving us with the expression 'draconian' as a memento.

In England as early as the fifth century BC, strangulation was used either as a form of punishment or ritual sacrifice. The method involved tying the hands of the

35

felon and throttling him, afterwards throwing his body into a quagmire. Several such corpses have been recovered, marvellously preserved by the peat bogs, usually with the leather throttling thong still around their necks. One such corpse, humorously christened 'Pete Marsh' by scientists, has been subjected to rigorous tests to determine the diet of the time and cause of death. The grooves of the strangling cord have been preserved in the neck.

Human societies failed to learn the lesson that ever more repressive tortures and punishments did not achieve their object. In England we continued to hang, apart from minor aberrations like the Halifax gibbet, which may still be examined *in situ*. It was a beheading machine, with a blade between wooden guides which was drawn up to fall on the neck of the felon. The parish register of Halifax lists the names of forty-nine people who were thus executed between 1541 and 1650.

Joseph Ignace Guillotin therefore did not *invent* the beheading machine which was named after him, but simply declared it to be the most efficient means of execution. Legend has it that it was Louis XVI who suggested that a triangular blade would be more effective. He would know – he was beheaded by it. The guillotine was first used in 1792.

Spain had the garrote. The USA had a variety of methods, including hanging, shooting, gassing and the electric chair. These did not seem to be very efficient. At one execution by shooting in Utah in 1951, all five marksmen in the firing-squad failed to hit a vital organ, and the prisoner bled to death. Electrocution was not too certain, several jolts of current sometimes having to be administered, and death in the gas chamber could last an agonizing eight minutes.

New York State abolished public executions in 1835, but they continued elsewhere. A public execution drew a crowd of twenty thousand in Kentucky as late as 1936, and the last public execution was performed in France in 1939.

The last public execution in Britain took place on 26 May 1868, when Michael Barrett, a Fenian, was hanged by Calcraft outside Newgate. The first person to be hanged privately within prison walls, under the new Act of 1868 which abolished public executions, was eighteen-year-old Thomas Wells, hanged at Maidstone Prison on 13 August 1868.

A Royal Commission into capital punishment in 1864 heard the lord chief justice of the time say in evidence that: 'in the course of forty years there were twenty-two persons sentenced to death who were afterwards proved to be innocent'. The 1949 Royal Commission into the same subject heard Sir David Maxwell Fyfe say: 'There is no practical possibility of an innocent man being hanged in this country, and anyone who thinks otherwise is moving in the realms of fantasy'. He was perhaps haunted by the case of Timothy Evans . . .

The pressure of evolution, of civilisation itself, was mounting. In 1942 Switzerland abolished capital punishment, followed by Italy in 1949, together with Finland and West Germany, and Austria in 1950. Britain held out. When statistics revealed that only forty-eight per cent of English murderers were being hanged, Lord Goddard complained bitterly: 'Too many people are being reprieved'. It was he who told the Royal Commission that in his opinion it was 'very right and proper to hang a madman'.

The 1949 Royal Commission heard evidence until 1953. They learned that fifteen people had been reprieved simply because their physical structure made it impossible to hang them with certainty, and there was no legal alternative method of execution. Four prison doctors assured the Commission that 'lethal injections were impractical'. They are now widely used in the

USA. The Commission also considered the facts. That during the years from 1900 to 1949, 1,210 persons (1,080 men and 170 women) were convicted of murder and sentenced to death in England and Wales, and 59 persons (54 men and 5 women) in Scotland. The conclusion of the Commission was that: 'It is evident that the death penalty has no effect on the murder rate'.

The Tower of London had continued to function as usual. During the First World War a German spy, Carl Lody, was executed there by firing-squad, followed by some fifteen others during the Second World War under the Treachery Act of 1940.

The practice of hanging aroused revulsion in some people, but its effect seemed to be brutalising on the hangman himself. Several English hangmen have themselves been hanged in our history, several have either gone mad or committed suicide. The most notable was the case of Hangman Ellis in our own century. It was said that his mind had become deranged after the horrific experience of hanging Mrs Thompson, who had to be dragged half-drugged to the scaffold. Ellis first tried to shoot himself, and later, after appearing in seaside shows demonstrating 'the art of the hangman' for sixpence admission, he finally cut his throat. The most sane and respected of all executioners, Albert Pierrepoint, said after his retirement: 'I do not believe that any one of the hundreds of executions I carried out has in any way acted as a deterrent against future murder. Capital punishment, in my view, achieved nothing except revenge.' It is a view worthy of consideration.

On 13 July 1955 the last woman was hanged in England, twenty-eight-year-old Ruth Ellis. In February 1956 English hangings were halted while Parliament debated the question of abolition, but the motion to abolish was finally defeated by thirty-one votes. In 1956 the Archbishop of Canterbury declared that the death penalty was not always wrong or unchristian. Hanging was resumed in July 1957.

The Homicide Act of 1957 allowed a plea of 'diminished responsibility' for the first time. Between the passing of this Act and December 1964, forty-eight persons were sentenced to death in England and Wales, but only twenty-nine were actually executed.

On 13 August 1964 the last executions in Britain took place when Gwynne Owen Evans and Peter Anthony Allen were hanged in separate prisons for the murder of a van driver in the 'furtherance of theft'. In 1965 the Murder (Abolition of Death Penalty) Act was passed, since when the only penalty for murder is one of life imprisonment.

An analysis of murder carried out in 1961 revealed that a quarter of murders were motivated by mental disorder, and a further half took place during fights or quarrels – when tempers were high – or during extreme depression. The revelations came as no surprise.

The ending of capital punishment marked a new and enlightened attitude towards crime. The emphasis was to be on the detection and reformation of the criminal.

This summary has of necessity involved looking at several notorious criminals. As Sir Leslie Stephen – himself a judge – said: 'The highwayman is often more interesting to the historians of society than the learned judge who hangs him.' That remains true today. We can learn more about crime from criminals than we can from judges. There is a plethora of books by former criminals which contain valuable insights, including the autobiographies of John McVicar, Jimmy Boyle and Walter 'Angel-Face' Probyn.

From them – and from history itself – we learn that the practice of imprisonment has never been an *efficient* answer to crime. It is costly and often brutalising. In some cases prison has created criminals who are released to commit even worse offences, driven by rage and resentment. Shakespeare summed up this type in his 1st Murderer in *Macbeth*: 'I am one, my liege/Whom the vile blows and buffets of the world/Have so incensed that I am reckless what/I do to spite the world.'

Society had always reacted to crime instead of trying to prevent it. In the early part of the nineteenth-century some eleven thousand murders a year were committed in the nation. There was no police force, and in London all that stood between the householder and the burglar was the Bow Street Runners, who were basically private detectives operating for private reward.

Gradually change came. The barbaric punishments of former centuries were abandoned as society attempted an *intelligent* response to crime. Transportation was an alternative to execution. Then came lengthy periods of imprisonment with a strict 'no talking' rule. Later came 'preventive detention', under which an old lag could be jailed for up to ten years for stealing a bottle of milk. There was the birch for young offenders and the cat for hardened criminals. Between the wars, the Borstal system was introduced, followed by probation. The prison system became relaxed, with talking permitted.

Now we have community service orders as an alternative to prison, and even in prison, prisoners can be released after serving half their sentence under the parole scheme. Future solutions include electronic tagging.

These changes started around the third decade of the nineteenth century, when society began to fight back against crime in a positive manner.

In 1829, the Metropolitan Police was founded. In 1835, Alfred Swaine Taylor, Professor of Medical Jurisprudence at Guy's Hospital, published his classic *Principles and Practices of Medical Jurisprudence*. The same year also saw the publication of *On Man* by Lambert Quételet, a Belgian astronomer who attempted to apply statistics to measure criminal activity. And in 1836 came the Marsh test for detecting minute quantities of arsenic in samples. These are all examples of enlightened men *thinking* of solutions to the problem of crime.

That, then, is a brief history of punishment. Crime continues with little variation. The old motives remain as potent as ever. The big change in the history of crime lies not with the criminal, but with the policeman. Crime is now detected with science, not crushed with brutality. This is best illustrated with two cases which, although widely separated by time, show a marked similarity in execution. The first was in 1847, the second in 1984.

Some three miles from Dewsbury and five miles north-east of Huddersfield, lies the pleasant Yorkshire town of Mirfield. Water Royd House is a large detached property which to this day is known to the locals as 'the murder house'. On 12 May 1847 all three occupants of that house – the master, his wife and the young servant girl – were brutally murdered, their blood literally running out under the front door. The murders were discovered by the great-nephew of the householder, and although he sent for the police, many neighbours trampled through the house to view the bodies, destroying any forensic evidence.

A large stone memorial stands at the roadside, in front of the Baptist Zion Chapel. Its inscription reads: 'In Memory of Caroline Ellis, Aged 21 years, Who with James Wraith, Gent., and Ann his wife, her Master and Mistress Comprising a Whole Family, was most Barbarously Murdered at Mid Day Ad 1847 at Water Royd House, situated 127 yards NE from this Place.' *The Leeds Mercury* (now defunct) reported the case as: 'A triple murder which surely cannot be equalled in England's "calendar of crime" for atrocity and brutality'. James Wraith, seventy-seven, his wife Ann, sixty-seven, and Caroline Ellis had been 'horribly murdered', with Caroline Ellis having 'her brains scattered over the floor and her teeth drawn out', while Mr and Mrs Wraith had also been savagely battered, afterwards having their throats cut.

Michael McCabe was a genial Irish hawker who had lived in England for twenty years. He plied his trade around the district, walking miles each day carrying his basket of pots from door to door. There existed an intense anti-Irish feeling in England at the time, but the thirty-five-year-old McCabe was welcomed at every door; in an age of limited travel and expensive newspapers, he was a source of news and gossip. But he had visited Water Royd House at the exact time of the murder; he had knocked at the door and had had the murderer partly open it to him; he had seen the blood coming from under the door. *He had seen too much.* He went away. He did not report what he had seen, but his incautious remarks in a local pub led to his arrest. He was arrested by the parish constable, to whom he told his unlikely story. As a result the real murderer, another Irish hawker named Peter Reid, was arrested.

McCabe refused to identify Reid through fear, and since the money and valuables stolen from the house were not found in their possession, both men were charged with the murders. The well which served the murder house was dragged and a heavy soldering iron was recovered – the murder weapon – plus the key to the back door. Witnesses testified to having sold Reid the iron, or having seen it in his possession.

At York Assizes on 19 July 1847, McCabe turned Queen's Informer against Reid, who stood charged only with the murder of James Wraith. The jury were puzzled; they knew three people had been murdered; who had committed the other two? They acquitted Reid. The authorities now placed both Reid and McCabe in the dock, jointly charged with the murder of Caroline Ellis. It was a 'cut-throat' defence, with Reid's lawyer trying to place the blame on McCabe. Both men were found guilty of murder and sentenced to hang. Immediately afterwards, Reid's lawyers told the judge that his client had made a written confession to the murders, which exonerated McCabe of any involvement. Reid had committed the murders because of a grudge he had against Caroline Ellis, who had once turned him away from the house. Reid's lawyer had had this confession in his pocket all through the trial.

After consultation with the Secretary of State, McCabe's death sentence was respited; but even with Reid's full confession, McCabe was transported for life. Reid was hanged outside York Castle by Howard, the county hangman, before a huge crowd. It was a badly bungled case, even if the real villain of the piece was detected and convicted.

By comparison, in Sheffield on the night of 23 October 1983, following the wedding of their eldest daughter, the Laitner family were savagely murdered in their home, leaving one sole survivor – the youngest daughter – who was forced to walk past the bloodied corpse of her father before being repeatedly raped.

The Laitner's were a wealthy and gifted Jewish family, living in a luxury home in the fashionable suburb of Dore. Basil Laitner, fifty-nine, was a solicitor; his wife Avril, fifty-five, was a doctor who had fought a battle against cancer, having both breasts removed. Richard, twenty-eight, the only son, was a brilliant young man, studying at university for the law but home for the wedding. All three were butchered within minutes by a knife-wielding maniac on the run from the police and with a long record of crime and punishment behind him.

While serving a prison sentence, Arthur Hutchinson, born illegitimate on 14 February 1941, had filled two exercise books with notes about women who were likely candidates for rape and robbery, using information culled from newspaper reports. He was an extremely violent man who had been convicted several times of sex offences.

Hutchinson viewed the world as a jungle, with himself as the predator. It was a world of cruel lusts to be instantly gratified – whatever the cost; truly a Sadean landscape. On his release from prison Hutchinson went straight to a woman's house and raped her. He was quickly arrested and taken to Selby police station. The keep-fit fanatic escaped from custody on 28 September, leaping a barbed-wire fence and gashing his leg badly in the process. He remained free for thirty days, during which time he became a killer.

Hutchinson was drifting across Yorkshire like a poisonous cloud. He broke into the Laitners' home through a faulty patio door, armed with an eight-inch bowie knife. In an upstairs bedroom he stabbed the sleeping Richard to death, and when the father came on the scene, alerted by the noise, Hutchinson plunged the knife into him. Then he killed the mother, stabbing her twenty-six times. He took the youngest daughter out to the marquee on the lawn, where he raped her all night. Next morning the hysterical girl was found by workmen who had come to dismantle the marquee.

On the run, Hutchinson booked into guesthouses using the name 'A. Fox'. He was captured in a turnip field as a result of a police trap. At his resulting trial at Sheffield Crown Court on 4 September 1984, Hutchinson was tried for three murders, rape and aggravated burglary. He pleaded not guilty. It was a long and complex trial.

The Crown presented its evidence. The surviving victim had identified Hutchinson as being the assailant. He had a rare blood group and had left bloodstains from his injured leg on the girl's nightdress and in her bed. He had left an impression of his training shoe in blood on the stairs. His palm-print was found on a bottle of champagne in the marquee, and two bite marks on a piece of cheese in the kitchen fridge matched his dental characteristics exactly. For the first time in a British murder trial the jury were shown a police video-tape of the murder scene, complete with bodies.

The jury took four hours to convict Hutchinson on all the charges. The judge read out a psychiatric report on Hutchinson which branded him a psychopath, before sentencing him to three life terms, eight years for rape, and five years for burglary.

Notice the difference? The second case is full of *science*. Bloodstains. Palm-prints. Footprints. Teeth impressions. Video recordings. Finally, a psychiatric report. As we shall see later, the psychiatrist can help identify a killer through the use of 'psychological profiling'. With the full use of all these forensic techniques, Britain's crime fighters have come of age.

There is one other significant difference: the motive. Killing for sex is a fairly modern phenomenon, as again we shall see later in the chapter on sex killers.

Of course, it could be argued that under the old system, Hutchinson would have been hanged years ago and so could have offended no more. That is a valid point, but it ignores the fact that all progress comes at a *price*; in this case it was the lives of three people.

2

THE HISTORY OF DETECTION

One murder case in recent years almost literally stopped me in my tracks, causing me to reflect on why I personally write about murder cases which contain so much pain and human misery – and why it is that so many cases are simply dull and banal, with a dearth of really good detection.

The murder in question took place in Los Angeles on 12 May 1984, and briefly the facts are these: in the middle of the night Terri Lynn Scrape, aged twenty seven, ran from her home screaming, pounding on neighbours' doors. While waiting for the police to arrive she told neighbours that her husband was badly hurt – maybe dead. She said she had woken up alone in bed and had gone downstairs to find him lying in a pool of blood in the living room. She had run out of the house *without touching anything.*

Homicide Detective Tom Cuillard duly arrived on the scene. He went first to the murder house. He noted that dew on the front lawn showed no footprints. At the rear of the house was a poker, bent and covered in blood. The ground beneath it was wet with dew, indicating that the poker had not lain there long. A thermometer on the patio read 60 degrees, a thermostat inside the house was set for 74 degrees, indicating that the patio door had been opened for a lengthy period, from the *inside.* It had not been forced. There was a single splash of blood on a closet door.

The victim, Lee Scrape, aged forty, lay sprawled nude on the living room floor. He was very dead, from multiple stab wounds and blows to the head. Defensive marks on his arms showed that he had fought fiercely for life. The detective's first thought was that there ought to be more blood. It looked as if someone had cleaned up afterwards...

A poker was missing from a set of fireplace tools in the hearth. It was presumably the weapon on the rear lawn. In the master bedroom the bed looked smooth, as if it hadn't been slept in, while the floor of the shower stall was still wet.

Cuillard then interviewed Mrs Scrape in a neighbour's home. She told him that she and her husband had drunk champagne, then made love on the living room floor. She had gone to bed at about twelve-thirty, showering before getting into bed. She fell asleep immediately. She woke at 3.20 a.m. to find that her husband had not joined her in bed. She went downstairs and found his body as described, touching only the light switch. In the words of the detective's report: 'Mrs Scrape ran outside screaming. She did not touch or examine the victim before she ran out of the house.'

Three days later the detective returned to the sealed house with a photographer and a forensic scientist. The scientist sprayed two chemicals around the house – orthotolidine and phenolphthalein, which reveal the presence of otherwise invisible bloodstains. The first turns blood bright green, the second turns it pink. There was reaction to human blood on the light switch in the living room and on a laundry basket in the bathroom. Cuillard wondered about the second weapon – the knife. He looked in the dishwater and saw clean plates, plus one dirty knife covered with butter. Why would the plates be clean but the knife dirty? When he had it checked with the chemicals it showed a positive reaction to blood.

That was enough for the detective. The wife had touched the light switch with bloody hands, yet insisted she had not touched the body. She said she had been asleep for three hours, but the shower floor was still wet – and her hair had been wet when first interviewed. The murder must have been noisy, yet the wife claimed to have slept through it.

Investigation into the wife's background revealed that she had a secret lover, who was never traced. Detective Cuillard theorised that Mrs Scrape and her lover had jointly killed the husband, the lover leaving by the patio door and driving away. Mrs Scrape had gone upstairs to shower the blood off, before staging her dramatic screaming run out into the night. Found guilty at her trial, she was sentenced to sixteen years to life, with the judge commenting: 'My only regret is that the law will not allow me to inflict a more severe punishment.'

It was, I think you will agree, a stunning piece of detection of a remarkable and detailed nature, but for which the wife might well have got away with murder. The case was an interesting mix of detection and forensic work. Yet without the detective's instincts telling him in the first place that something was wrong, the forensic people would never have been called in. This standard of detection is almost unparalleled in recent years, and the purpose of this chapter is to ask why.

I write about murder because I firmly believe that the reporting and collecting of true crime cases serves an important social function. It gives us a kind of running commentary on the state of our nation, and it is of invaluable use to future historians. Thus the foul murder of PC Blakelock, along with a twenty-nine per cent increase in rape alone, serves to illustrate the downward spiral into violence and anarchy that Britain is now experiencing.

But invaluable as the collating of these crimes is, what the true connoisseur of crime really wants to read about is a fine piece of detection like the case quoted. We owe our ideas of the 'great detective' to fiction. It is well known that Conan Doyle was inspired to create Sherlock Holmes because he admired Edgar Allan Poe's character Dupin, who made his first appearance in *The Murders in the Rue Morgue* (1841). The plot revolves around a body found in a locked room, with the murder weapon missing. Dupin solves the problem by deducing that since the killer could not have left by the door – it was locked from the inside – then he must have entered and left by an apparently nailed-shut window. Sure enough, Dupin discovers that the nails are fake, the window being held shut by a concealed spring. It is the most famous of the early detective stories, but by no means the first.

In real life, however, there has in recent years been an absence of the brilliant detective. More and more the detective leans on the forensic laboratory to provide him with clues and answers. A half-eaten apple enables the scientist to describe the suspect in detail. A laundry mark revealed under ultraviolet light leads the detective to the killer. There is an almost *mechanical* aspect about this, as if the detective no longer trusts his brain, his intuition, his deductive thinking processes to solve the case, but looks to scientific instruments to provide answers.

This was not always the case. For over half a century, Scotland Yard's Murder Squad was famed all over the world. Any mysterious murder in the provinces almost automatically ensured a call to the Yard to send one of the big-name murder detectives to solve the case. But times have changed. The various police forces asserted that they had officers quite capable of investigating murders, thank you very much. And in any case, they argued, they knew their own patch and local villains. Any Yard man would find himself in unfamiliar territory, faced by strangers. It might have seemed a persuasive argument, but it simply wasn't true. Let us examine the history of criminal detection.

Professional police officers tend to look with disdain on the private detective, yet the 'private eye' existed in fact long before any policeman. In 1729 Thomas de Veil was appointed magistrate for Westminster and Middlesex. He seemed an unlikely lawman, having twenty-five legitimate children and a score of bastards. An incorrigible womaniser, he was always heavily in debt. He frankly accepted the post because of the opportunity to expand his income by accepting bribes, but discovered that he had a real talent for detection.

In 1739 De Veil transferred his office to a house in Bow Street, where he consolidated his reputation as a detective by solving robberies and murders by the application of simple logic. He became a 'consulting detective' long before Conan Doyle invented Sherlock Holmes.

When he died in 1746, his position and house in Bow Street were taken over by the playwright Henry Fielding, who, despite the success of his play *Jonathan Wild* accepted the post of justice of the peace. Fielding threw himself into his new task with zeal, and founded what was to become known as the Bow Street Runners. He had just half a dozen men, all former parish constables who knew the local thieves by sight. When someone was robbed, they went to Bow Street to report it, together with a description of the robber. The Runners then set off in pursuit of the suspect. It sounds absurd, almost like the Keystone Cops, but it worked. Scores of criminals were arrested, and the crime rate dropped rapidly. The government had given Fielding a £600 grant to fund his experiment, but in the event he spent only half of it. When Fielding died in 1754, his blind brother John took over his work, investigating murders all over the country and putting an end to the careers of hundreds of highwaymen.

The success of the Bow Street Runners had impressed the government, and Sir Robert Peel, the Home Secretary, pushed a Bill through Parliament to establish the first police force. The Metropolitan Police set up its headquarters at Scotland Yard in 1829. The public did not like the idea of 'bobbies', considering them to be an infringement of civil liberties. When the first policeman was murdered on duty in 1830, kicked to death by two drunken Irishmen he was trying to separate in Somers Town, no one came to his aid and the killers escaped. When a policeman was stabbed to death while trying to disperse a crowd at a political meeting in the 1830s, the jury brought in a verdict of 'justifiable homicide'.

But within twenty years the police had won the respect − if not the admiration − of the public. This acceptance was brought about in part by the author Charles Dickens, who was very enthusiastic about the police, often going on patrols with them. He seems to have invented the term 'detective police' in his magazine *Household Words*. He also invented the first Professional detective in fiction, Inspector Bucket in *Bleak House* (1853). But Dickens had not invented the detective *genre*. That distinction belongs to Edgar Allen Poe (1809–49), who had in turn been influenced by the real-life exploits of Eugène François Vidocq (1775–1857).

Vidocq was a French criminal who while in prison offered his services as a police spy and informer. So great was his success as a manhunter that in 1811 he became the first chief of the Sûreté, with a staff of four men, eventually increased to twenty-eight. The members of the newly formed Sûreté received no salary, but were paid a fee for every arrest. Most of Vidocq's agents were ex-criminals like himself, but Vidocq quickly established the Sûreté as the premier crime office in Paris, complete with a card-index system with descriptions of criminals. He also took plaster impressions of feet marks.

Vidocq was a remarkable character, proving the truth of the old adage 'Set a thief to catch a thief'. A master of disguise, he became a close friend of the writer Balzac, who based the character of Vautrin in *Père Goriot* on him. In 1827 Vidocq was forced to resign from the Sûreté, following allegations that he had engineered the robberies he was investigating. He was reinstated in 1832 but was never really trusted again, and resigned in November 1832. He set up the first modern detective agency, Le Bureau des Renseignements, but was harassed by the authorities. He published his *Memoires*, which captured the European imagination and established him as being the 'greatest living detective'.

Poe wrote his first detective stories before the Detective Office was established at Scotland Yard in 1842 – but he had read Vidocq. *The Murders in the Rue Morgue* (1841) appeared before Dickens had invented the term 'detective officer'. In the third of his Dupin stories, *The Purloined Letter* (1844), the missing letter is hidden in full view of searching police officers, in so obvious a place that the officers cannot see it. Dupin was a wonderful creation, the prototype for Sherlock Holmes, who was to follow him – Conan Doyle had in turn been influenced by Poe – and Poe had created him in the USA, a country lacking real police or detective forces.

Yet America was not lacking in enterprise. Oddly enough, the first great detectives were American. Jacob Hays (1772–1850) was High Constable of New York from 1801 until his death in 1850. With only six deputies, 'Old Hays' controlled New York with an iron grip. He knew his city intimately – and its villains. He tracked them down through the warren of slums. His fame was to spread around the world.

In 1820 he suspected a boarding-house keeper of the murder of a sailor. He forced the suspect to view the corpse, asking him: 'Have you seen this man before?' The suspect answered like a rabbit hypnotised by a stoat. 'Yes, Mr Hays,' he said. 'I murdered him.' In 1831 Hays solved the robbery of the City Bank of $1,200,000 by trailing a suspect as far as Philadelphia. Hays boasted that he knew every rogue in his city.

It is interesting to speculate what might have happened had the Jack the Ripper murders occurred in his city. Certainly it is evident that the London police did not know all *their* rogues. From 6 August 1888 to the end of the year, the Whitechapel area of London was terrorised by the unknown killer, who butchered at least five women. So badly bungled was the investigation that the Commissioner of the Metropolitan Police, Sir Charles Warren, was forced to resign. There were cheers in Parliament when this was announced.

Another great detective was Allan Pinkerton, an immigrant from Glasgow who fled to America to avoid arrest – he had been involved in radical political activities. He arrived in America in 1842, aged twenty-three, and was the first detective officer in the Chicago police force, before resigning in 1850 to found his own private detective agency, the famed Pinkertons, which was to have offices in every major US city. His logo, the wide-open eye with the motto 'We Never Sleep', gave rise to the expression 'private eye'.

Pinkerton was noted for his remarkable memory for faces. When bandits started robbing trains carrying money, Pinkerton and his men were hired to guard them. Often he would track outlaws as far as Canada to arrest them. What really made his reputation as a manhunter was his smashing of the Reno gang, probably America's first group of organised criminals.

The five Reno brothers, Frank, John, Simeon, Clinton and William, were the sons of a farmer from Seymour,

Indiana. They served in the army in the Civil War, where they became familiar with the use of firearms to achieve short-term ends. They invented the trade of train robbing; other outlaws like Jesse James and Cole Younger had robbed banks. The first train robbed by the Reno gang was on the Ohio and Mississippi railroad. They got away with $10,000.

The Pinkerton agency was asked to take on the case. Although the raiders had worn masks, it was fairly obvious that they were the Reno brothers. The problem was that they had made their base in the town of Seymour, which had become virtually an armed garrison run by outlaws.

Allan Pinkerton now displayed his usual cunning. Within days a photographic salon opened up for business in Seymour, and the Reno brothers were keen to try out this new-fangled invention. They happily posed for a group photograph – just as Pinkerton had intended. The man operating the salon was one of his agents, a man called Dick Winscott. The photograph was circulated to other law agencies in case sheriffs around the country could identify the brothers for crimes committed in their areas. This was possibly a historic 'first' in the history of crime fighting. The brothers were identified from the photograph as being the men who had robbed a bank in Missouri.

One day a train pulled into the station at Seymour. Dick Winscott was on the platform, talking to John Reno. Pinkerton and his men, plus a sheriff from Missouri, left the train and grabbed John Reno, bundling him into the train and abducting him. He was sentenced to twenty-five years in jail in Missouri. The remaining brothers were furious.

The gang was now led by Frank Reno, and they reacted by robbing the treasury at Harrison County, Iowa, getting away with $14,000. Pinkerton tracked them down to a house in Council Bluffs and arrested them, locking them in the local jail for the night. But when the sheriff arrived at the jail next morning he found they had escaped from the flimsy structures, leaving behind a chalked message on a cell wall: 'April Fool'. It was 1 April 1868.

Pinkerton had to catch them all over again. He now laid a cunning trap, circulating rumours that a train would be pulling into Seymour carrying $100,000 in gold. The Renos duly stopped the train and broke open the baggage car, only to be met with a volley of shots from a Pinkerton posse hiding inside. Three of the gang were captured, and the rest met with increasing hostility from the honest townsfolk in Seymour. When the remaining Reno brothers found themselves again in jail, this time in New Albany, a gang of vigilantes broke in, overpowered the sheriff, and dragged the prisoners out of their cells, hanging Frank, Simeon and William without ceremony.

Pinkerton had less success in his attempts to smash the James gang, led by brothers Jesse and Frank. They too had been blooded in the Civil War. They robbed banks with seeming impunity and when Pinkerton managed to infiltrate one of his agents into the gang, the man was detected and murdered.

When Pinkerton received a tip-off that Jesse James was visiting his mother, his agents surrounded her house and tossed in a 'smoke-bomb', which killed Jesse's half-brother, aged eight, and blew off his mother's arm. It served to generate sympathy for the James brothers, and hostility towards the Pinkertons, who were savagely criticised for their brutality. Jesse James was so angry that he tracked Allan Pinkerton to Chicago and hung around for four months, hoping to catch him alone so that he could kill him, but without success.

Jesse James was finally shot in the back by a member of his gang, Bob Ford, for the reward money, and died aged thirty-four, a folk hero. Frank benefited from this sympathy and was acquitted of charges he faced, although patently guilty. He died an old man in 1915.

Allan Pinkerton went from strength to strength, defeating an attempt to assassinate President Lincoln in 1861. The Pinkertons were detested in some quarters in the United States because of their involvement in strike-breaking, when they used heavy-handed tactics. Allan Pinkerton died two years after Jesse James, aged sixty-five, but sons and grandsons continued to operate the agency, which survives and flourishes.

Indirectly the Pinkertons were responsible for the arrest of one of the worst mass murderers in American history. Allan Pinkerton's son William, now head of the agency, had effected the arrest of Marion Hedgepeth, a train robber from Colorado noted for being a very handsome man. Hedgepeth was jailed for twenty-five years at hard labour. After two years in prison he got a new cell mate, a mild-looking man with faded blue eyes who introduced himself as Mr Holmes. He was a druggist with winning ways. He asked Hedgepeth if he could recommend a good – but crooked – lawyer, explaining that he had a scheme to swindle an insurance company of $10,000. He would insure the life of a friend, and then have his friend meet with a fatal accident. Holmes told Hedgepeth the full details and promised him a cut from the insurance money.

Holmes was soon released on bail, and Hedgepeth learned that the 'friend' had indeed been killed in an explosion. When Holmes failed to send him his cut or get in touch, the aggrieved Hedgepeth wrote a letter to the insurance company denouncing the swindle. The Pinkertons were hired to find out if there was any truth in the allegations.

They discovered that Holmes' real name was Herman Webster Mudgett, and further inquiries into his background revealed that he had had a large house built on Chicago's 63rd Street which he called his 'castle'.

During the Chicago Exposition of 1893, Holmes – or Mudgett – had killed over twenty people there. The castle was a strange structure, consisting of hidden doors, secret passages and trap doors leading to chutes. One room was a furnace in which people were burned alive, another was airtight so that deadly gas could be pumped into it. There was acid and quicklime in the basement for the disposal of bodies, and a dissecting table. Mudgett was tried in October 1895, found guilty and sentenced to hang. The remains of some two hundred corpses had been found in the castle, and Mudgett confessed to all the killings and began a detailed confession, citing all the bodies in turn. He had reached number twenty-seven when he was hanged on 7 May 1896.

Meanwhile, the Bow Street Runners had not ceased operating with the founding of the official police in 1829. They survived for a further dozen years, and were replaced in 1842 by the Detective Office, consisting of two inspectors and six sergeants. The first head of the department was Henry Goddard.

He had been a Bow Street Runner and had distinguished himself in 1835 as a sergeant, when he was called to a house in Southampton which had been burgled. The butler said that two men in masks had forced their way into the house and fired a pistol at him, the bullet missing him by inches. Goddard examined the jemmy marks on the window and came to the conclusion that they were inconsistent with a real break-in. It had to be an inside job, and the butler was the chief suspect. He retrieved from the woodwork the bullet which was alleged to have been fired at the butler, and compared it with bullets from the butler's own pistol. They were an exact match, down to a small pimple caused in the moulding process. A gunsmith later testified that the bullets had come from the same mould, and the butler confessed and was convicted. It was a fine piece of detection, and in the course of it, almost incidentally, Goddard had laid the foundations for the science of ballistics.

In 1890 the headquarters of the Metropolitan Police were moved to a new site and called New Scotland Yard. Originally the Yard had been controlled by two commissioners, but in 1856 Parliament ordered that the force should be placed under the command of a single commissioner, responsible to the Home Secretary. From its new headquarters, the Yard was the centre of a vast spider's web controlling 23 police divisions, with some 27,000 officers covering 740 square miles.

The first Yard detective ever sent outside London on a case was Detective Inspector Whicher. It was on the morning of Saturday, 30 June 1860 that little Francis Saville Kent, aged four, was found to be missing from his cot in the family mansion, Road Hill House, ten miles from Bath. The Kent family comprised three girls and two boys, all over fifteen years of age, from Mr Kent's first marriage; by his second wife – who had been his mistress when employed as the family governess – he had two girls and a boy, all aged under five, and she was again pregnant at the time of the murder. The entire family and three servants had been asleep in the house and had heard nothing amiss.

The police were summoned and made a search of the premises, finding the child's body in an outside lavatory. He had been stabbed in the side, and his throat was cut so deeply he had almost been decapitated. There had been other cut-throat murders in the area in previous years, and the father was convinced that his son was the victim of some unknown intruder; the police thought otherwise. There were no signs of a break-in, suggesting that the killer had been one of the household. A blood-stained chemise was found hidden in a boiler flue. However, the blood was of menstrual origin, and it is likely that it belonged to a servant girl who was frightened she might be a suspect and so had hidden it. It turned out to be irrelevant anyway, since the police managed to lose the chemise.

Another item of clothing was found, however. A chest-flannel in the lavatory bowl belonged to the nurse, Elizabeth Gough. She was taken into custody as a suspect but was released for lack of evidence. But while in custody she had remarked that one of Miss Constance's nightdresses was missing . . .

The doctor who had examined the corpse of the little boy remembered that the nightdress worn by sixteen-year-old Constance had seemed suspiciously clean, since she said she had been wearing it for several days.

Two weeks after the murder, Inspector Jonathan Whicher arrived on the scene from the Yard to take over the case. Wilkie Collins, the author, had based his Sergeant Cuff – in *The Moonstone* and earlier articles – on Whicher, having been impressed by him when he was a sergeant in the Detective Department. His skills were such that he gained a reputation as being the 'Prince of Detectives'. This case was to shatter his career.

A few days after his arrival, he arrested Constance Kent for the murder of her half-brother. He had discovered that she had come from school with three nightdresses, but now had only two, and he did not believe her explanation that one had been lost in the wash. Whoever killed the boy must have been covered with blood. If she had done it, Constance would have had to destroy that damning nightdress.

Constance Kent appeared before the local magistrates, who decided the evidence was too flimsy and released her on 27 July. Loyal villagers stood behind Constance, and Whicher was heavily criticised by the press for daring to arrest a tragic young girl. Three months later Elizabeth Gough was again arrested, and despite 'grave suspicion' against her she too was released.

Whicher returned to the Yard with his tail between his legs, his career blighted. It didn't help when in 1861 he again arrested an innocent man for murder. He retired from the force prematurely, but the damage had also stained the Yard's reputation. A year later the Kent family moved to Wales, and Constance was sent to a convent in France. She returned to England in August 1863 and went into a convent at Brighton. Having had a religious conversion during the Easter of 1865, she confessed to the Rev. Arthur Wagner to having murdered her half-brother to 'punish' her stepmother, whom she hated. She appeared at the Salisbury Assizes and pleaded guilty and was sentenced to hang. This was commuted to life imprisonment, and after spending twenty years in Millbank Prison she was released in 1885, dying in 1944.

Her belated confession vindicated Whicher – too late. When the Criminal Investigation Department was founded at Scotland Yard in 1878, it was not Whicher, but one of his protégés, Superintendent Adolphus Williamson, who was chosen to head it. By the turn of the century the Yard had extensive *modus-operandi* files, along with thousands of photographs of known criminals.

There never was, or has been, an official 'Murder Squad', even though its members wear a specially designed tie; simply a team of CID officers at the Yard who investigated all serious crime. It was founded in 1907 by the Home Office, who decided that these very experienced officers should be available to assist local forces in county areas. (This was long before the formation of regional crime squads.) Even then the Home Office predicted that the Yard men would probably be met with 'great jealousy and very little help' from local policemen. Sadly, this turned out to be true in many cases. And yet in its seventy-four years, the squad has a ninety per cent clear-up record, which is pretty good by any standards.

The first detective officers from the central office of the CID at the Yard were soon in demand in the provinces to help solve murders, and they were soon dubbed the 'Murder Squad' by the press. Its first chief was Detective Superintendent Frank Froest – his photograph still hangs at the Yard. This elite squad quickly captured the public imagination, and its officers, men like Edward Greeno, Jack Capstick, Fred Cherrill, William Chapman, Reg Spooner, Peter Beveridge and Robert Fabian, became household names. One of Frank Froest's officers was Detective Chief Inspector Walter Dew who achieved fame by arresting Crippen at sea aboard the SS *Montrose*. In 1913 the first detective training school was opened.

The first great Yard detective was Frederick Porter Wensley. He joined the Metropolitan Police in 1888 and was appointed to the CID in 1895, retiring in July 1929 as its Chief Constable. One of his early cases was the arrest of brothers Mark and Morris Reubens in 1909 for the murder of a sailor in a room where one of the prostitutes they controlled worked. Wensley had the bloodstained door produced in evidence at the Old Bailey trial. The brothers were convicted and hanged.

Wensley was also involved in the famous Siege of Sidney Street, while in 1911 he solved the murder of Leon Beron by Steini Morrison – whose details he had remembered from the Convict Register. When he joined the Murder Squad in 1916 (ironically, he did not believe in capital punishment) he had a record of having solved every murder case in which he had been involved.

A good example of his keen deductive powers was illustrated in the case of Emilienne Gerard, a French-woman found dismembered in a sack in Regent Street in November 1917. Also in the sack was a scrap of brown paper on which the words 'Blodie Belgiam' had been scribbled. After identifying the headless torso, Wensley discovered that she had been the mistress of a man called Louis Voisin, who happened to be a butcher by trade. Wensley asked Voisin to write the words 'bloody Belgium' four times on a piece of paper. Each time Voisin spelled the words incorrectly – as they had been on the scrap of paper found with the body. Voisin was duly hanged at Pentonville.

As students of crime know, the importance of the informer cannot be overemphasised. Often the solving of a case depends on a tip-off. Smith, the infamous 'Brides in the Bath' murderer, would probably have gone on killing undetected, but for a letter to the Yard from a suspicious Mrs Crossley, who kept a boarding house in Blackpool.

In 1922 the first women constables were sworn in, twenty of them. That same year someone tried to poison the Commissioner of Police by sending him a box of poisoned chocolates through the post. The Commissioner ate two and collapsed. Only prompt medical attention saved his life. The sender of the chocolates was later committed to Broadmoor.

In 1921 Fred Wensley, by then the head of the Murder Squad, was sent to investigate a murder attempt in Wales. He subsequently arrested solicitor Major Herbert Rowse Armstrong for attempted murder by poisoned chocolates of a fellow solicitor – and also had Armstrong's dead wife exhumed. She too had been poisoned. Armstrong was hanged at Gloucester Prison.

Wensley was also involved in The Crumbles murder case, although he delegated the investigation to Detective Chief Inspector Percy Savage. The latter was soon to arrest Patrick Mahon for the murder of Emily Kaye, whose dismembered body had been thrown from the trains between Waterloo and Richmond, after parts of her had been boiled. The remainder of the body was found at a bungalow known as The Crumbles near Pevensey Bay. This case led to the introduction of the famous 'Murder Bag', after pathologist Bernard Spilsbury complained about the lack of rubber gloves. The Murder Bag contains medical equipment, test-tubes, tweezers and other forensic aids.

It took the Murder Squad just three months to find the killer in the Charing Cross trunk murder of 1927. Although a laundry mark helped solve the case, Detective Chief Inspector George Cornish used his instincts in first identifying the victim as Minnie Bonati, then following the trail which led to John Robinson. Cornish found a vital clue in a waste-paper basket in Robinson's office – a bloodstained match. When Robinson was hanged on 12 August 1927, that matchstick went into the Yard's Black Museum.

In 1929 Detective Chief Inspector John Protheroe was sent to Southampton following a request by the Chief Constable who sent the following telegram to the Yard: 'A case of murder has occurred here. A man has been found shot dead in a room, the door of which was padlocked. The body was found today and has probably been in the room for some eight or nine weeks. Please send an officer down to investigate the matter.' Protheroe found the murderer of Vivian Messiter – he was William Henry Podmore, hiding behind a string of aliases – but not before following a long and involved trail. Podmore was hanged on 22 April 1930, due to the diligence and expertise of a very good detective.

Hans Gross was one of the first 'scientific detectives', and his book *Criminal Investigation* (1907) started a revolution in police work. Soon afterwards the police laboratory in Lyons, France, was founded, as was the school of scientific police in Lausanne, Switzerland, a similar institute in Vienna, and the Institute of Scientific Police in Brussels. England was slow to assimilate the new discoveries, but the first police laboratory in this country was established in Nottingham by Chief Constable Popkess. In 1934, after much agonising, our first national police laboratory was founded at Hendon by Lord Trenchard. The laboratory, divided into five sections – biology, chemistry, photography, documents and firearms – was formally opened by the commissioner. Since then we have not lagged behind so much in the use of new scientific techniques to detect the criminal.

Detective Inspector Leonard Burt found the new laboratory very useful when he took over the investigation into the death of Walter Dinivan, a wealthy retired garage owner battered to death at his villa in Bournemouth on 21 May 1939. The evidence at the scene included a thumb-print from a beer glass, plus saliva from cork-tipped cigarette ends. It was enough to arrest Joseph Williams, sixty-nine, whose saliva and that on the cigarette ends belonged to a blood group found in only three per cent of the population.

Williams was tried at Dorchester in October 1939, and, to police astonishment, the jury acquitted him. It was not until 1951, when Williams died, that a journalist was able to publish the true story; after his acquittal Williams boasted to him: 'I did it. The jury got it wrong. It was me.'

In November 1941, DCI George Hatherill was sent to Buckinghamshire to investigate the murders of two little girls – eight-year-old Doreen Heare and Kathleen Trendle, aged six. Both girls had been stabbed repeatedly in the throat, then left in some woods. Hatherill traced vehicle tyre-marks found near the bodies to an army truck. He subsequently arrested Gunner Harold Hill, who was hanged for the murders in April 1942. It had been a classic and meticulous investigation.

Detective Inspector Fred Cherrill solved London's wartime 'Ripper Murders' when he deduced that the killer of three women within a five-day period was left-handed. After a fourth victim was discovered, DCI Edward Greeno was sent to assist him. When the killer tried unsuccessfully to attack a fifth woman, he was forced to leave his service gasmask behind. Its serial number was quickly traced as belonging to one Gordon Frederick Cummins, aged twenty-eight. The airman was left-handed – he even signed his statement denying the murders with his left hand – but a jury found otherwise and he was duly hanged. Greeno also solved the 'Wigwam' murder of Joan Pearl Wolfe, when he arrested a Canadian-Indian soldier, August Sangret, twenty-eight, who was hanged at Wandsworth Prison in April 1943.

In May 1948, DCI John Capstick went to Lancashire at the request of the Chief Constable to investigate the murder of June Ann Devany, aged three. The baby had been snatched from a hospital cot during the night, to be killed in the hospital grounds by a sex maniac. The killer had left just one fingerprint, which was not on file at the Criminal Records Office at the Yard. Capstick caused consternation when he announced his intention of fingerprinting every man and boy in Blackburn. Thousands of prints later he was able to arrest Peter Griffiths, aged twenty-two and charge him with the murder, for which he was subsequently hanged.

These were the golden years of the Yard's Murder Squad. In 1949 came the John George Haigh case of human vampirism. The year 1946 had already seen the shocking case of sexual psychopath Neville Heath. In 1953 the nation shuddered at the revelations of necrophilia in the Christie case.

In 1953 Detective Superintendent John Ball was sent from the Yard to Halifax, Yorkshire, to help the enquiry into a suspected murder there. Mary Hackett, aged six, had been missing from home for over two weeks. Despite massive searches, she could not be found and had to be presumed dead. Ball arrived on the scene, and within twenty-four hours had arrested the caretaker of the Congregational church near the missing girl's home. The caretaker had been just too helpful and inquisitive. When the crypt of the church was searched, the girl's body was found hidden under a pile of chairs. Found guilty of murder, Albert George Hall was hanged at Leeds in April 1954.

Meanwhile, in the United States, the Federal Bureau of Investigation had been established by Act of Congress in 1908 to be an investigative arm of the Justice Department; but it did not really get into its stride until the appointment of J. Edgar Hoover as Director in 1924. His reign was to last an incredible forty-eight years. It was he who began the FBI's collection of two hundred million photographs, although it was not until 1928 that New York State passed legislation requiring all criminals convicted of felonies to be fingerprinted. Eventually the FBI was to rival, then outstrip, Scotland Yard as the world's leading criminal investigation agency.

By the 1960s the criminal intelligence unit at the Yard, C.II., was operating a 'target criminal' policy, whereby the dossiers of the nation's top one-hundred criminals were kept constantly updated with such information as telephone numbers, mistresses, hobbies, vehicles and favourite pubs, and at random several of these criminals were subjected to round-the-clock surveillance to detect them in the act of planning or committing robberies.

In 1966 the Yard smashed the Richardson gang, and on 7 May 1968 they crushed the Kray empire. But if we have to search for a date to mark the end of Scotland Yard as a national force in the investigation of murder, then it was perhaps the 'Black Panther' case in 1975.

Donald Neilson was a small-time crook from Bradford, Yorkshire. In February 1974 he went on a murder spree, carrying out robberies at sub-post offices. His method was to break in, his face obscured with a sinister black hood, then attempt to force the postmaster at shotgun-point to open the safe. But Neilson showed a predilection for shooting the postmasters even when they offered no resistance. His first victim was Donald Skepper, aged fifty-four, at Harrogate.

He struck again on 6 September 1974, robbing a sub-post office in Accrington, Lancashire, where he blasted forty-four-year-old Derek Astin with his own shotgun. Dying from two shotgun wounds, Mr Astin was still able to fling the intruder down the stairs, but Neilson rolled lithely to his feet and coolly shot again, using a .22 automatic pistol attached to a lanyard around his neck.

Just over a month later he struck again in Langley, Worcestershire shooting the sub-postmaster Sidney Grayland dead with a pistol. Mrs Grayland, pistol-whipped by the gunman, was able to give the police a description of the killer. Police now knew quite a lot about this callous gunman who always wore black and had the agility of a panther. He was in his forties, with dark hair and of medium build. He spoke in monosyllables, in an obvious effort to hide his native accent.

The three murder-robberies were linked by the same MO – two holes bored in the window frames to enable the killer to lift the latch and make entry. With police from three counties involved in the hunt, a reward of £25,000 was on offer for his capture. Without the use of computers, the hunt for the killer was necessarily laborious and time-consuming, relying on officers manually checking a massive card-index system of cross-referencing. And with three separate police forces involved, command and liaison was difficult.

The Black Panther's most ambitious – and ruthless – crime took place on 14 January 1975 when he kidnapped seventeen-year-old heiress Lesley Whittle from her family's home in Highley, Shropshire, during the night. She was wearing only her nightdress. Next morning her father found a ransom demand printed on Dyno tape, stuck to a vase. The ransom demand was for £50,000. The message emphasised: 'If police or tricks – death.' The message also included details of the arrangement for a member of the family to wait by a certain telephone kiosk for further details. Neilson had read about Lesley in a newspaper – presumably he got his kidnap plans from reading a thriller.

The officer initially in charge of this case was DCS Robert Booth, head of West Mercia CID. He did not feel disposed to seek the aid of Scotland Yard. But on 7 March 1975 the missing girl was found dead – sixty feet below ground in a circular concrete shaft leading to sewers. She was naked, hanging from a thirty-foot long wire rope around her neck, her hands tied behind her back. The site of the murder was in Bathpool Park, Kidsgrove, Staffordshire. Since the responsibility had shifted to a different police area, the Chief Constable of Staffordshire called in the Yard's Murder Squad.

Commander John Morrison, with DI Walter Boreham as his assistant, arrived at the scene. Morrison's first act was to confer with DCS Booth. The meeting was acrimonious, with Booth apparently feeling that he should retain control of the inquiry. However, the two Yard men continued their investigation.

The killer had left many clues in the sewer shaft, including a pair of binoculars, a notebook, a sleeping bag and a pair of shoes, size seven. It also helped that, soon after Lesley's kidnapping, a stolen car was found parked at Dudley, near to where a security guard had been fatally wounded by gunshots. He had apparently stumbled across the kidnapper. The car contained a tape recorder with Lesley's voice on the spool; that and other clues linked the post-office killings and the murder of Lesley Whittle as being the work of the same man. The police began the task of trying to track down the items found in the sewer and in the car, and teams of detectives were detailed to find out where each item had been bought.

The binoculars had been bought in Manchester, the sleeping bag in Stafford, some of the clothing in Leeds. The wire had been acquired locally, while the shoes came from a market stall in Leicester. It was a nightmare trying to trace the unknown killer.

What had happened after Lesley's kidnapping and before the involvement of the Yard was to play a crucial role in the ensuing rancour and discord. DCS Booth had encouraged the family to pay the ransom money, the plan being that his team would keep constant surveillance on the handover, then arrest the kidnapper in the act of receiving the money. Lesley's brother Ronald drew £50,000 from the local bank, which DCS Booth carefully marked.

The following day a message arrived from the kidnapper. Ronald was to go to Bathpool Park at midnight, then follow a flashing light. But the kidnapper never showed up because at midnight a police patrol car drove slowly through the park, scaring him off. Booth was furious, convinced that the Staffordshire police were trying to sabotage his case. After that, the trail went cold.

The massive investigation had resulted in 28,000 statements being taken, 60,000 people being interviewed and millions of checks made on driving licence applications to check the handwriting against that found in the notebook. It also took considerable time and money. In the event, Donald Neilson was caught almost by accident.

On 11 December 1975, eleven months after Lesley was kidnapped, two police constables were on patrol in a panda car in Nottinghamshire. They became suspicious of a man walking late at night, carrying a bag. When they stopped him for questioning he produced a shotgun and kidnapped the officers, forcing them to drive him away. Six miles later the officers managed to overpower the man, but not before the gun was discharged, wounding one officer in the hand.

Donald Neilson had finally come to the end of the road. Police found a mass of incriminating evidence in his Bradford home, including spare hoods, weapons, books on the SAS and commandos. Neilson made a full confession and was tried at Oxford in July 1976, pleading not guilty to murder, claiming that his gun had gone off accidentally – at all five murders! The jury did not believe him and he was jailed for life, Mr Justice Mars-Jones telling him: 'In your case life must mean life. If ever you are released from prison, it should only be on account of great age or infirmity.'

The definitive statement about Neilson came from his own defence counsel during his trial. He said of the former soldier who had hunted Mau-Mau in Kenya and EOKA in Cyprus, and who had subsequently waged a one-man war against society: 'He is a jobbing joiner from Bradford. He regards himself as being to crime what Sherlock Holmes was to detection – thorough, painstaking and logical. But whereas Holmes' confidence was well-founded, this man's was not. There was conceit in it. There were also mistakes. He was not an intellectual giant, he was a jobbing joiner, failed. He was a little man with big ideas. That's the mark of Donald Neilson, not a superior criminal who went out to kill, but a burglar who blundered, for all his intelligence and obsession with detail.' (Incidentally, Neilson is now studying for an Open University degree at Wakefield Prison.)

Later, former DCS Booth wrote a bitter attack on police officers which was published in the *Mail on Sunday* on 15 January 1984. Titled: 'Police Blunders Led To Lesley Whittle's Murder', it blamed inter-force rivalries for the tragedy. He accused five senior officers of botching the investigation.

He was particularly scathing about the Yard involvement in the inquiry. Booth claimed that after the case he was forced back into uniform, transferred sixty miles away and ordered not to return home to his wife at night. He also claimed that he was declared *persona non grata* by the Staffordshire police and by Scotland Yard.

It seems after this that the Yard's position as being the elite murder team was over. Individual police forces are too jealous of their own competence ever to consider calling in outsiders. But are they really so competent?

The hunt for the Yorkshire Ripper – from October 1975 to his eventual arrest on 2 January 1981 – is too long a story to be examined here. But readers will be aware that the hunt for the killer of thirteen women was too protracted, and too fraught with blunders. Peter Sutcliffe's name had come up at least fifty times during the investigation. He was interviewed nine times – once while actually wearing the boots of which police had plaster-cast impressions, found near one of the victims. One young detective sent a memo to his chiefs urging them to pull Sutcliffe in for an in-depth interview. He felt instinctively that Sutcliffe was the killer. That memo got lost in the paperwork mountain which had built up. The officer in charge, George Oldfield, confided to newsmen: 'It's personal between him and me.' It was *too* personal. Oldfield was side-tracked by a hoax tape, and he later suffered a breakdown.

Peter Sutcliffe's arrest, it will be remembered, came about by accident when two vice squad officers picked him up in Sheffield for having false number-plates on his car. But nobody will ever forget those TV pictures of Yorkshire police jubilation at Sutcliffe's arrest, as if they had scored a winning goal in the World Cup. And this well before Sutcliffe had appeared in court.

The Ripper case was simply too big for the West Yorkshire police force to handle, but they did not even consider calling in the Yard. They were condemned by public opinion – and by some prestigious journals – for being incompetent, stupid, and guilty of bureaucratic arrogance.

Other, more recent, cases have displayed what at best might be described as poor detection, or at worst just plain bungling. The 'Bambi' case was so badly handled that even the trial judge criticised the police for losing valuable forensic evidence. Jeremy Bamber might well have got away with slaughtering his entire family – father, mother, sister and her twin sons – since police accepted it as a case of murder by Sheila 'Bambi' Cafell, followed by her own suicide, and duly burned all the evidence, including bloodstained carpets. Only the fact that Bamber's girl friend informed on him, a month after the funeral of the massacred family, led to an evil killer being unmasked.

Farmer Graham Backhouse was able to pull the wool over police eyes for long enough, and in the recent 'sleeping beauty' case, where Tessa Howden was found cruelly murdered in her own bed, was it really necessary to grill the father for eleven hours as a prime suspect, when killer Gary Taken had left his fingerprints in Tessa's blood? Not to mention other clues in the murder bedroom, including his sunglasses . . . (The Backhouse case is examined in detail later.)

The evidence presented here would seem to indicate that no individual police force is big enough – or *good* enough – to cope with the new threats to society, the supercriminals of murder, drug-trafficking and terrorism. Inter-force rivalries simply cannot be tolerated – they obstruct the investigation of crime.

It is surely time once again to establish the Murder Squad at Scotland Yard as the *national* murder inquiry team. They have the expertise, the training, that streak of intuitive genius, which is the vital ingredient of any great detective agency.

Despite all the scientific advances, then, the police still sometimes get it wrong. We will be looking at the successes – and failures – of the police in this scientific age in a separate chapter.

3

BLOOD TRACES

Blood is the great bedrock of forensic science, the foundation of murder detection itself. When a body is found, very often death from natural causes can be assumed. But if blood is discovered on the corpse, then the ugly question of murder arises.

Most murders involve the spilling of blood, and from earliest times the written records abound with references to that red substance which pumps through all our veins and arteries. The Bible is full of allusions to blood: the spilling of blood, blood sacrifice and so on. Shakespeare too had his way with blood – blood feuds, ties of blood, blood-lust, blood money – and who can forget Lady Macbeth's obsession with the blood of her victim?

In practical terms, we all have about ten pints of the stuff inside us, accounting for some nine per cent of the average body weight. Inside the envelope of our bodies it is barely noticeable, except when we blush, but when a little is spilled it makes an awful mess. It is very difficult to clean off clothing and fabrics, or to remove completely from floors. It has a habit of hiding in cracks, and many a killer has been trapped by the minute particles of blood left behind at the murder scene, when he was convinced he had removed all incriminating traces.

Anthropologists have found remote societies and tribes who have never recognised the link between the act of sex and the birth of babies. But all societies and tribes at all times have recognised the life-preserving properties of blood. Once that envelope is punctured and enough blood leaks out, death follows inevitably. Small wonder, then, that early scientists tried to find ways of putting the blood *back* into the envelope and so restore life. These first experiments in blood transfusion invariably resulted in the death of the patient, because not enough was known about the properties of blood. It is all red, it all looks alike, yet it is, as we now know, as unique to the individual as a fingerprint.

Blood has always been, and remains, a potent motif in all religions – and in magical practice. It is either drunk, as in Christianity, or sacrificed. Warriors used to drink the blood of their slain enemies to give them strength, and it is not hard to see how the belief came about; since one dies from lack of blood, it is logical to think that one can live again by drinking it.

This is the basic motivation for the acts of a killer like John George Haigh; such killers are, without realising it, acting out an ancient and deep-seated magic ritual. We are carnivores, natural meat-eaters, and cannibalism was once natural practice. In times of famine people ate one another. As we became more civilised, those who clung to ancient habits were labelled 'sick', 'mentally ill' and so on. In reacting with horror against such grisly behaviour, we are reacting against our own heritage. Our rage is that of a Caliban.

This is part of the confession of Haigh, relating what he did to his victims after death. Of the killing of Swan he said: 'When he found himself alone with me that autumn evening, I knocked him out with the leg of a chair. Then I slit his throat open with a penknife. I tried to drink his blood but it wasn't easy. I didn't know yet what was the best way to go about it. I held him over the kitchen sink and tried somehow to gather the red liquid. In the end I managed to drink directly from the wound with a sense of deep satisfaction.'

Of his final victim, Mrs Olive Durand-Deacon, he confessed: 'Then I went out and fetched a drinking glass and made an incision in the side of her neck and collected a glass of blood, which I drank.' Tried at Sussex Assizes in July 1949, the former choirboy was sentenced to be hanged.

We now describe 'vampire killers' as being psychotic, yet the annals of crime are littered with cases of blood-drinkers. The legendary Sawney Beane with his family of eighteen sons and six daughters lived in a cave in East Lothian in the fifteenth century. They preyed on passing travellers, robbing them and then eating the corpses. It was probably a practical way of obtaining nutrition, rather than for any magical reasons. The cave was found to be filled with hanging corpses being cured over smoking fires. The entire Beane family were executed with great sadism in Edinburgh in 1435. Yet even their execution implied a belief in magical powers. The very reason why a murderer was hanged, drawn and quartered – the body being cut into pieces – was precisely so that he could not return as a malevolent ghost to haunt people.

The link between vampirism and black magic is amply demonstrated in the case of Elizabeth of Bathory in 1611. She was a Hungarian countess who slaughtered six hundred young girls for her pleasure. An account of her arrest states: 'On 30 December 1610, the governor of the province accompanied by soldiers raided the castle and arrested everyone in it. They had interrupted an orgy of blood. In the main hall of the castle they found one girl drained of blood and dead, another living girl whose body had been pierced with tiny holes, another who had just been tortured. In the dungeons and cellars they found and liberated a number of other girls, some of whose bodies had already been pierced and "milked". Others intact, plump, well-fed, like well-fed cattle in their stalls. The dead bodies of some fifty more were subsequently exhumed.'

The court records of her trial reveal the various methods she employed to harvest human blood. One was to 'put a terrified naked girl in a narrow iron cage furnished with pointed nails turned inwards, hang it from the ceiling and sit beneath it, enjoying the rain of blood which came down'.

She was tried at Bitce in 1611. King Matthias II of Hungary commuted the death penalty to one of life imprisonment, and ordered her to be walled up in her own castle.

This hunger for human blood was exhibited by both the unknown Jack the Ripper and Haigh. But it is probable that the vampire legend which was firmly believed in the Middle Ages arose out of the practice of burying people alive – and then finding corpses ripped and torn. What happened was that people in catatonic trances were mistakenly thought dead, and buried. When the person in the trance revived in the coffin, not unnaturally they would claw at the lid to try and get out, thus tearing their nails.

Fritz Hartman published a book called *Premature Burial* in 1896 to warn about this, and suggested that everyone ought to be buried with a bottle of chloroform with which to commit suicide should they wake up in a coffin.

In the early 1900s the statistics show that every week a case of premature burial was discovered. There is a monument at St Giles Cripplegate in London to a lady called Constance Whitney. She was buried in a trance state, but when the sexton opened the coffin to steal a ring from her finger the fresh air revived her.

That is an objective theory to account for the vampire legend; the fact remains that we still have our killers who lust for human blood. Peter Kürten, the Monster of Düsseldorf, is a case in point. Born in 1883, he was executed in 1931 for twenty-seven murders. Contemporary newspaper accounts described how he 'gained intense pleasure from receiving the stream of blood that gushed from his victim's wounds into his mouth'. He wrote from prison to the mother of one of his victims, who had reproached him: 'What do you want, madam? I need blood as others need alcohol.'

Bloodstains enter the history of crime detection at an early age. When a blood-spattered corpse was found, and a man nearby seen with his clothing covered in blood, that was proof enough of his guilt. It was a very unscientific – and injudicial – method of proceeding. Many a man was executed for a nosebleed, or because of blood on his clothing for which there was an innocent explanation. William Shaw of Edinburgh was hanged in 1721 after his daughter was found lying in a pool of blood. Unable to speak, when asked if her father was responsible for her condition, she nodded. (The father was known to be on bad terms with his daughter because of her association with a man he despised.) After the execution a suicide note was found in the chimney of her room, in which the girl said she was going to kill herself because she could not marry the man she loved. *It was her father's fault*, she stressed.

The presence of blood in itself could be used constructively by a cunning detective, as the case of the French murderer, Voirbo, demonstrates. In January 1869 a drinking well in Paris was found to be contaminated with human remains – two legs, to be precise. Gustave Macé – later to become head of the Paris detective office – was put in charge of the inquiry. The legs were identified as having belonged to a man who was a friend of a tailor called Pierre Voirbo who lived nearby. Voirbo was questioned and denied the murder, but a search of his room revealed valuables belonging to the murdered man.

Macé wanted a full confession, and he played out a hunch. Certain that Voirbo must have dissected the victim in his room, he examined the tiled floor and noticed what appeared to be dried blood in the crevices around the tiles.

Macé tells us in his autobiography *My First Crime* that he spun Voirbo a dramatic story, telling him that an 'accessory' was going to reveal the name of the murderer. Picking up a carafe of water, he told Voirbo to watch the slight slope in the floor. 'The blood would have run down like this,' he continued, letting the water pour on to the floor. As Voirbo watched, the water coated the tiles, which were removed one by one, clearly showing dried blood on the undersides. Trembling with terror, Voirbo confessed, saying: 'I am guilty. I will tell you everything. But take me away from this accursed place!' Voirbo did not die on the guillotine. In his cell he cut his throat with a razor smuggled in in a loaf of bread, and must have spent some time watching his own blood drain away. . . .

There had been earlier experiments with blood. Sir Christopher Wren invented the first syringe, basically a sharpened quill with a bladder attached, and by 1665 Jean Denys was curing some of his patients in France by injecting them with lamb's blood. But when a patient died, he was forced to stop. In England as early as 1814 Dr James Blundell was experimenting with dogs; draining them of blood and reviving them with injections of blood from another dog. But if he used the blood of any other animal but a dog, the dog died. He began experimenting with humans. Some survived, some died. He could not explain why.

The answer came in 1875 when German scientist Leonard Landois discovered that there were several *types* of human blood. It was left to Karl Landsteiner, an assistant professor in Vienna, to carry out the conclusive tests, which he did in 1900. He separated the colourless serum from the red blood cells in a centrifuge, then found that by adding red blood cells from different people to the serum, different reactions followed. In some cases the serum seemed to attract the red blood cells like a magnet, but others it repelled, forming a porridge-like mixture. One lot of cells agglutinated – or clumped together – others didn't. Landsteiner realised that there was something in the serum which reacted against certain blood cells, and he called this factor 'agglutinin' and the factors they disliked he termed 'agglutinogens'.

With two distinct reactions, it was easy to label the blood types A and B; but it wasn't that easy in practice, and he had to assume that blood came in three types, A, B and C. This was because he found a third type which didn't react like either A or B, but showed characteristics of both. Later C became known as O. Two years later one of his assistants discovered yet another type of serum which did not agglutinate with either A or B and was 'typeless'. This was labelled AB.

This steady scientific progress must have been known to Conan Doyle, who had after all qualified as a doctor. In *A Study In Scarlet* (1886) he has Watson approach Holmes in the laboratory at Bart's, with Holmes introducing himself by exclaiming: 'I've found it! I've found it!' What he had found was an infallible test for bloodstains. The problem was that no such test existed. It was not until 1901 that another German doctor, Paul Uhlenhuth, discovered how to distinguish between animal and human blood. He had developed the precipitin test. However, the Belgian Jules Bordet had founded the science of serology – the study of blood fluids – and had done the groundwork for Uhlenhuth's discovery. Rather unfairly, the test became known as the Bordet test, and Uhlenhuth had to wait until 1930 before receiving a Nobel Prize for his work.

By 1902 a French murderer had been sent to the

guillotine by the use of the Bordet test. He claimed blood on his clothing came from skinning a rabbit; the test showed the blood was of human origin.

The first 'great' case with which guilt was proved with the test was that of Ludwig Tessnow, a German murderer who killed two small girls on 9 September 1898 near Osnabrück. He had dismembered and mutilated the bodies. He killed again on Sunday, 1 July 1901, in another village, this time murdering two small boys. Witnesses had seen him in the area with suspicious stains on his overalls. When questioned he claimed that the marks came from woodstain he had been using. The examining magistrate sent for Paul Uhlenhuth, who examined the stains carefully. It took him four days to examine over one hundred stains. The overalls were indeed covered with woodstain, he concluded – but he had also found seventeen stains of human blood. Tessnow was convicted and sentenced to execution as a result.

In England, scientists had begun using a substance called benzidine. Developed around 1900, it turned blue in the presence of blood. (Later found to be a carcinogenic, it was replaced by the Kastle-Meyer test, which uses a solution of phenolphthalein which turns pink in contact with the minutest trace of blood.

Dr William Willcox was the Home Office expert on bloodstains at the beginning of this century. He gave evidence at the Crippen trial. He was also involved in the first British murder case in which the identification of blood played a vital and convicting role. The murder took place in Slough in 1910. Seventy-year-old Isabella Wilson was discovered in the back room of her second-hand shop in the High Street. She had been severely beaten and suffocated. The motive was robbery, and William Broome, aged twenty-five, was the chief suspect. He had moved away from Slough, but on the day of the murder-robbery he had been seen by several witnesses in the town. He was tracked down to Harlesden and taken in for questioning. He said he had been in London all that day, and had been nowhere near Slough. The dead woman had managed to scratch his face in the struggle, and Dr Willcox found human blood on his boots and under the dead woman's fingernails. Broome was convicted and hanged.

In 1915 Dr Leone Lattes was the first to establish the group of an *old* bloodstain – in his case three months old. In 1922 he published *The Individuality of Blood*, which established him as the leading serologist. By now it was known that 40 per cent of people are group A, 40 per cent group O, 15 per cent group B, and 5 per cent group AB.

Fritz Schiff, a Berlin serologist, was dissatisfied with the Lattes test. In time all groups lose their antibodies and can easily be mistaken for one another. He decided to try adding fresh serum to the cells of old bloodstains to see if they attracted. They did, but Schiff was unable to measure the exact amount. This was achieved by Franz Josef Holzer, who in 1931 demonstrated his new test at a murder trial and gained a conviction as a result.

But the problem remained that if both killer and victim were of the same blood group, there was no way to tell them apart. Progress came slowly but surely. It was found that group A is made up of two different strengths, for example, and could be labelled A1 and A2. Then in the mid-twenties Landsteiner discovered another blood-group system as a result of injecting rabbits with human blood. This produced M and N groups; a person could be either M or N, or a combination of the two, MN. Further experiments on rhesus monkeys in 1940 by Landsteiner led to the discovery of the 'rhesus factor'.

Discoveries followed quickly, as more scientists began to realise the importance of this work. In 1946 the Kell factor was found, followed by the Lewis, Kidd, Duffy

and Diego factors – named after the men who discovered them – between 1946, and 1955. In 1949 two
British scientists observed that the nuclei in cells of
female tissue usually contain a distinctive structure
which is rare in males. It was called the Barr body, after
one of its discoverers, and is most noticeable in white
blood cells. The presence of this 'female only' structure
is accounted for by the difference in chromosomes
between males and females. It was a useful discovery.

It now meant that when blood was found at a crime
scene, scientists could first tell if it was blood by the
Kastle-Meyer test. Then by using the precipitin test they
could tell if it was animal or human blood. And finally,
they could tell the blood group and the sex of the victim.

Another useful aid had been the work on blood-spots
by the French criminologist Lacassagne, who plotted
the correlation between blood-spots and the position of
the victim. Blood dropped vertically from a stationary
object makes a circular spot with crenellated edges. The
higher the distance between the victim and the floor,
the more drawn-out the crenellations. If the blood falls
from a moving object, it leaves spots like exclamation
marks, indicating the direction of travel, and so on. It
made it possible to develop a blood-spot chart, so that
detectives at the scene of a bloody murder could recon-
struct what had happened. This was to be of crucial
importance in the Backhouse case, as we shall see.

A new kind of 'blood fingerprint' system was emerging, all of which culminated in the discovery in 1984
of DNA fingerprinting. But a lot was to happen before
that.

In Britain the first major case solved by forensic serology occurred in 1934. A girl called Helen Priestley was
murdered in Aberdeen on 20 April 1934, and her body
stuffed in the recess under the stairs of a building. The
girl's knickers were missing, and blood around the
vaginal area suggested a sexual attack. But there was

83

no sperm present, which indicated the injuries had been caused deliberately as a cover for the real motive. The police suspicions centred on Jeannie Donald, who lived next to the stairwell where the body had been found. She was known to have a violent temper, and had recently quarrelled with the Priestley family. When her flat was searched blood of the same group as Helen's – group 0 – was found. Donald was subsequently convicted. Her death sentence was commuted to life imprisonment, of which she served ten years. Professor Sydney Smith was the expert witness in this case.

In 1939 it was the turn of the formidable Bernard Spilsbury. He was involved in the case of the murdered Walter Dinivan, already mentioned, where the clues at the scene were prints on a beer glass and cigarette ends. The prints on the glass belonged to Joseph Williams, and from the saliva in the cigarette ends it was possible to determine the blood group – also Williams's. It all seemed rather a waste of time and effort when Williams was acquitted – only to confess to a newspaper reporter in a fit of pique that evening that he had indeed killed Walter Dinivan.

Serology has never been a headline-grabbing science, unlike other branches which can convict a man on a hair, from traces of glass particles, fibres, ballast from a safe or traces of explosives on his hands. What has happened is that forensic science has become 'atomised' over the years. Originally, almost every aspect of a murder investigation was the province of the pathologist: he did the lot, from establishing time and cause of death to microscopic examination of substances. But with each new discovery the greater part of forensic science became unrelated to medicine. The examination of hairs, fibres, bullets, toxins, bloodstains – all these became split up among many different specialists.

The Americans call that part of forensics which is not related to medicine 'criminalistics'. That in itself is divided up among specialists, but even forensic medicine split to produce pathologists, dental experts, psychiatrists, anthropologists and so on. Serologists and toxicologists both belong in the laboratory and remain closer to medicine than the other sciences. There is no connection between medicine and ballistics, for example.

In criminal cases the job of the pathologist, serologist and toxicologist is to confirm whether certain suspected substances are present in the evidence or not. Was the victim poisoned? Had the victim received any drugs or medication prior to death?

In criminalistics, the work consists of comparing one thing to another. Does the bullet recovered from the victim come from that gun? Does the fibre found on the victim come from the suspect's clothing? Did that knife inflict this wound?

Serology has now almost completely defined blood grouping. An individual can be placed with certainty in one of 288 different groupings, and since eighty per cent of the population are 'secretors' – their blood cells are present in body fluids like semen and saliva – it is possible to determine the blood group of a perpetrator simply by examining these fluids.

Although serology has never captured the public imagination, or indeed been as successful in solving violent crime as fingerprinting, it still has its uses. One case was solved because of *lack* of bloodstains.

On 29 July 1950 the body of forty-three-year-old Catherine McCluskey was found lying in the middle of a road in south Glasgow. The victim appeared to have been knocked down by a lorry, and a trail of blood along the road suggested that she had been dragged by the vehicle for a distance. The body was examined by the pathologist, Professor Andrew Alison, who concluded that the injuries were not consistent with the victim having been knocked down. There were no leg injuries. It looked very much as if she had been run over while lying on the ground – which made it murder.

The victim was an attractive blonde with many boy-friends and two illegitimate children. One boyfriend was a policeman, James Ronald Robertson. He had confided to a colleague that he was meeting a blonde on the night of the killing. He had told another officer that although on night duty, he had taken time off to run a friend home in his car.

Robertson was arrested and his home was searched. Much stolen property was found, and it was discovered that his black Austin car was also stolen. Under questioning Robertson admitted having met the victim on the night of her murder. He said they had quarrelled and she got out of the car to walk home. He reversed to offer her a lift, but accidentally knocked her down. He tried to drag her out from under the car, but her clothing was caught in the prop-shaft. So he moved the car backwards and forwards until she was free.

It was a nice convincing story, but there were several objections to its being the truth. The principal one was that the victim had no injuries to her legs, not a smear of blood – she couldn't have been knocked down. And the prop-shaft was boxed in and couldn't have caught her clothing.

Professor John Glaister had no doubt that it was a case of deliberate murder. There was blood on a cosh found on Robertson when he was arrested, but not enough to test. But there was no blood on Robertson's trousers, and there should have been if he had indeed attempted to drag the body out from under his car. Detectives established that Robertson had first coshed the woman unconscious, and then deliberately driven his car over her to kill her. His motive for murder was to avoid paying maintenance for a child he had fathered by her. Robertson was duly hanged. He was convicted because there was no blood on his trousers . . .

The murder of the Laitner family in Sheffield on 23 October 1983 has already been discussed in chapter one, but it is worth pointing out the value of the scientific evidence gathered against Arthur Hutchinson. The blood on the bed of the sole survivor interested detectives: she hadn't been cut, so the blood must have come from the killer. It was sent to Mr Alfred Faragher, Principal Scientific Officer at the forensic science laboratory at Wetherby. As soon as he tested it and discovered it belonged to a very rare blood group found in only one in fifty thousand of the population, it rang a bell with him. Just a month earlier he had been sent a similar sample for analysis. It had come from a petty thief called Arthur Hutchinson who had escaped from a police station. The scientist compared the two samples and was able to give detectives the *name* of the killer long before the fingerprints had been checked out. Once Hutchinson was captured, of course, his teeth could be compared with the bite-marks found in cheese in the Laitner kitchen.

This quick identification of Hutchinson was made possible by the new discoveries constantly being made in blood typing. Although it was still impossible to prove that blood had come from a particular individual, the new discoveries included variations in red blood cells – 'polymorphisms' – and haemoglobin variations. Mr Faragher had decided to concentrate on six factors in the sample sent to him, for which the statistical frequency in the population were as low as 7.6 per cent, rising to 32 per cent.

Graham Backhouse was a farmer who devised an extremely cunning murder plot. He was in financial trouble, his Widden Hall farm near the village of Horton, some ten miles from Bristol, having run him up a £70,000 overdraft at the bank. On 30 March 1984 one of his herdsmen found a sheep's head impaled on a fence, with a note attached warning: 'You Next'.

Backhouse went to the police station to complain, saying it was just the latest incident in a hate campaign against him which included threatening phone calls and poison-pen letters.

Backhouse had set the scene. On the morning of 9 April Backhouse asked his wife to drive into town to pick up some medicine for the livestock. She took his Volvo car because her own wouldn't start. When she turned the ignition key there was a loud explosion. A home-made bomb under the driver's seat had exploded, ripping off half of Margaret Backhouse's thigh and embedding hundreds of fragments of shrapnel in her body. Even so, she was lucky to be alive.

Forensic experts examined the wreckage and discovered that the bomb had been made from a length of steel pipe packed with nitroglycerine and shotgun pellets, wired to the ignition. Luckily, most of the force of the explosion had been deflected downwards by the seat. Shortly after she had been taken to hospital, Backhouse received another threatening letter.

The police naturally took a very serious view of the whole situation. The letter was sent to Birmingham, where Mike Hall, the document examiner at the forensic laboratory there, quickly realised that it would be useless for trying to establish the identity of the writer. Each letter had been gone over forwards and backwards to disguise the hand. Of far more interest to Mike Hall was the 'You Next' note. On the back of it was the impression of a doodle made on a covering sheet.

Backhouse told police that he had no enemies, but then named a neighbour, Colyn Bedale-Taylor, as a likely suspect. He and Backhouse had had a violent row over a right of way, and Mr Bedale-Taylor had been extremely depressed ever since his son died in a car crash two years previously.

For nine days Backhouse was given police protection, which had to be withdrawn when Backhouse made an angry phone call to Detective Chief Inspector Peter Brock, telling him to get his men off his land. Backhouse was in possession of a shotgun, like most farmers, and the alarm on his house was wired to the local police station.

It sounded on the evening of 30 April 1984. Police who rushed to the farm found a scene of carnage. Backhouse was standing covered in blood, with horrific cuts to his face and a deep gash which extended from his left shoulder down across his body. At his feet lay Mr Bedale-Taylor, shot dead with two shotgun cartridges.

Backhouse told the police that the dead man had called for a cup of coffee, but then, after announcing that God had sent him, began accusing Backhouse of being responsible for the death of his son. During an angry exchange he admitted planting the bomb, and then attacked Backhouse with a Stanley knife, cutting him badly. Backhouse turned and fled down the hall, grabbing his shotgun from the stairs and shooting his demented neighbour in self-defence.

It sounded a plausible explanation, given recent events, and when police searched the neighbour's house they found the very length of steel pipe from which the bomb length had been cut. The Stanley knife bore the initials 'BT'. But they had been crudely scratched, and other tools in the man's workshop – he had been a carpenter – were neatly engraved.

Dr Geoff Robinson, the forensic biologist who studied the crime scene, was the first to point out inconsistencies. The drops of blood on the kitchen floor were of the *wrong shape*; they were round, suggesting they had fallen from a man standing motionless. Yet Backhouse said he had been running. . . . And Backhouse had no typical defensive wounds on his hands, nor was there any trail of blood leading down the hall to the shotgun. Backhouse had to be lying.

The forensic pathologist, Dr William Kennard,

agreed. That Stanley knife should have been lying on the floor – not still clutched in the dead man's hands; and most of the blood on the victim's shirt front had come from Backhouse. He had obviously stood over the man, allowing his blood to drip on to him.

Geoff Robinson now examined the envelope which had contained the first threatening letter sent to Backhouse. He had hoped to be able to test the saliva on the gummed flap for blood grouping. What he did find was a tiny wool fibre which had come from Backhouse's sweater. He had sent the letter to himself. . . . The farmhouse was searched and in a drawer detectives discovered a notebook. They found the page which still bore the original doodle found impressed on the 'You Next' note.

Now it all fell into place. Backhouse had lured Bedale-Taylor to his house on some pretext, with the express intention of murdering him to cover up his own botched murder attempt on his wife. Only a month before the car-bombing, he had increased the insurance on his wife's life from £50,000 to £100,000. And to ensure that the police would be fooled, he had inflicted those cuts on himself with a stoical fanaticism. It had taken the combined efforts of a pathologist, a biologist, a document examiner and a bomb expert to establish Backhouse's guilt. On 18 February 1985 Graham Backhouse was sentenced to two terms of life imprisonment.

Perhaps the most useful invention of the post-war period had been the 'absorption elution' test devised by Stuart S. Kind of the forensic science laboratory at Harrogate. It is now standard in all labs, having replaced the old Holzer test. Basically, it is a very simple method of testing old bloodstains. Blood cells contain antigens and antibodies. If the old bloodstain is diluted to liquid form and then placed in two containers, by adding A group cells to one sample and B group cells to the other, the group can be established by seeing which sample 'clumps'. (This is a greatly simplified explanation of a very complicated scientific process.) But it was Kind's test which was used to determine the ABO characteristics of the bloodstains found in Miss Laitner's bed, for example.

Then in 1984 the ultimate goal of the serologist was achieved. It proved to be the biggest single advance in forensic science since the adoption of fingerprinting in 1901.

As early as 1911 it was known that human beings, individually, are made up of about a hundred million million cells, each comprising a protein surrounding a nucleus, the nucleus consisting of a substance called nucleic acid. In 1911 the biochemist P. Levene discovered that there are two types of nucleic acid, RNA and DNA, according to whether they contain ribose or deoxyribose. When the cell nucleus is stained with a dye it displays the chromosomes, thread-like objects. Every cell has 46 chromosomes: 23 from the father's sperm and 23 from the mother's egg, and the chromosomes are made up of DNA . . .

By the 1940s it was realised that DNA was the magic building block of life, the substance which prints out the secret code which determines if we are to be born with red hair or black, brown eyes or blue – in fact the very blueprint for everything we are to become. If you are left-handed it is because your DNA code dictated that you should be so. The instructions are very precise.

But exactly how does DNA issue its instructions? Scientists knew it had to be a code, similar to a series of dots and dashes like Morse. Every code is unique to every individual – rather like the bar code seen on groceries – which is why no two individuals are exactly alike, save for identical twins, who share the same DNA code. Since the code determines the characteristics of a human being, in a sense we are all 'programmed' before birth. In the cloistered world of the scientists the race was on to crack the code.

Crick and Watson solved the problem in the early 1950s, winning the Nobel Prize in the process. They demonstrated that DNA consists of a structure resembling two interlocking spirals – the double helix. This is made up of four types of chemicals in different permutations: adenine, guanine, cytosine and thymine – these are the magic ingredients. Any permutation of these – for example GGGTTCACA – determines the characteristics of any human being, just as the letters of the alphabet determine a word or sentence. Since all of Shakespeare's work is composed of variations of just twenty-six letters, it is not unreasonable to imagine a human being made up from a combination of four different chemicals.

It was an interesting discovery without much practical application that the code comes in short bursts or sequences rather like Morse, with no two people receiving exactly the same message. It is important to remember that long sections of the DNA code *must* be the same for every human being, since we all have two arms, one head and so on. But certain stretches of the three-foot-long DNA code show dramatic differences (except in the case of identical twins) and these are called the 'hypervariable regions' and consist of short bursts of code repeated over and over again.

And so in September 1984 Dr Alec Jeffreys was in his laboratory at Leicester University, working on all the pioneering discoveries which had gone before. He was to devise a completely new method of 'typing' an individual: the genetic fingerprint, as it has become popularly known. Dr Jeffreys was studying the gene coding for myoglobin proteins, which carry oxygen to the muscles. In the course of this work he discovered a building block made up of repeated sequences within the DNA, each ten or fifteen sections long. Like any curious scientist he was keen to 'read' the secret message.

He isolated two of these blocks by cloning, then made them radioactive with an isotope so that he could 'track' them. When he introduced his treated blocks to other materials – like human blood – he was able to follow the progress of the blocks as they homed in on similar blocks to themselves, remembering that like attracts like.

Basically what Dr Jeffreys did was to isolate the DNA from the proteins which surround the nucleus. Then he chopped the DNA material into tiny pieces, using an enzyme as a catalyst, and sorted the chopped-up material into various sizes on to a base made of gel electrophoresis. This produced bands of material, which he stuck to a nylon membrane, before adding his radioactive probes. He placed a radio-sensitive film over the membrane, and it registered marks where each probe had combined specifically with the highly variable DNA. This produced an 'autograph' – unique for every individual on earth.

By having the probes in gel form imprinted on X-ray film, Dr Jeffreys was able to produce long columns of dark and light patches, each of different lengths and thicknesses, and different spaces apart. It was the human bar code. With identical twins, a blood sample from each displayed as a 'genetic fingerprint' and placed side by side will show the light and dark patches in exactly matching positions. With other individuals – even siblings – no two columns or bands will be the same. The odds against any two people in the world having matching patterns is astronomical. In a letter to the author Dr Jeffreys explains: 'We have developed two independent multi-locus probes, and on good quality DNA using both probes, we estimate the chance that two unrelated people have the same pattern at less than

1 part in a 1,000,000,000,000,000,000,000,000,000,
000.'

The first use made of Dr Jeffreys' discovery was in
paternity cases, where his test could prove beyond
doubt that a particular man or woman was the parent
of a particular child. Dr Jeffreys' process is now patented and operated under licence by ICI.

The police first made use of Dr Jeffreys' technique in
November 1987. In June of that year a burglar broke
into a house in Avonmouth, Bristol, and raped a forty-
five-year-old disabled woman, stealing her jewellery in
the process. Later, a man called Robert Melias was
arrested for burglary, and the rape victim picked him
out from an identity parade. Semen stains from the
woman's clothing were subjected to Dr Jeffreys' 'bar-
code' test and matched exactly with the print of Melias'
blood. He was jailed on 13 November 1987 for rape
and robbery; the DNA fingerprint had secured its first
conviction.

However, the next use police made of it had even
more interesting implications. When the police suspect
in the Enderby murders had his genetic fingerprint
tested at Leicester University – Dr Jeffreys was
requested to carry out the test – the result was that
Jeffreys was able to tell police that the man they had in
custody was not the killer-rapist. The bar code obtained
from his blood samples were in a completely different
order. The suspect had to be released – an innocent
man caught up in a murder hunt.

That hunt had begun in November 1983, when fifteen-year-old Lynda Mann, set out from her home in
Narborough, near Leicester, to visit a friend in the
nearby village of Enderby, taking a short cut through a
footpath known as Black Pad. The following morning
her body was found lying near the path: she had been
strangled and raped. The killer's semen stains were preserved. Police inquiries came to nothing.

Three years later, in July 1986, the killer struck again. This time the victim was Dawn Ashworth, another fifteen-year-old schoolgirl who lived in Enderby. Her body was found less than a mile away from the spot where Lynda Mann had been found. She had been brutally battered and raped. This time a suspect had been arrested, but because of the results of Dr Jeffreys' test, he had to be released.

For the police the result was bad news, since it meant that the inquiry which had been brought to a halt by the arrest of a suspect had to be restarted in the autumn of 1986 from scratch. But the work had not been for nothing: the implication of Dr Jeffreys' revolutionary new technique was that not only could it determine a suspect's guilt, it could also *prove his innocence.*

The senior officer in charge of the Enderby murders inquiry decided to take blood samples from every male in the area for DNA testing, certain that the killer was a local man. Over five thousand blood samples were analysed, but the result was disappointing. The killer was not among them.

Then an indiscreet remark in a Leicester pub revealed that twenty-seven-year-old Colin Pitchfork, of Little Thorpe, had paid a fellow worker in a bakery to act as his 'stand-in' and give a sample in his place. The police computer showed that Pitchfork had a conviction for indecent exposure. He was quickly arrested and a blood sample taken. It was rushed to Dr Jeffreys' lab, where his 'bar code' proved to be identical to that of the DNA samples from the killer-rapist. Pitchfork admitted both murders and on 27 January 1987 he was sentenced at Leicester Crown Court to two life terms and ten years for the rapes. The stand-in got an eighteen-month suspended sentence. Trial judge Mr Justice Otton remarked that if it had not been for genetic fingerprinting, Pitchfork might still be at large. The judge said of the test: 'In this case it not only led to the apprehension of the correct murderer, but also ensured that suspicion was removed from an innocent man.' Colin Pitchfork was truly a killer trapped by science.

The first USA conviction by DNA fingerprint followed soon afterwards. The case began on 9 May 1986 when Nancy Hodge was raped in her apartment in Orlando, Florida. It was the first in a series of similar cases which involved break-ins, rape and robbery. On 22 February 1987 the unknown assailant broke into the home of another twenty-seven-year-old woman and raped her, cutting her with a knife. He left behind two fingerprints.

On 1 March a prowler was reported on Candlestick Street. A patrol car chased a blue car, which crashed. The man driving was twenty-four-year-old Tommie Lee Andrews, who lived just three miles from the scene of the original rape. When put on an identity parade, Andrews was picked out by Nancy Hodge, but since she had only seen him for a few seconds, a clever defence lawyer could shake her testimony. As things stood, Andrews was positively linked with the rape where he left his fingerprints. No other victim could identify him, and when his blood sample was compared with the semen deposited in the victims, it showed a blood group common to thirty per cent of American males.

In August 1987 the prosecution had heard about the Pitchfork case in England and wondered if the new DNA fingerprint could help their case. Lifecodes laboratory in New York were offering the test under licence, and when approached agreed to test the semen stains and the blood of the accused man. They got a perfect match.

On 27 October 1987 Andrews stood trial for the rape of Nancy Hodge. He denied the charge, and she went into the witness box to identify him. Andrew's defence was an alibi: he had been home all that night. The alibi was supported by his girl friend and sister. The prosecution then presented the DNA evidence, stating that there was only one chance in ten billion that Andrews was not the rapist. When challenged by the defence to prove this claim, the prosecutor, lacking expert knowledge, dithered, and the judge declared a mistrial. Meanwhile Andrews was tried for the rape case where he had left fingerprints, was convicted, and sentenced to 22 years. At a retrial of the Nancy Hodge case the prosecutor made sure he had expert witnesses to explain DNA fingerprinting and confirm the accuracy of the statistics quoted. The jury convicted Andrews on the DNA evidence, and he was sentenced to an additional 28 years for rape, 22 years for robbery and 15 years for burglary, giving him a total sentence of over one hundred years.

A series of historic 'firsts' followed, starting with the first English murder conviction with the use of DNA 'by proxy'. On Tuesday 9 February 1988, twenty-two-year-old Helen McCourt vanished in the three hundred yards between the bus stop in the village of Billinge, near St Helen's and her home. All premises on that route were searched, particularly the village pub, the George and Dragon, where Helen spent much of her free time. The landlord, thirty-two-year-old Ian Simms, was questioned, his name having been found in Helen's diary.

Three weeks later Helen's clothing and purse were found on the banks of the River Irwell, near Manchester. Police searched the area, and three miles away found men's clothes dumped on a slag heap. They were heavily bloodstained, and proved to belong to Ian Simms. He denied having murdered the girl, and said his clothing could have been taken and used by the real killer.

Scientists now came up with a bright idea. Helen's body was never found, so they could not take her blood and match it against that on Simm's clothing. But they *could* take the blood samples from her mother and father. Their conclusion was, after testing, that the DNA make-up of the blood on the clothing was 126,000 times more likely to come from an offspring of Mr Williams and Mrs Mary McCourt than from a random member of the population. On Tuesday 14 March 1989, Simms was found guilty of murder and sentenced at Liverpool Crown Court to life imprisonment. All along, Simms had insisted that someone had 'framed' him. But it was the DNA fingerprint which condemned him.

Another first came on 16 June 1989, when for the first time in British legal history a rapist was convicted with the help of 'genetic fingerprint' evidence obtained by comparing samples of hair from his head with semen stains left at the scene of the crime. DNA tests showed that the chances of the hair and semen coming from a different person was 150 million to one, and thirty-five-year-old Lawrence Connors was convicted at St Albans Crown Court for the rape of two elderly women. He was jailed for eighteen years by Mr Justice McKinnon.

Genetic fingerprinting can only improve in technique, especially since agreement has been reached among leading countries about the exact nature of the catalyst enzyme to be used to standardise tests between nations. It is a source of endless speculation to look back over the famous 'unsolved' murders and see which the genetic fingerprint would have solved. It would certainly have proved beyond all doubt exactly who murdered Mary Ashford in Birmingham in the early hours of 27 May 1817. It remains Birmingham's best-known murder precisely because the identity of her killer was never established, although all the clues were there.

Mary Ashford left the Tyburn pub at 1 a.m. arm in arm with Abraham Thornton, a local bricklayer. The couple were observed by other witnesses kissing at 3 a.m. At 6.30 a.m. a farmer found suspicious footprints across a newly ploughed field, those of a woman running, with a man chasing. The footprints ended in a depression where bodies had lain. The soil was discoloured with blood and with the marks of a man's knees. A trail of blood led from that spot to a cess-pit a hundred yards away. In the cess-pit was Mary Ashford. She had been raped and battered.

Thornton was put on trial at Warwick Assizes on 8 August 1917. The jury found him not guilty – much to the disgust of local newspapers, who condemned the verdict as allowing a guilty man to go free. The dead girl's brother William had been studying the law books and discovered that he had the right to 'name' Thornton as the killer and challenge him to mortal combat. Thornton was arrested again and held in custody while the Court of King's Bench decided the matter. The Lord Chief Justice observed that the law had never been repealed and he saw no reason why trial by combat should not take place, William Ashford having indicated that he was willing to fight Thornton to the death. There had been no trial by challenge since 1638, and finally the judges freed Thornton unconditionally.

What the judges and mortal combat could not do, Dr Alec Jeffreys can do. By examining the semen in the murdered girl's body, he could have named the killer.

We have not heard the last of the DNA fingerprint. There have been over sixty successful rape convictions by its use in the USA already, and several murder convictions. The story – and history – of blood is by no means over.

4

POISON: MURDER WITH VENOM

Poisoning is a method of murdering a person without leaving any inconvenient and incriminating clues like bloodstains, knife-wounds, marks of strangulation or crude bludgeoning. With luck, the murder might even be put down to death from natural causes. That, quite simply, is the reason why poisoning was the favourite method of murder for thousands of years: because it was virtually undetectable, its effects indistinguishable from a heart attack or a stroke.

That is, until science had progressed to the point where to use poison was as obvious as using a knife or gun. Then poisoning virtually ceased, until today it accounts for only six per cent of all murders. This is one area where forensic science can be said to have had a positive deterrent effect.

Ancient Rome is the first society on record where poison was used on a large scale, almost indiscriminately, as a matter of policy by the rulers. But we know that the Greeks used poison much earlier, referring to aconite as the 'queen of poisons', for example. And certainly poison was known and widely used in the East, the Arabs and Indians in particular being great practitioners in the deadly uses of venom.

The practice of what we call 'witchcraft' made extensive use of poisons, and may well have been the first 'science' to discover the properties of various vegetable poisons. Witches knew all about herbs and their uses, and were in fact early doctors, treating ailments with their potions, just as witch doctors do in many countries today. The 'medicine-men' of Red Indian tribes knew how to induce trance states by the use of certain drugs, and the Incas chewed coca leaves as a matter of course, which made them happy and tended to induce hallucinations. It was Sigmund Freud who discovered the anaesthetic properties of *Erythroxylon coca* plants, and so gave us cocaine.

In ancient times people were literally surrounded by vegetable poisons – as indeed we are today. Poison grew all around in various plant, leaf or berry form. Aconite comes from monkshood; a virulent poison, it can be absorbed through the skin. Atropine is the drug which comes from deadly nightshade, and is a related substance to hyoscine, which is extracted from henbane. George Henry Lamson used aconite to commit murder in 1881; Hawley Harvey Crippen chose hyoscine in 1910. Both men were doctors.

Bryony has attractive berries which can kill, as does the thorn apple. Among poisonous funguses are fly agaric and the death cap mushroom. And plants give us abundant poisons. Water hemlock produces cicutoxin, which can cause death within half an hour. Meadow saffron produces colchicine in its seeds. Several varieties of fruit stones produce cyanide, including plum, cherry and apple pips; it can also be distilled from laurel leaves. Coniine, used to poison Socrates, also comes from water hemlock. Curare, the exotic poison used to tip arrows by South American Indians, is extracted from plants of the genus *Chondrodenron* and paralyses the central nervous system. It is used during hospital operations to keep the patient absolutely still. Digitalis comes from the foxglove, mescaline from the cactus peyote, and ricin – the poison used to kill Georgi Markov (see p. 126) – comes from caster-oil seeds. Even the green parts on potatoes are poisonous, and ergot, a fungus which grows on cereals, causes madness and death. Strychnine, favoured by so many poisoners, is extracted from the nux vomica and other plants.

The metallic poisons, extracted from ores, consist of another great favourite, arsenic, used for centuries as a potion to improve the complexion, antimony, beryllium and thallium – used by Graham Young in 1971 to poison over seventy of his workmates, killing two of them, before his own vanity led to his detection.

Poison first played an important role in witchcraft rites. Witches used to make an ointment from henbane and thorn apples which produced hallucinations coupled with a warm tingling feeling. Witches would coat a stick with the substance and then 'ride' it, the effect on sensitive places giving them a feeling of flying – hence the 'witches on a broomstick' legend.

In ancient Rome poison was used for far more sinister purposes than merely to get 'high'. It became a tool of political expediency, as one rival murdered another, like so many gangsters fighting for supremacy. Tacitus tells us of a woman called Locusta, a professional poisoner of great skill, who had been condemned to death. Her talents were too valuable to lose, so she was reprieved to work for wealthy clients. It was she who prepared the poison to kill the emperor Claudius. A dish of mushrooms was soused in her concoction, but when it took too long to work – Claudius simply complaining of a stomach ache – his physician persuaded him to vomit, tickling his throat with a poisoned feather. Claudius promptly died. Nero, his successor, was so amused by this that forever afterwards he referred to mushrooms as 'a dish fit for the gods'. (Claudius had been proclaimed a god.)

Nero made use of Locusta to poison Claudius's fourteen-year-old son Britannicus. When the boy fell dead at a feast, Nero simply shook his head sadly, remarking that the boy was a victim to epilepsy. The guests continued eating without pause. But emperors like Nero and Caligula were only following in the footsteps of Livia (Julia Drusilla), who poisoned everybody who stood in the way of her offspring's succession.

Rome and Venice in the sixteenth century continued the tradition, poisoning having become a favourite method of disposing of rivals and enemies. Although the Borgias are credited with being masters of the art – Lucrezia Borgia has gone down in history as the 'Queen of Poison' – there is little substantiating evidence. Cesare Borgia certainly killed many men, but he preferred the knife or garotte, and almost died of arsenical poisoning himself. However, many fortune-tellers also specialised in selling poisons to wealthy women who wanted either an abortion or to dispose of a husband. Thus the element of witchcraft continued.

What is certain is that wealthy men in the Middle Ages paid fortunes for supposed 'antidotes' against poison, such as bezoar stones – simply animal gall stones – or cups made from unicorn horn from which they could drink without fear. They must have been an extremely credulous lot, since the supply of unicorn horn never seemed to dry up. But then, Mithridates, King of Pontus (120–63 BC) took a daily concoction containing seventy-two separate poisons in order to build up a resistance to them and so protect himself against any poisoning attempt. Legend has it he was so successful that when in danger of capture by the Romans, he found it impossible to poison himself.

Stories about the prolific use of poison in Italy alarmed the English aristocracy, and something of a 'poison scare' began. The Poisoning Act of 1531 was passed in the reign of Henry VIII for the specific purpose of ensuring that a cook named Rose, employed in the household of the Bishop of Rochester and suspected of poisoning the porridge, should be boiled alive instead of enjoying the luxury of being hanged. The boiling took place in Smithfield. That same year saw a servant girl in King's Lynn boiled to death for poisoning her mistress. Queen Elizabeth had her physician castrated and disembowelled on the mere suspicion that he was plotting to poison her. The great and good did not feel safe with poison about; it was a great equaliser, and a mere scullery maid could get even with a Queen.

In the seventeenth century, when a brothel-keeper called Mother Turner approached the apothecary James Franklin in London and requested an undetectable poison, it led to a scandal which involved the throne. The poison was required to murder Sir Thomas Overbury, a homosexual poet and courtier lying prisoner in the Tower. Overbury's former lover, Robert Carr, who was now James I's favourite, was bisexual and had a mistress called Lady Frances Howard, whom he wanted to marry. Overbury had objected, and for this he now found himself in the Tower, imprisoned on false charges by the king. Now the mistress wanted to ensure he died in there.

She had caused the governor of the Tower to be replaced with one of her friends, Sir Gervase Elwes, and it was a simple matter to smuggle in the poisons to Overbury's food until he finally succumbed. However, two years later the chemist's assistant, who had helped prepare the poisons, lay dying and confessed the whole matter to a priest, who lost no time in informing the authorities. The King had tired of Carr and had a new lover, George Villiers, and so ordered the entire matter to be investigated. All the conspirators were sentenced to death, although Carr and his wife were merely imprisoned in the Tower for six years.

The poison scene now switched to France. Paris had the international reputation of being the venom centre of Europe, and its supreme exponent being the incredible Marquise de Brinvilliers, a woman whose life and character seemed like a chapter from De Sade.

To set the scene we have to remember that arsenic was freely available in France and was believed to enhance the complexion. But arsenic, a sweetish white powder, was also undetectable in food. In 1572 there were at least thirty thousand apothecaries in France, who sold remedies to produce abortion and dispose of unwanted spouses.

Perhaps the fashion for poisoning in France began with the fact that two French Queens actually came from Italy; Catherine de Medici married the Valois Henry II, while Marie de Medici married Henry IV. In 1670 the daughter of the English King Charles I, Henriette, who had married Philippe Duc d'Orleans, was poisoned by him. The chicory water she drank was not poisoned – it was the cup itself, which had been coated inside with arsenic.

Then in 1676 all the rumours about poisonings, the fact that arsenic was openly referred to as 'poudre de succession' – 'inheritance powder' – became an open scandal when the pretty Marquise de Brinvilliers was put on trial for the murder of her father, two brothers and her husband, among others. It was alleged that she was guilty of some hundred murders. Her story deserves to be told in full.

Born Marie Madeleine d'Aubray in July 1630, nature had gifted her with blue eyes, glossy hair and an insatiable sexual appetite, together with a convenient lack of morals. The daughter of a wealthy Paris magistrate, she had a dowry of some two hundred thousand pounds and attracted many suitors. She chose to marry a minor nobleman, Baron Antoine Gobelin de Brinvilliers, because of the social cachet, but unfortunately the Baron had no money. Now a Marquise, Marie now indulged herself in a long round of pleasure which soon got rid of her money. She was also having an open affair with a young cavalry officer, Godin de Sainte-Croix, who was a friend of her husband's and had morals to match her own.

The husband didn't mind about his wife's affair, but her father was outraged and got a *lettre de cachet* from King Louis XIV to have Sainte-Croix thrown into the Bastille for a few months to cool his ardour. Unfortunately, Sainte-Croix's cell-mate was a skilled Italian poisoner, who whiled away the hours teaching his new friend the secrets of the deadly art. Sainte-Croix came out of prison a skilled toxicologist himself, and became friendly with a chemist called Glaser who had a shop in the rue du Petit Lion. There Sainte-Croix set up his laboratory.

Using poisons supplied by her lover and Glaser, the Marquise began visiting charity hospitals, tending to the poor and sick and feeding them food laced with poison. Her trips were a trial run to test out the poisons and discover what dosage to administer.

In 1666 she visited her father at his estate and fed him poisoned soup. He fell ill and she nursed him for six months, dosing him with further potions of arsenic until he died. She had now come into her inheritance and began enjoying herself once more, seducing her husband's cousin, her own cousin – by whom she had a child – and finally the tutor of her children. However, by 1670 she was broke again. Her two brothers had each inherited a third of her father's estate, and much as she loved them, the Marquise decided she needed it all.

The elder brother died in June 1670, the second brother following him in September. By now the Marquise had developed a taste for this method of smoothing out life's little obstacles, and she decided that her husband had to die so that she could marry Sainte-Croix. However, the husband proved difficult to kill. She kept increasing the doses but the husband, although constantly ill, obstinately refused to die. Eventually she discovered that her lover had no wish to marry her and had been secretly feeding the husband with antidotes to her poison. He was also attempting to blackmail her. The Marquise was furious at discovering a rattlesnake worse than herself and promptly poisoned him. Sainte-Croix died suddenly in July 1672.

It was her undoing. In his room was found a trunk containing phials of poison and incriminating letters from the Marquise full of clinical notes about the effects of the poisons she had administered to her victims. Promissory notes in the box proved that the Marquise had owed Sainte-Croix thirty thousand francs, and other prominent citizens who owed their sudden rise in society to the death of someone standing in their way also owed Sainte-Croix money.

The Marquise tried desperately to gain possession of the trunk, but it was taken into custody by a new Chief of Police, Nicolas Gabriel de la Reynie. The Marquise had used a valet known as La Chausée to help in the poisonings, and also the tutor she had seduced, Briancourt. The Marquise fled to England and was tried in her absence when La Chausée was taken into custody and found to have his pockets stuffed with poisons. He was broken on the rack and confessed everything, implicating the Marquise. He was sentenced to be beheaded.

When Louis XIV was told of the affair he announced that no matter how exalted the rank of the offenders, they must all be brought to justice. (Wiser heads had counselled keeping the whole scandal secret.) An extradition from England was arranged – very novel for the time – but the Marquise fled to Belgium, hiding away in a convent. Her whereabouts became known and she was arrested in Liège in 1676. She protested: 'Half the people I know, important people, are involved in the same sort of thing. I could bring them all down with me if I confessed everything.'

That was precisely what the Paris Parlement wanted – a full confession. They were determined to put a stop to poisoning lest others take up her career. A Jesuit priest was appointed to be her confessor. When she was tortured by being stripped naked and bent backwards over a wooden hurdle while gallons of water were poured down her throat with a funnel, he was always there afterwards to soothe her, persuading her that God would forgive her if only she would tell all.

The trial of the Marquise de Brinvilliers lasted from 29 April to 16 July 1676, her testimony scandalising all Paris. She talked freely about her relations with her two brothers, both of whom she had initiated sexually (including sodomy) before she was seven. Sentenced to death, she was taken to the Place de Gréve and beheaded, and afterwards her body was burned before the mob.

There had been previous poison scandals. In the latter part of 1668 priests began reporting to the police that a surprising number of women were confessing to poisoning their husbands and asking for absolution. The police investigated. A fortune-teller called Marie Bosse had been heard to boast: 'What a marvellous trade! What a clientele I have! Duchesses, Marquises, Princesses! Only three more poisonings and I can retire!' On 4 January 1669 she was arrested while sharing a bed with her two sons and daughters. (It was believed that magical powers could be passed on within a family by incest.) Another fortune-teller, La Vigoreux, had also been arrested, and the two women quickly began to talk.

At first they confessed to supplying the love potions and other occult spells. Then they began revealing the names of the highest in the land to whom they had supplied poisons. They also named a further accomplice, another fortune-teller named La Voison, real name Catherine Deshayes. A search of these women's houses turned up the usual stock in trade of the necromancer, but there were also laboratories for turning out arsenic and other poisons. Magistrates, Dukes, even a close friend of the King's mistress, Madame de Montespan – all had been named as clients of the fortune-tellers.

In fact, the trail the police followed led into the Palace of Versailles itself. In order to protect the reputation of the French aristocracy – many of whom were implicated – the King ordered the hearing to take place in secret. *La Chambre Ardente* began hearing evidence which was startling in the extreme. La Voison's garden had been dug up and the remains of many unwanted children born to ladies of the Court had been found. But even worse, Madame de Montespan had taken part in sexual black-magic orgies and Black Masses where a live baby had had its throat slit. She had been the King's mistress for thirteen years, but the King had tired of her, taking a new mistress, a seventeen-year-old blonde named Mademoiselle de Fontanges. The thirty-eight-year-old Madame de Montespan was determined to use black magic, and if that failed, poison, to get rid of her rival. In fact she succeeded: Fontanges died before the court even sat.

As a result of the court's findings of just how widespread black magic was in France, with many priests involved in the obscene rituals, thirty-six people were sentenced to death, four were confined for life in the galleys, and a further thirty-four were banished. Madame de Montespan was allowed to retire to a convent. The findings of the court in document form were handed over to the King, who very wisely burned them before the council without a word being spoken. The court's secrets were kept safely for a long time, but incredibly the minute-book of the clerk of the court had not been included in the documents, and when it surfaced in the nineteenth century it was published, causing a sensation.

Typical of the lack of any science to combat the poisoner was the case of Mary Blandy, tried in 1752 for the murder of her father by arsenic. Her lover had supplied her with 'magic potions' to sprinkle on her father's food to make him agreeable to their union. When the father died, the lover fled to France. Mary was left to face the music, a servant having retrieved incriminating letters from the lover to Mary, and a quantity of white powder. At her trial on 3 March 1752 four doctors testified that the white powder was arsenic – but they had only been able to come to this decision by applying a red-hot poker to the powder and sniffing the fumes given off. The jury took just five minutes to find Mary guilty and she was hanged outside Newgate Prison, her last words to the hangman being a request that he should not hang her too high – 'for the sake of decency'.

It was a very unscientific age, the only test for poison being to feed it to an animal and see if it died. But the men of science were now emerging, men like Joseph Priestley and Henry Cavendish. Around 1790 Johann Metzger discovered the 'arsenic mirror'. He found that if substances containing arsenic were heated and a cold plate held over the vapours, a white layer of arsenious oxide would form on the plate. This could prove that food had been doused with arsenic, but it could not tell if the body had already absorbed arsenic.

Dr Valentine Rose of the Berlin Medical Faculty solved this little problem in 1806. If the corpse's stomach with its contents were cut up and boiled, when the resulting liquid had been filtered and treated with nitric acid to remove any remaining flesh and to convert any arsenic into arsenic acid, it could be subjected to Metzger's 'mirror' in the usual way to detect any arsenic. Rose's discovery came in time to convict one of the worst murderers in German history, Anna Zwanziger, daughter of a Nuremberg innkeeper. She poisoned without motive, simply for the sheer sadistic pleasure of watching her victims suffer. It was said of her that she trembled with joy when she looked at the white powder of arsenic, describing it as 'her truest friend'.

When she got a job as a housekeeper to a judge named Glaser, she poisoned his wife in the hope that he might marry her. She poisoned another judge, and a magistrate, before attempting to poison an entire family. When she was arrested on 18 October 1809 a packet of white arsenic was found in her pocket. She refused to admit anything for six months, but when Rose's test proved her guilt she confessed to eleven murders. She was executed by beheading with the sword in 1811.

The most important step in the history of forensic toxicology was the arrival on the scene of the Spaniard named Matthieu Joseph Bonaventure Orfila, born 24 April 1787. He had studied at the Paris School of Medicine, obtaining his degree and becoming a lecturer. He soon became aware – to his astonishment – that there existed no standard tests to detect many poisons, and he decided to remedy this. When he published his *Traites des poisons* in 1813 he found himself famous at the age of twenty-six, and his book marked the end for the poisoner.

Orfila himself had to become a scientist-detective, involved in many police cases of suspected poisoning. In 1824 he cleared a woman of suspicion of murder after a local chemist had said that he had detected arsenic in her husband's remains. The contents of the dead man's stomach were sent to Orfila, now a full professor in Paris, and he carried out exhaustive tests before reporting that he could find no trace of any poison. In other cases his expertise helped convict.

The next turning point in the detection of murder by poisoning came in 1836 when James Marsh, a middle-aged alcoholic, published his incredibly sensitive test to detect the smallest quantity of arsenic. It was a refinement on the Metzger test. Instead of allowing the vapours to rise up to the cold metal plate – with most of the gases escaping into thin air – the whole process took place in a sealed apparatus in which the vapours could only exit via a small nozzle. The suspect material was dropped into a solution of zinc and sulphuric acid to produce hydrogen. Any arsine gas was then heated as it passed along a glass tube, condensing when it reached a cold part of the tube to form the 'arsenic mirror'. It was simple yet effective. The Marsh test is still used, although modern analysts prefer to use the Reinsch and Gutzeit tests. Hugo Reinsch developed his test in 1842, and although an improvement on the Marsh test, great care has to be taken to ensure that the reagent is itself arsenic-free. Failure to ensure this botched the Smethurst case, as will be seen later.

Orfila had not faded from the annals of detection, and 1840 saw his greatest triumph at the trial of Marie Lafarge. Her husband had died on 16 January 1840 aged twenty-nine, of a gastric ailment after eating a slice of his newly wedded wife's cake. But even before this alarming incident a maidservant had seen Marie stirring a white powder into a glass of milk she gave to her husband. The maidservant told the doctor, and nine days after her husband's death Marie Lafarge was arrested and charged with murder.

Her trial began on 3 September 1840, with the prosecution relating how she had watched her husband die in agony because of her sadistic murder plot. Her defence was that the white powder she had put in her husband's drink and on his food was gum arabic. But the evidence was that she had purchased arsenic on at least two occasions, and the local chemist had detected arsenic in the milk and in the dead man's vomit.

Orfila appeared for the defence. He pointed out that the prosecution had never even heard of the Marsh Test, let alone used it. The prosecutor then demanded that Orfila should examine the contents of the dead man's stomach in the courtroom and in the presence of local chemists. Orfila accepted the challenge, performing a Marsh test that night. The following day he went into the witness box to state that he had found arsenic in the stomach, liver, thorax, heart and brain. On 19 September 1840 Marie Lafarge was found guilty and was condemned to hard labour for life.

In England the Arsenic Act of 1851 laid down that no arsenic compound was to be sold unless the seller knew the buyer, and it also insisted that all arsenic compounds had to be coloured either with soot, or with half an ounce of blue indigo per pound of arsenic. No longer was arsenic to be confused with sugar or flour. The Pharmacy Act of 1852 brought in regulations making it compulsory for purchasers of poisons to sign a Poison Register. And in 1933 the Pharmacy and Poisons Act tightened matters still further, with the Dangerous Drugs Act of 1951, and further legislation in 1968 and 1971 making it virtually impossible for anyone but a doctor to obtain poisons.

Doctors, of course, tended to use other poisons than arsenic. And if the names of doctors as poisoners seem to abound in the annals of murder, it is simply because doctors have access to poisons as painters have access to paint, and a doctor can give poison in the form of medicine. He can also usually find a friendly colleague to sign the death certificate. Dr Pritchard used antimony; Dr Palmer used antimony and strychnine; Dr Cream used strychnine alone, while Dr Lamson used aconite. Dr Crippen used hyoscine.

While doctors were aware of the success of the Marsh

test, news of its infallibility took a long time to get through to the general public, and for decades to come poisoners would obtain arsenic by any means – even if it meant boiling down flypapers – in the hope of getting away with murder by its use.

In France, Hélène Jegado went on using arsenic, Marsh test or no. She could hardly have been aware of it anyway, being an illiterate Breton peasant woman. She travelled across France working as a domestic servant, usually for clergymen, and was frequently dismissed for stealing. But she left behind her a trail of mysterious deaths over a twenty-year period, none of which was suspected as being murder. In fact Jegado once said dolefully: 'Wherever I go, people die.' They certainly did – some twenty-three of them.

She poisoned with arsenic, apparently for no motive other than a grim secret pleasure. It may be that when scolded for theft, or facing dismissal, she poisoned fellow servants as an act of revenge. For a while she went into a convent, but then nuns began falling ill . . .

Her career came to an end when she began working for Professor Theophile Bidard, a university lecturer at Rennes. He was a trained surgeon. When a junior servant died after a mystery illness, Jegado said she would willingly do the work of two servants, but the Professor hired another woman, Rosalie Sarrazin, and when she too died suddenly in the summer of 1851, the Professor was immediately alerted to the possibility of poisoning. The symptoms were only too familiar: the stomach pains and vomiting. The police were called in and Hélène Jegado opened the door to them saying: 'I am innocent!' To which a magistrate replied: 'Of what? Nobody has accused you.'

An in-depth investigation of her past was begun and her murderous career was unmasked. Tried at Rennes in December 1851 for three murders and three attempted murders, the prosecution could not prove she had ever

114

been in possession of arsenic, but the circumstantial evidence of her having been connected with twenty-three deaths from arsenical poisoning was enough, and she was sentenced to the guillotine.

What the case did illustrate is that poisoning is the most difficult crime to prove because it is carried out in secret, and therefore only circumstantial evidence is usually available. The mere fact that poison is found in the stomach contents does not rule out the possibility of suicide or accidental death.

The Madeleine Smith case was a British *cause célèbre* in 1857, when the lover of this nineteen-year-old Glasgow girl, a Frenchman called Pierre L'Angelier, died in March of that year in extreme agony after drinking a cup of cocoa prepared by her.

Madeleine Smith had taken a new lover and told L'Angelier that their romance was over. His response was to threaten to send her extremely candid love letters to her father. It was emotional blackmail. Madeleine Smith then wrote him affectionate letters inviting him to tea. But when he arrived at her house it was to be met with poisoned cocoa. The postmortem on L'Angelier revealed the presence of eighty-seven grains of arsenic in his stomach – a fatal dose being three grains. Madeleine's letters were found in his room and she was arrested on 31 March. At her trial she insisted that L'Angelier regularly took small quantities of arsenic to improve his complexion, and the arsenic found in the dead man's stomach bore no trace of the statutory blue indigo. The jury brought in the Scottish verdict of Not Proven and she walked free. She died in America aged ninety-one.

Arsenic was the favourite poison of the Victorian era – what George Orwell termed the 'golden age of English murder', – because it was so readily available as a rat-killer. The Marsh test was useful for the metallic poisons, but there were plenty of vegetable poisons

which could not be detected so readily, including aconite, belladonna, strychnine, opium and nicotine. And
other deadly poisons like mercury, phosphorus and
chloroform were equally undetectable. As late as 1847
the great Orfila admitted that it was possible that the
vegetable poisons would remain undetectable.

But in 1850 the murder of Gustave Fougnies in
Belgium led to Jean Stas, a disciple of Orfila, devising
a test to detect nicotine poisoning. The Stas test is still
used today.

Another landmark in the history of forensic medicine
had come in 1835 with the publication of Alfred Swaine
Taylor's *Principles and Practices of Medical Jurisprudence*. Professor Taylor had studied under Orfila. The
first major poisoning case with which Taylor was
involved was that of Dr William Palmer of Rugeley,
Staffordshire, who poisoned his friends and relatives
wholesale with strychnine for profit. He poisoned his
children, his mother-in-law, and uncle and various
creditors. In 1853 Palmer insured his wife for £13,000.
She promptly died. He then insured the life of his
brother, Walter, for £82,000, but when Walter died
suddenly the insurance company refused to pay up.
Undeterred, Palmer next insured a friend, George Bates,
for £25,000 and then poisoned him. Again the
insurance company refused to pay out, having hired a
detective to investigate the circumstances, but incredibly, they did not inform the police of their suspicions.

Palmer was arrested when a friend called John
Parsons Cook died after drinking brandy with him following a day at the races. Even as Cook writhed in
agony, Palmer forged a document showing that Cook
owed him £4,000 and forged Cook's signature on a
cheque for £350.

Cook's stepfather demanded an autopsy. Palmer, out
on bail, attended the autopsy and was actually caught
sneaking out of the room with the jar containing the

contents of Cook's stomach. Palmer had obviously thought that poisoning was a marvellous way of making money, and resorted to strychnine and antimony as a spendthrift today resorts to card cash-dispensers. Professor Taylor testified to the poison found, and Palmer was convicted. He was hanged in public at Stafford on 14 June 1856 before a huge crowd.

The case of Dr Smethurst illustrated the need for caution in forensic medicine. This fifty-four-year-old doctor fell in love with his lodger, Isabella Bankes, in 1858. The forty-three-year-old spinster had money. . . . When Miss Bankes moved to new lodgings in Richmond, Smethurst abandoned his invalid wife to go and live with her, bigamously marrying her. In March 1859 Miss Bankes was taken ill with severe stomach pains. Smethurst gave every appearance of innocence by calling in another doctor to tend to her. Poisoning was suspected, but even as she lay dying, Miss Bankes signed a will leaving all her property to 'my sincere and beloved friend Thomas Smethurst'. The patient's vomit was analysed and arsenic was detected. Dr Smethurst was arrested on 2 May and charged with administering poison, but when Miss Bankes died the following day the charge was changed to one of murder.

Dr Alfred Swaine Taylor, the chief Home Office analyst, testified before the magistrates that he had used the Marsh test and found arsenic. However, at the resulting Old Bailey trial in July 1859 he was forced to admit that he had conducted the test improperly, having found impurities in the copper gauze he had used; copper containing natural arsenic of its own. Two separate trials were held, the jury failing to agree at the first. There was no proof that Smethurst had ever possessed arsenic, and the Crown's expert witness having admitted negligence by contaminating the sample, an acquittal might have been expected. However, Smethurst was found guilty and sentenced to death. The judge was disturbed by the quality of the medical evidence and asked the Home Secretary to refer the evidence to an independent scientific finding. Sir Benjamin Brodie headed that inquiry, being the most eminent surgeon of his time. He reported that there were six reasons for believing Smethurst guilty, and eight for doubting his guilt. The Home Secretary granted Smethurst a free pardon. He was then tried for bigamy and received a sentence of one year at hard labour. Later he impudently fought and won an action to prove the will of his deceased bigamous wife.

Dr Ambois Tardieu was one of France's foremost experts on toxicology when he became involved in a celebrated poison case. On 17 November 1863 a woman called Madame de Pauw died, apparently from cholera. She was the former mistress of a country doctor called Pommerais. Chief Inspector Claude of the Sûreté received an anonymous letter suggesting that Pommerais had murdered the woman for gain. The Chief Inspector investigated and discovered that Pommerais had indeed insured the dead woman for five hundred thousand francs and was about to receive that amount from the insurance company. The body of Madame de Pauw was exhumed and Dr Tardieu had the task of finding out which poison had been used.

It certainly wasn't a metallic poison; the standard tests ruled that out. The concentrated extract from the stomach contents were then injected into a dog, and the animal's heartbeat slowed until it nearly stopped. The poison had been digitalis, an extract of foxglove, and when Pommerais's mother-in-law was exhumed it was found that she too had been poisoned with this substance. Pommerais was convicted and executed in June 1864, and Tardieu's test for digitalis, using a frog, is still the standard test in use.

The state of knowledge in the field of forensic toxicology at this time was limited but improving. There were hundreds of poisons for which no test as yet existed, but broadly speaking poisons could now be grouped into four categories according to their effects. First those poisons which affect the oxygen-carrying capability of the blood – typically cyanide. Then the acids and alkalis which are corrosive and usually burn the mouth. Chloroform is one example. The third group consists of those poisons which destroy the entire body system by absorption, either slowly or quickly, such as arsenic, antimony, mercury and the vegetable poisons, like strychnine, morphine and hyoscine. The fourth group comprises poisons which leave no trace of entry – no obvious lesions – but kill after being absorbed by the body. Ricin, arsine and nitrobenzine fall into this category.

But new drugs were being developed almost daily which could also be used as poisons – including morphine, strychnine and hyoscyamine – faster than the toxicologists could develop tests for them. In 1880 Dr Stevenson, the chief Home Office expert on the subject, admitted in court that the method he used to detect vegetable poisons was to taste them. He had some seventy samples in his possession, and had tasted them all. When faced with a suspect poison, he first tasted it, then compared it with his collection to find a match. It was a very crude and unscientific system.

Still poisoners persisted with arsenic. Mary Ann Cotton holds the title of Britain's greatest mass murderer, having disposed of some twenty victims in her career. Born in 1832 in Durham, she married aged twenty and had five children, of which three died. She had another three children, all of whom died, before her husband died of a mystery illness. She married again in 1865, to George Ward, but fourteen months later he too died. She then took a job as housekeeper to John Robinson. In 1867 his son John died, followed by two other children within twelve days, and then her own surviving children died.

Mary then introduced the widowed Margaret Robinson to her brother Frederick Cotton. Margaret then died – perhaps because she knew Mary was married to Robinson – and Mary bigamously married Frederick in 1871. Frederick, who was thirty-nine, soon died suddenly of 'gastric fever'. A lover then moved in, one Joseph Nattrass. In March and April of 1872 Nattrass died, followed by Mary's baby by Cotton, and Cotton's ten-year-old-son. In July Cotton's remaining son died.

It was one death too many. The doctor refused to issue a death certificate and the police were called in. Arsenic was found in the child's stomach, and Nattrass's corpse was exhumed and it too showed the presence of arsenic, as did one of the other dead children.

Mary Cotton's defence at her trial in March 1873 was that the child licked arsenic from the wallpaper – which it did indeed contain. The prosecution proved her purchases of arsenic. While in prison Mary had given birth to another child by yet another lover. Mary Cotton's motive for murder was the few shillings' insurance money she had coming from each victim. She was found guilty and sentenced to death, hanged on 24 March 1873 at Durham Gaol, the hangman botching the job so that she dangled twitching on the rope for a full three minutes before death intervened.

The ingenuity and persistence of poisoners has no limit, but arsenic seems to be a particularly popular choice.

Dr Edward William Pritchard was a Glasgow doctor who was suspected of murdering one of his housemaids in 1863. The girl was burned to death when his house caught fire; she had been locked in the attic and was naked and pregnant. Rumour had it that the amorous doctor had drugged her unconscious before setting the fire. The insurance company only paid out when Pritchard threatened legal action. Then in October 1865 he systematically poisoned his wife with antimony. A crowd of a hundred thousand turned up to see him publicly hanged in Glasgow.

Dr George Henry Lamson, himself a morphia addict, was heavily in debt in 1881 and decided to poison his eighteen-year-old brother-in-law Percy for gain. The boy lived at Blenheim House School in Wimbledon. On 3 December Dr Lamson visited the school, and in the presence of the principal brazenly offered Percy a slice of Dundee cake which he had brought with him. The cake, already cut into slices, had one slice dosed with aconite – the slice which Percy ate. He promptly died. Twenty-nine-year-old Lamson was tried at the Old Bailey in March 1882 and was found guilty. He was executed at Wandsworth Prison, after confessing his guilt to the chaplain, on 28 April 1882.

Prior to this, a Dutch woman called Van der Linden of Leyden in Holland had attempted to poison 102 people between 1833 and 1851, of whom 27 died. And in Geneva in 1880 a nurse, Jeanne Raies, was convicted of poisoning twelve people simply because the local undertaker paid her a small commission for each death she notified to him, so that he could be first in with a funeral quote.

Adelaide Bartlett was a fascinating character. Unhappily married, she had an affair with a local preacher, the Reverend George Dyson. Her husband Edwin died on 1 January 1886 at their Pimlico home, a huge quantity of chloroform being found in his stomach. But there was no trace of any burns to the mouth or gullet. She was acquitted on this count, a noted surgeon of the time saying: 'Now that she has got away with it, in the interests of science she should tell us how she did it.'

Florence Elizabeth Maybrick, a thirty-six-year-old American woman, was convicted of poisoning her English husband with arsenic at Liverpool in 1889. Evidence was given that the husband was in the habit of taking regular doses of arsenic as an aphrodisiac. But evidence was also given that Florence had purchased three dozen arsenic-coated flypapers immediately prior to his death. The judge's summing-up was heavily biased against her and she was sentenced to hang. Following many public petitions the sentence was commuted to life imprisonment and Florence was released from prison in 1904, dying in the USA in 1941 aged seventy-six.

The case of Dr Hawley Harvey Crippen is almost too well known to bear repeating. American-born, he poisoned his wife at their home at 39 Hilldrop Crescent in London in 1910, fleeing to Canada aboard the SS *Montrose* with his mistress, Ethel le Neve, dressed as a boy, after Chief Inspector Walter Dew of Scotland Yard had visited his home and made it clear he intended to find the wife.

The captain of the ship radioed his suspicions of the couple to London – the first time radio had been used in a murder hunt – and by taking a faster vessel Dew was able to arrest the couple when their ship docked. What remained of Mrs Crippen was found in the cellar at Hilldrop Crescent: dismembered flesh, the head, skeleton and limbs never being found. Hyoscine was found in the flesh and Dr Spilsbury identified the body from an abdominal scar. Crippen was found guilty and hanged, his mistress being acquitted.

The Bingham poisonings remain a classic unsolved case. Over a period of nine months in 1911 three members of the same family died from arsenical poisoning at Lancaster Castle, where James Bingham was the caretaker. He and two sisters died; the third sister Edith, was tried at Lancaster Assizes – held at the castle – in October 1911 but was acquitted.

Frederick Seddon was a London insurance agent who murdered for greed. In July 1910 he and his wife took in a lodger, Miss Barrow, who signed all her assets over to Seddon in exchange for an annuity of £3 a week. On 1 September 1911 she fell ill with severe vomiting, dying two weeks later. Suspicious relatives demanded an autopsy and the victim was exhumed – with typical meanness Seddon had her buried at the cheapest cost in a common grave – and arsenic was found in the remains. Mr and Mrs Seddon were tried at the Old Bailey in March 1912. During the ten-day trial evidence was heard that Mrs Seddon had bought flypapers. Marshall Hall, for Mrs Seddon, successfully attacked the prosecution's forensic method of multiplying samples: the pathologist had found one grain in one organ and then multiplied that by the total body weight. The wife was acquitted. Seddon, after revealing to the judge that he was a Mason, was sentenced to death by a distressed judge who was himself a Mason. Seddon was hanged at Pentonville Prison on 18 April 1912.

Harold Greenwood, a forty-five-year-old solicitor from Wales, was tried for murder in 1921 after his wife died from arsenical poisoning. The prosecution argued that the arsenic had been in a bottle of Burgundy from which she had drank; Marshall Hall, defending Greenwood, put Greenwood's daughter in the witness box to testify that she had drunk from the same bottle with no ill effects. Greenwood was acquitted.

Herbert Rowse Armstrong was another Welsh solicitor, who in July 1920 poisoned his wife. Her death was attributed to natural causes. Armstrong then tried to poison a rival solicitor with arsenic-filled chocolates. The local chemist was suspicious, as Armstrong had recently purchased quite a lot of arsenic. The wife's body was exhumed and Spilsbury found arsenic in great quantity. When arrested Armstrong had a packet of arsenic in his pocket. He was hanged at Gloucester Prison on 31 May 1927.

Jean-Pierre Vaquier, a forty-five-year-old Frenchman

domiciled in England, poisoned the husband of his mistress with strychnine on 29 March 1924. The husband was the landlord of the Blue Anchor pub at Byfleet, Surrey, where Vaquier was staying as a guest. He had put the strychnine in a bottle of Bromo-Selzer from which the husband always drank following a hangover. Vaquier protested his innocence, but when photographs were published in the newspapers, a London chemist identified him as a 'Mr Vanker' who had bought strychnine at his shop. Vaquier was hanged at Wandsworth Prison on 12 August 1924.

The Croydon poisonings remain an unsolved mystery. Between April 1928 and March 1929, three members of the same family all died from arsenical poisoning. Fifty-nine-year-old Edward Creighton Duff, died on 27 April 1928. Vera Sidney, his forty-year-old sister-in-law, died on 15 February 1929, and on 5 March Mrs Violet Sidney, mother of Vera, died. All three victims lived close to one another in Croydon, and the murderer must have been a close family relative. A pathologist's mistake was revealed in this case; while analysing the organs of Mr Duff he got them mixed up with those from another corpse, leading to confusion about the cause of death and allowing the poisoner that much longer to do his or her deadly work.

Annie Hearn, a middle-aged Cornish widow, was tried in June 1931 for the murder of her friend and neighbour, Annie Thomas, by feeding her a salmon sandwich liberally dosed with arsenic. Sir Norman Birkett, defending, argued that it was a simple case of food poisoning, and that in any case the local soil was heavy in arsenic content, and so could have entered the coffin and body through the graveyard soil. Mrs Hearn was acquitted.

Dorothea Waddingham, a thirty-six-year-old widow and 'nurse' without any qualifications, opened her own private nursing home in Nottingham in the 1930s.

When patients made out wills in her favour, she killed them with injections of morphine. On 12 May 1935 a Mrs Baguley died at the age of eighty-nine, followed four months later by her fifty-year-old sister Ada. At the postmortem morphia was found. Waddingham was tried at Nottingham Assizes in February 1936, found guilty, and hanged at Winson Green Prison, Birmingham, on 16 April 1936.

Although modern forensic toxicology has made great strides, with the result that poisoning now accounts for only six per cent of all murders, the fact remains that almost anything can be a 'poison' if enough is used. Nurses, like doctors, tend to turn to drugs when driven to kill. In 1956 John Armstrong, a naval sickbay attendant, murdered his five-and-a-half-month-old son using seconal, a sleeping capsule. In 1957 Kenneth Barlow, a male nurse, killed his wife by injecting her with insulin, which is quickly absorbed by the body and leaves no traces. However, since he had boasted to a colleague of his idea for the 'perfect murder', the police were suspicious and a pathologist found a tiny pinprick in the buttocks. The pathologist carried out tests on mice, injecting extracts from the victim's body into them. All the mice died from the typical reactions of insulin overdose. Barlow served twenty-seven-years of a life sentence.

Graham Young was an obsessive poisoner who fitted into no category. Sent to Broadmoor in his teens for poisoning his family, he was released nine years later and got a job at a photographic supplies firm in Hertfordshire. In June 1971 a storeman died, aged sixty. Young went to the funeral. There followed a spate of mysterious illnesses at the firm, with over seventy employees being affected by the 'bug' as they called it. Young was the tea-boy. He liked to refer to himself as 'your friendly neighbourhood Frankenstein'. In October 1971 another workman died. Two more were in agony.

When a medical team arrived at the factory to investigate, Young asked the doctor in charge if he had considered the possibility of thallium poisoning. Thallium is odourless, colourless and tasteless. Its symptoms include loss of hair, numbness of the limbs, blurred vision and shaking of the hands. When arrested, Young had a packet of thallium in his pocket, and police found his diary containing the names of actual and intended victims. Young claimed the notes in his diary were ideas for a novel he wanted to write.

As the bodies of both his victims had been cremated, there seemed little chance of proving thallium poisoning. But thallium is a metal, and in a 'first' for forensic medicine the ashes of the victims were examined by atomic absorption spectrometry and found to contain five micrograms of thallium per gram of ash. Tried for the murder of two of his workmates and the attempted murder of six others, he was found guilty at St Albans in July 1972 and sentenced to life imprisonment.

We turn now to the stuff of spy fiction. On 7 September 1978 Georgi Markov, a Bulgarian defector working for the BBC in London, felt a sharp jab on his leg in a crowded street. He turned to see a man with an umbrella hailing a cab, and thought he had been 'spiked' accidentally. Markov fell violently ill. The symptoms puzzled the doctors, and when he died on 11 September of toxaemia, his blood count was the highest ever recorded.

A careful postmortem revealed the presence of a tiny metal pellet in his leg. Scientists from Porton Down, the Ministry of Defence Chemical Defence Establishment were called in to examine the pellet and advise on the cause of death. They found it to be a case of ricin poisoning. Ricin, a deadly poison, is isolated from the castor-oil bean and is one of the most toxic poisons known, being almost impossible to detect and having no antidote. It was considered as a possible chemical weapon during the Second World War. It is known that Eastern Bloc secret service assassins favour the use of the 'umbrella gun' and had killed another Bulgarian defector in Paris by the same method.

The tiny platinum sphere, just 1.77 millimetres in diameter and drilled through with two tiny 0.35 millimetre holes to carry the ricin, is now in the Black Museum at Scotland Yard.

The poisoner is detested because she or he works in secret, often over a long period, pretending to nurse the victim they are slowly murdering, and so poison has become known as the 'coward's weapon'. Mr Justice Avory sternly intoned in 1924: 'Of all the forms by which human nature may be overcome, the most detestable is that of poison, because it can of all others be the least prevented by manhood or forethought.' Traditionally, the Attorney-General prosecutes poisoning cases personally, which may not always be a good idea. He certainly botched the prosecution of Dr Bodkin Adams, who was indeed innocent of murder but, in the words of Mr Justice Devlin, may well have 'eased the passing' of his aged patients.

The scientific advances in forensic medicine of this century have made the task of identifying poisons relatively simple. First came the discovery that many vegetable or alkaloid poisons form distinctive crystals which can be identified under the microscope, with each crystal having its own specific melting point. Far more effective was the discovery of column chromatography. This is simply an upright glass tube filled with fine chalk, the filtering process allowing pure water to run out of the bottom. When the suspect poison is put in the top and fresh water added, the chalk becomes coloured. The colour layer descends and splits into different layers corresponding to the dyes and components in the poison. This process was refined in the 1930s.

Then came the spectroscope. When any substance is

heated it gives off emissions of light which vary according to the substance. The spectrum of the light given off can be measured and charted against known poisons. Now we have reagents which can routinely test for many different poisons – some two thousand of them.

By the 1950s nuclear physics was helping to test for poisons; bombarding suspect substances with neutrons makes the poison radioactive enough to be measured on a Geiger counter.

We have come a long way, but make no mistake: poisoners will persist!

5
BALLISTICS: THE NAME ON THE BULLET . . .

The history of man the killer, can be traced by examining the development of his weapons. First came the club, then the knife, spear, bow and arrow, and so on, right up to the latest nuclear weapons. As man has evolved he has become a far more efficient killer.

The invention of gunpowder in China around AD 1000 marked a revolution in world history, changing the course of the centuries to come. By as early as AD 1200 the Arabs had invented the first handgun, with the result that knights in their heavy armour became obsolete, although they continued to be used in battle because firearms were scarce, being owned by the very wealthy. By the Elizabethan era the gentry were using guns for hunting, while the heavy cannon was still basically a siege weapon, not being very effective against troops because of the time it took to reload.

The various wars of the seventeenth century brought firearms into the possession of the peasant class, who learned how to shoot a pistol or rifle, and when their particular war ended were reluctant to return to being peasants, and so invented the trade of highwayman. Those early flintlock pistols had to be loaded by pouring gunpowder down the barrel, followed by the lead ball, and then a paper wad was forced down the barrel with a ramrod to keep the charge tightly packed. Gunpowder then had to be poured into the pan to 'prime' it, and was ignited either by a string soaked in saltpetre called a 'match', or by a spark from the flint. The powder in the pan flashed off, and the resulting flame passed through the ignition hole in the pan and so set off the main charge. Sometimes the powder would flash without igniting the main charge – hence our expression 'flash in the pan'.

These pistols could fire only one bullet, of course, and then required laborious reloading. Muzzle-loaders were very inefficient, relying heavily on the paper wad to keep the charge in place. But highwaymen and others killed many people with this relatively new weapon before anyone thought to try and match a particular shot to a particular suspect.

This happened in 1794, and is perhaps the first recorded example of forensic ballistics in history. (Forensic ballistics is the study of projectiles related to legal questions, and can include arrows, spears and even rockets. There have been quite a few recent murders by means of crossbow bolts. However, in practice ballistics is limited to firearms, and strictly speaking is called 'firearms evidence'. Ballistics, however, has become the popularly accepted term.)

In 1794 a man named Edward Culshaw was shot in the head at Prescot in Lancashire, and when the surgeon examined the body he found the wad of paper which had been used to pack the shot in the wound itself. When unwrapped this proved to be an extract from a street ballad, and when a suspect, eighteen-year-old John Toms, was arrested, the remaining piece of the ballad was found in his coat pocket. This was enough to impress the jury, and he was sentenced to death at Lancaster Assizes on 23 March 1794.

There are records of at least two other cases of murder by firearms being solved in this same manner. In 1860 a policeman was killed with a double-barrelled pistol, and the paper wad found in the wound had come from a copy of *The Times* for 27 March 1854. When a suspect called Richardson was taken into custody and a paper wad from *The Times* was found in the unfired barrel of his pistol, police contacted the editor of the newspaper, who was able to confirm that both pieces of paper had come from the same issue. Richardson was convicted and hanged.

In 1891 in France, a man named Charles Guesner was shot in bed as he lay sleeping beside his wife. The paper wad in the wound had come from the *Lorraine Almanach*, and was the only clue to the killer's identity. Since the victim had no known enemies, police investigated the case as a *crime passionnel* and interviewed a man called Bivert, who had courted Madame Guesner prior to her marriage. A search of his room revealed a copy of the *Almanach* with the relevant page missing. Bivert served twenty years' hard labour for his crime.

There were several such cases of murder by shooting solved by fluke solutions, where the ball could be matched to comparison balls in the suspect's possession, and so on. And we have seen how Henry Goddard, the Bow Street Runner, solved a crime as early as 1835 by matching the butler's pistol to the ball found in the wall and so exposed the alleged burglary as an 'inside job'.

Muzzle-loaders became obsolete in the mid-eighteenth century, when manufacturers began making rifles which could be 'broken' in the middle – like the modern shotgun – and so could be reloaded easily. This led to the invention of the bullet: a projectile which carried its own gunpowder charge and which in effect acted like a rocket, the lead front portion being projected out of the gun by exploding gases, while the 'second stage' booster is left behind in the gun in the form of the cartridge case. With this method the bullet could be made an exact fit, making full use of the exploding gases and becoming more powerful as a result.

In 1820 the percussion cap was invented, usually

containing fulminate of mercury, which exploded when struck with a hammer and so set off the main charge. But the real revolution in handguns came when the sixteen-year-old Samuel Colt began carving a revolver out of wood to see if a revolving chamber worked. It did, and when he was twenty-one he patented the idea. After modifications the Colt revolver, with only five simple working parts and cheap in price, became the weapon which ruled and eventually tamed the West. It became standard issue for the Texas Rangers – and any bandit who could get his hands on one.

Not for nothing was it known as the 'equaliser'. With this cheap mass-produced weapon a little man could defeat a much bigger one. The poor could kill the rich, giving it revolutionary qualities, which was ironic, since its invention had made Colt a millionaire. It came quickly to Europe and started a crime revolution of its own, becoming a very real menace to the police.

It was realised as early as the sixteenth century that if a gun barrel was rifled it imparted spin to the projectile and gave it much greater accuracy. This rifling – or spiral groove – leaves distinctive marks on the bullet itself which are called striations. The raised part of the rifling is called lands, the lower part grooves.

Every different manufacturer – and hundreds flocked to copy Colt and produce cheap handguns – uses his own particular system of lands and grooves, machined to different depths and widths, with the spiral either to right or left, the pitch or degree of rifling varying from one complete turn in eight inches to one in thirty-two inches.

Quite apart from these distinct variations, the calibre of the bullet varies from weapon to weapon, so that a .38 Smith and Wesson revolver has five lands to the right, while a .38 Colt revolver has six lands to the left. The shotgun, of course, is a smooth-bore weapon with no rifling, but still uses wads to pack the cartridges, which may be found in wounds if fired at close range.

The revolver has five or six cartridges with a rimmed base, which are hand-loaded into the revolving cylinder, and providing he does not reload, the firer takes the cartridge cases away with him still in the gun. The automatic pistol varies in that the cartridge has no rimmed base, but has an ejector groove. The bullets are magazine-fed to the breech, where the firing mechanism is recocked by the action of firing itself, so that as long as the trigger remains depressed the bullets keep firing automatically until the magazine is empty. But since each spent cartridge case is automatically ejected, the firer leaves the evidence of the cartridge cases behind him. These cases will bear the marks of the ejector, breech-face, firing pin and even the maker's name. As for the bullet itself, this will bear the striations caused by the rifling as it passed through the barrel when discharged.

The whole basis of ballistics is that no two guns are exactly alike, and in theory, if one bought two brand-new guns from the factory bearing consecutive serial numbers and fired them at a target, the ballistics expert could tell which gun fired which bullet. It sounds like fantasy, but the fact is that no two articles are ever exactly alike, even if manufactured on a production line. The tool making them wears, and imparts its degree of wear on the article. The greater sophistication of the gunmakers had led to bullets being that much more easily identifiable.

But to get to this stage of sophistication, with mechanism marks being left on the bullet and cartridge case, the integral cartridge had first to be invented. This was done in France in 1835, followed by Smith and Wesson in the USA in 1857. This cartridge, which is the modern bullet, is a self-enclosed round of ammunition consisting of a metal case designed to fit the chamber of a particular gun. This case contains the propellant charge and in its base is a soft metal cap holding the primer charge. When struck by the gun's firing pin it sets off the main charge, expelling the lead bullet – nowadays metal-jacketed – from the gun and leaving the case behind. The bullet is crimped into the top of the cartridge case by a circumferential groove called a cannelure. Some types of ammunition have two or more grooves, one of which contains a lubricant. This lubricant too can be chemically analysed to determine the maker.

The invention of smokeless powder by 1900 led to the introduction of the metal-jacketed bullet. Since it had a greater propellant velocity, lead bullets were too soft to be gripped by the rifling in the barrel and tended to get stripped, fouling the barrel. The modern bullet has an outer jacket of cupronickel.

The old black powder bullets used to leave distinctive marks around the wound if fired close enough, and on the hands of the firer. But the modern smokeless powder leaves traces which can be chemically detected. The hands of a suspect used to be subjected to the 'paraffin test' to detect minute nitrate traces and show if the suspect had fired a weapon recently. This test has since become suspect.

But this was all in the future. It was Professor Alexandre Lacassagne who first turned his attention to matching a bullet to a particular gun when in 1889 he noticed the grooves in the bullet extracted from the corpse in the Echallier case. A revolver was found under the floorboards of the room occupied by the suspected murderer, and although of the same calibre as the bullet removed from the victim, by itself it proved nothing. Lacassagne studied the bullet under the microscope and discovered it had seven grooves, the same as the suspect's revolver. As a result of his primitive comparison tests the suspect was convicted of the murder. Before this pioneering effort, every bullet had seemed anonymous. Now Lacassagne had gone a long way towards proving that every bullet bears its own 'fingerprint'.

But this early attempt to apply scientific methods to ballistics went unnoticed at the time, and 'firearms experts' were still pretty crude. Edward J. Churchill, the ballistics expert of his day, testifying at the Moat Farm trial, stated that the victim had been shot at close range in the head. The hole in the skull was fragmented and messy, and Churchill asserted that had the bullet been fired from a distance, the wound would have exhibited a clean round hole because the bullet would have had time to attain a greater speed. Nobody thought to challenge this absurd concept; a bullet can only *lose* speed after it leaves the barrel.

Gradually, however, advances were made in the scientific identification of bullets, and at the Congress of Legal Medicine held in Paris in May 1912, ballistics was accepted as a new branch of forensic science in its own right, mainly because of the work of Professor Victor Balthazard, an eminent medico-legal expert. He gave a lecture about a case in which he had been involved in which a man called Guillotin had been killed by several bullets. The chief suspect, Houssard, owned a revolver of the same calibre. Local firearms experts could not say with certainty that the bullets taken from the corpse had been fired from Houssard's revolver, and so Professor Balthazard became involved. He made enlarged photographs of bullets test-fired from the gun and bullets taken from the corpse and was able to point out no less than eighty-five similarities between them. As a result Houssard was convicted. When Balthazard published his findings the following year, he established his claim to be the founding father of modern scientific ballistics.

Edward J. Churchill died in 1910, and his nephew Robert Churchill, then twenty-three, took over the family gunsmith business and in the process devoted his life to the study of ballistics. He began making an inventory of the rifling in various makes of guns, and from his extensive knowledge of the direction, width, depth and pitch of the rifling, Churchill was able to tell at a glance from which make of gun a bullet had been fired. He became the premier expert witness on firearms, far more efficient and scientific than his uncle had ever been.

But even Churchill could still not prove that a particular bullet had come from a particular gun; he could only state the *probability*. In this capacity he testified as an expert witness in several notable murder trials, including the 'Hooded Man' case of 1912. (So-called because the suspect was hooded with an apron by the police after being taken into custody, for fear that press photographs might influence a potential identification witness.)

On 9 October 1912, police at Eastbourne were called to a large house in South Cliff Avenue. The coachman had spotted a burglar hiding on the wooden porch above the front door and alerted his mistress, who telephoned the police. Inspector Albert Walls arrived on the scene and shouted: 'Now then, my man, just you come down.' The reply came in the form of two shots which killed the inspector, the burglar-turned-killer fleeing the scene.

The only clues to the killer were the two bullets removed from the victim, but an informer turned in the name of John Williams as being the killer. The informer's motive appeared to be that he wanted to seduce Williams' girl friend, Florence Seymour, who was staying with Williams at Eastbourne.

Williams's real name was George McKay, but his extensive record for burglary had made a change of name essential. Williams was duly arrested when he fled to London, and was 'hooded' as he left the train in Eastbourne, handcuffed to a police officer. He was put up on an identity parade but witnesses failed to pick him out. There was nothing to connect Williams with the murder.

Now the informer once again came to the aid of the police. He persuaded Florence Seymour to show him where Williams had buried his revolver on Eastbourne beach, on the pretext that it was vital to hide it in a safer place. Once the police had the revolver they interrogated the woman, who made statements incriminating Williams.

The revolver was handed over to Robert Churchill, who test-fired a bullet from it. He was able to state that the bullet which killed Inspector Walls had been fired from a revolver of the same calibre and make – which was not proof that it had been Williams's revolver which had fired the fatal shots.

Chief Inspector Bower, the officer in charge of the case, persuaded Churchill of the need to be more 'scientific' and loaned him a police photographer for the purpose of photographing the inside of the revolver barrel. Since the necessary equipment had not yet been invented, the task was well-nigh impossible, but Churchill improvised. He coated the inside of the barrel with melted dental wax, then carefully removed it and photographed the impression of the lands and grooves it depicted. It was hardly 'scientific' but it served to impress the jury, and Williams was hanged.

It is possible – even likely – that Williams was innocent. As he explained at his trial, as a professional burglar he would never enter a house while the occupant was still at home. He had fled from Eastbourne only because he owned a revolver and had a criminal record. A modern jury would probably have acquitted him for lack of evidence, but the case made Churchill's name as an infallible ballistics expert, and he was to enjoy the same kind of reputation as did Sir Bernard

Spilsbury as a pathologist. The pair even worked together.

England still enjoyed the reputation of leading the world in all areas of criminal investigation, thanks mainly to the mythological status of the name 'Scotland Yard'. But the USA was in the process of rapidly overtaking the Yard in the application of forensic science, aided by sheer Yankee ingenuity. Curiously enough, one of the major characters in the case which was to change the history of ballistics had brought fingerprint techniques to America from Scotland Yard. He was Inspector Joseph Faurot of the New York State Police.

The case involved Charles Stielow, a farmhand of German extraction who spoke English poorly. On the early morning of 22 March 1915 he discovered that his employer, Charles Phelps, and the housekeeper, Margaret Walcott, had been shot to death. The motive had clearly been robbery, and the weapon used was a .22 revolver. Stielow stated at the inquest that he had never possessed a revolver, but a private detective discovered that Stielow owned a .22, which was found in his possession.

Under 'third degree' interrogation Stielow, who was mentally retarded, made a confession to the murders. At his trial, however, he withdrew it, claiming that it had been extracted by force. The prosecution relied upon a firearms expert named Dr Albert Hamilton, who knew precious little about ballistics. He photographed the *wrong* side of bullets test-fired from Stielow's revolver, and pointed out scratch marks which were clearly not visible. However, the jury was swayed by this 'scientific' evidence and convicted Stielow, who was sentenced to death.

The deputy warden of the prison where Stielow was being held became convinced of Stielow's innocence, and persuaded society ladies in New York to finance an investigation into the case. A private detective ascertained that two tramps named King and O'Connell had been seen in the area of Phelps' farm in Orleans County, New York, on the day of the murder, and both men were now serving prison sentences for theft.

A lawyer acting for the New York humanitarians got King to confess that he and O'Connell had committed the murders, but police in Orleans County were horrified – it would reveal their incompetence and mean another expensive trial. So they persuaded King to withdraw his confession.

When the Governor of New York heard about this, he asked a lawyer named George H. Bond to carry out a thorough investigation into the case. Bond's assistant was an employee of the New York State Prosecutor, Charles A. Waite.

Bond and Waite questioned Stielow and became convinced of his innocence. Waite then got Inspector Faurot, the State's firearms expert, to examine Stielow's revolver. Faurot reported that the weapon had not been fired in years – the barrel was thick with grease and dust. When he test-fired a bullet and compared it with the murder bullets, he found that the lands in the murder weapon had been twice as wide as those in Stielow's revolver. The difference was visible to the naked eye.

Faced with this conclusive evidence of Stielow's innocence, Governor Whitman granted him a free pardon – he had now served three years in prison. King again confessed to the murders, and once again Orleans County officials declined to prosecute him.

It was the obvious injustice of the case and the sheer lack of scientific discipline which motivated Waite to devote the rest of his life to firearms investigation. In 1912 in Britain, Robert Churchill had listed 119 pistols with a calibre of .25, noting the peculiarities of each. Waite decided to do the same thing, and began the mammoth task of cataloguing all the handguns in use in the USA. He took the simple step of approaching all the gun manufacturers for help and information.

In 1922 Waite had nearly finished his task, when he was disheartened to realise that thousands of European weapons of different makes and calibres flooded into the USA every year. Bravely, Waite visited all the European manufacturers and finally managed to catalogue thousands of weapons; he had fifteen hundred in his own collection.

The next step was to refine the method of matching the bullet to its gun. He got the Bausch and Lomb Optical Company to make him a microscope for comparing bullets. Philip Gravelle invented the comparison microscope, which could place a single test-bullet next to a murder bullet together in a single image so that the various marks could be compared and if possible matched. The physicist John H. Fischer then developed an instrument called a helixometer, which was a hollow probe with a light and a magnifying glass for examining the inside of a gun barrel, and together with Calvin Goddard, a former army doctor with a passionate interest in firearms, Waite set up the Bureau of Forensic Ballistics in New York in 1923.

Now ballistics had been set on a pure scientific footing in the laboratory, and when Waite died in 1926, Goddard took over from him and soon established himself as the world's leading firearms expert. His *History of Firearms Identification*, published in 1936, established his reputation internationally. Because of the indiscriminate use of firearms in Chicago under the rule of Al Capone, Goddard was asked to set up a crime laboratory at Chicago University, and became its first director. He did not lack for work, and one of his notable successes was in actually identifying the submachine gun which had been used in the notorious St Valentine's Day Massacre.

The first real test of ballistics as a *science* had come

in the Sacco and Vanzetti case in 1920. This case arouses strong emotions to this day, and countless books and articles have been written claiming that the two Italian immigrants, both self-confessed anarchists, were innocent martyrs to the cause of radical liberalism. The facts tell a different story.

On 15 April 1920 two payroll guards were shot dead in South Braintree, Massachusetts, while carrying boxes containing sixteen thousand dollars into the local shoe factory. Two men loitering outside committed the murders, then carried the cash boxes into a waiting car containing three other men, and made their escape. One of the killers had a heavy moustache.

The sheer brutality of the crime – one of the guards had had two bullets fired into his body as he lay on the ground – shocked the nation, and police pulled out all the stops to apprehend the killers. The first lead was the abandoned Buick car used in the raid, found two days later in woods. It had been stolen. A tip-off revealed that an Italian named Boda had been seen near the car.

Boda and his companions escaped on a motorcycle, but two men who had been with him were arrested on a streetcar. Twenty-nine-year-old Nicolo Sacco, and Bartolomeo Vanzetti, aged thirty-two, were both found to be carrying revolvers. Sacco's was a .32, the same calibre as that used to kill the guards, and Vanzetti had a heavy moustache, as described by witnesses to the robbery.

Both men were members of the anarchist movement and there was a great deal of resentment against them on this account, since there had been bomb outrages in many European capitals as well as the USA, with presidents and leaders being assassinated. It was alleged that Sacco and Vanzetti were tried for what they were rather than for what they did; a case of racial and political discrimination.

Sacco and Vanzetti were tried at Deham, Massachusetts, on 31 May 1921 before Judge Webster Thayer, who made no secret of his prejudice against the accused men, having described them in his club as 'those anarchist bastards'. District Attorney Frederick Katzmann also made no secret of his contempt for anarchists, and defence counsel Fred Moore made the most of this, implying that his clients were the victims of a witchhunt.

It was a poorly conducted trial. Witnesses for the prosecution, fifty-nine of them, placed Sacco and Vanzetti at the scene of the crime; but ninety-nine witnesses for the defence placed them elsewhere. The firearms experts were divided. One of them said that the bullet which had killed one of the guards had definitely come from Sacco's revolver, the other said it *could* have. (This was three years before the invention of the comparison microscope.) Two firearms experts for the defence said the bullet had not been fired from Sacco's revolver. The judge's summing-up was hardly a model of impartiality, and it came as no surprise when the jury convicted both men of murder on 14 July 1921, and Judge Thayer sentenced them to death.

The result was a worldwide outcry from the left-wing political parties of all nations, with the Red-Aid Committee raising money for a retrial, and millions of people signing petitions begging for Sacco and Vanzetti to be spared. The two men, who spoke poor English, waited on death row for the next six years.

In June 1927 a committee was appointed to examine the whole case, and this time Calvin Goddard was called in. With a defence firearms expert watching, he test-fired a bullet from Sacco's revolver into cotton wool and then placed it under the comparison microscope together with the murder bullet. After careful examination he declared that the bullet had indeed been fired from Sacco's revolver, and the defence expert was forced to agree. Whether or not Vanzetti was guilty, Sacco certainly was. The committee reported its results, and on 23 August 1927 Sacco and Vanzetti died in the electric chair.

The result was never accepted and controversy has raged ever since. Judge Thayer's house was bombed by angry sympathisers with the two 'martyrs'. But in 1961 another ballistics team examined Sacco's revolver and the murder bullet and concluded that there had been no mistake: that bullet had been fired from that revolver. This plain scientific fact should end all controversy, but of course it will not. It is in the nature of things that Sacco and Vanzetti will always be remembered as folk heroes in the fight for freedom, rather than as brutal killers who murdered for gain.

Also in 1927, a murder case gained the British public's recognition of the importance of ballistics evidence. On 26 September of that year a village policeman, PC George William Gutteridge, was shot dead in a remote country lane in Billericay in Essex. One horrific aspect of the murder lay in the fact that the killer or killers had shot out both the constable's eyes – no doubt because it was thought that a dead man's eyes retained the image of the last thing he saw, and could somehow be photographed to reveal the image of the culprit. The police even had the eyes of one of the Ripper's victims photographed in 1888, displaying the same mythical belief.

It was obvious that the constable had been shot because he had tried to stop a stolen car; his lantern was found in the road and there were tyremarks on the grass verge. He also had his notebook in his hand, but had recorded no details. The car was later found abandoned in Brixton, London, and so the case came under the command of Chief Inspector James Berrett of Scotland Yard. He knew the local villains, and one of his key suspects was a forty-six-year-old man named Frederick Guy Browne, who had violently attacked warders while in Parkhurst and was now running a garage business in Northcote Road, Battersea. However, there was no evidence to link Browne to the killing, and he continued his career of car thefts and burglaries.

Police had one vital clue which would nail the killer if he and his revolver were ever found. Inside the abandoned car they had found a cartridge case which was recognised as being ammunition for a Mark IV Webley manufactured at Woolwich Arsenal at the beginning of the war. It was the same make and calibre as the bullets removed from PC Gutteridge's body. The base of the cartridge case revealed a tiny blister caused by a fault on the breech-shield of the gun which had fired it.

Browne, along with a well-known local thief, was halted for a traffic accident in Sheffield while driving a stolen car, and gave the officer who stopped him a false name and address. When Sheffield Police tried to serve the summons and found the address didn't exist, they lost no time in tracing the passenger, whose real name and address were only too familiar to them. He said the driver had been Frederick Browne, and volunteered the information that Browne and his associate William Kennedy were the men who had shot PC Gutteridge.

On 20 January 1928 ten police officers lay in wait outside Browne's garage. As he drove into the ambush, they seized him immediately, before his hands could leave the wheel. This was fortunate, because in his pocket they found a revolver, and he subsequently claimed that it had been his intention to shoot as many policemen as possible before taking his own life.

Kennedy was arrested in Liverpool. He tried to shoot the detective who made the arrest, but his automatic pistol jammed. Kennedy made a full statement about the murder of PC Gutteridge, claiming that at first he had taken no part in the killing and had been shocked when Browne shot the officer; but then, standing over the officer and noticing that his eyes were open, he had

asked him: 'What are you looking at me like that for?'
– and shot him through both eyes.

Browne's Webley revolver proved to be the murder
weapon. An enlarged photograph showed clearly the
fault in the breech-block, and Robert Churchill testified
that it was indeed the weapon which had killed Gutteridge. His testimony in the trial of Browne and Kennedy
in April 1928 was crucial to their conviction, and both
men were hanged. It was the first British case in which
ballistics evidence played a central role, and it helped
establish the science in the public mind as another step
forward in the fight against crime.

The case was widely reported in European newspapers, and as a result within two years every major
forensic laboratory in Europe had been equipped with
comparison microscopes, helixometers, and special
equipment for micro-photography.

However, the dangers of relying too heavily on expert
witnesses was demonstrated in the case of John Donald
Merrett, an eighteen-year-old youth who was a spoilt
brat and a wastrel, having been expelled from Malvern
College following a sex scandal. His mother, who continued to indulge the boy, decided to go and live in
Edinburgh so that her son could attend university there.
She moved into a ground-floor apartment at 31 Buck-
ingham Terrace, keeping house and waiting for her son
to return home from his studies each evening. Return
home he did, but he had not been to university; he
spent his days playing truant and lavishing money on
girls.

On the morning of 17 March 1926, the daily help
heard a gunshot in the house, and Donald Merrett ran
into the kitchen saying: 'My mother's shot herself!' His
mother lay unconscious with blood oozing from a bullet
wound behind her ear. She was rushed to hospital and
treated as an attempted suicide. The .22 Spanish automatic pistol with which she was supposed to have shot

herself had been purchased by Donald Merrett a few days previously. Although unconscious when taken to hospital, Mrs Merrett regained consciousness sufficiently to sign cheques. She told a nurse that she had been writing a letter while her son was standing looking over her shoulder, and she had said to him: 'Go away, Donald, and don't annoy me.' She then heard a loud bang and lost consciousness. She asked the nurse: 'Did Donald do it? He's such a naughty boy.' On 1 April 1926 Mrs Merrett died.

Her estate, worth some £700 a year, went in trust for her son, but his behaviour remained as erratic as ever, and relatives who had moved into the house to look after him were so concerned that they had him examined by a psychiatrist, who pronounced him to be perfectly sane. Months later it was discovered that he had been systematically forging his mother's name on cheques, spending large sums of money on a dance hostess. The forged cheques amounted to £450, and were the first hint that the boy might well have had a motive for murdering his mother. In November 1926, some eight months after his mother's death, he was charged with her murder.

The prosecution had a very weak case. No attempt had been made to gather evidence, and any evidence which might have existed had long since disappeared. Professor Harvey Littlejohn had carried out the post-mortem and had concluded that the bullet wound behind the right ear of the victim, slanting upwards, was consistent with suicide. But after hearing of Merrett's forgeries and erratic behaviour, he became suspicious. There had been no powder burns around the wound, which he would have expected to find in a point-blank shooting.

Sydney Smith was in Edinburgh, and was something of an expert on ballistics as well as being an eminent pathologist. Professor Littlejohn consulted him about the death of Bertha Merrett, and they carried out experiments with the little Spanish pistol, discovering that it left powder burns at any distance less than eight inches. Professor Glaister was also consulted and was also of the opinion that Mrs Merrett had been murdered. Three top pathologists for the prosecution . . .

But the defence had engaged Sir Bernard Spilsbury as their expert witness, and he in turn consulted Robert Churchill. Churchill carried out experiments not with the Spanish pistol, but a pistol of the same calibre, and concluded that it did not necessarily leave powder burns, and even if there had been slight traces of spent powder, this could easily have been washed off.

The duo of Spilsbury and Churchill put up an impressive performance in court, demonstrating how Mrs Merrett would have held the pistol and emphasising that it did not leave powder burns. No one thought to point out that as their experiments had not been carried out with the Spanish pistol, their conclusions were irrelevant.

The judge was impressed and his summing-up was favourable to the defence. The jury brought in a verdict of not proven, although Merrett was jailed for twelve months for forgery. After his release from prison he changed his name to Chesney and began a life of petty crime, serving at least two prison terms in the course of squandering his mother's legacy. In 1952 he found himself broke and began thinking how he could acquire the wealth his estranged wife possessed. He had married her when she was sixteen, but she had refused to divorce him because she was a Catholic.

His wife and her mother, Lady Mary Menzies, were running an old people's home in Ealing. As part of an ingenious murder plot, Merrett stole a passport from a man in a pub and travelled to England from Germany on false papers. On 11 February 1954 he drowned his wife in the bath in an attempt to commit the 'perfect murder', but ran into his mother-in-law, whom he was obliged to strangle. He then returned to Germany, believing he had the ideal alibi, as no one could prove he had ever been in England.

The police were not that easily fooled, and within twenty-four hours of the double murder being discovered they announced that they were anxious to interview Ronald Chesney, formerly John Donald Merrett. Interpol was alerted, and four days later, on 16 February, Merrett shot himself through the head in a park in Cologne. This time it was a genuine suicide. Merrett, having been acquitted of one murder, had been freed to go on and commit another, proving perhaps that murder can become a habit. The case demonstrates the fact that outstanding advocacy and experts with reputations for being infallible can, despite the forensic evidence, gain an acquittal for a guilty man. The brilliant barrister Marshall Hall did it all the time.

The Spilsbury-Churchill team were involved in the sensational case of Elvira Barney, a wealthy twenty-seven-year-old nymphomaniac who lived in a London mews flat and took young lovers from the fringe of the homosexual underworld. By 1932 her latest lover was a man called Michael Scott Stephen, the son of a wealthy banker. He lived with Mrs Barney despite their frequent furious quarrels because he had nowhere left to go. His father had stopped his allowance.

At some time around 4 a.m. on the morning of 31 May 1932, neighbours heard the couple quarrelling loudly, and then the sound of a gunshot. Mrs Barney telephoned her doctor and said: 'Come at once – there's been a terrible accident.' Stephen lay dead, shot in the chest. Mrs Barney went to the police station to make a statement about the matter, and explained that she had threatened to kill herself in the course of a quarrel, and when her lover attempted to take her revolver away from her it went off, killing him. It had all been the most dreadful accident. . . . She was allowed to return home after signing her statement.

Churchill and Spilsbury were asked by the police to examine the evidence in the case. They went to the crime scene at the mews flat and quickly concluded that it was a case of murder. The deciding factor was that the trigger-pull on the death weapon, a .32 revolver, was fourteen pounds – far too strong for it to have gone off accidentally as claimed. And there was no powder scorching on Stephen's clothing, which there should have been if the gun had gone off at point-blank range.

Neighbours testified to hearing Mrs Barney say: 'I'll shoot you,' and one had heard more than one shot fired. Curiously, there were two empty chambers in the cylinder, but the other bullet was never found. Three days later Mrs Barney was arrested. When her trial began on 4 July 1932, policemen had to hold back the crowd of society women anxious to get a seat in court. The defence counsel was the adroit Sir Patrick Hastings, who realised from the outset that the man he had to defeat was Sir Bernard Spilsbury. If Spilsbury gave his evidence and was then asked if the defence story of an accidental shooting was possible, it would seal Mrs Barney's fate if he said 'no'. But if Spilsbury were not in court to give his evidence, then that question could not be put to him. Hastings made the unusual request that Spilsbury should not be allowed in court to hear the evidence, and the trial judge agreed. Hastings had won the first round.

When Churchill testified that it was impossible to fire the revolver accidentally since it required such a strong pull, Hastings fired it rapidly, click after click echoing around the courtroom. Churchill protested that it would require a stronger pull if held loosely. Hastings then held the revolver negligently and fired it again at the same speed. It was an impressive demonstration –

149

even if afterwards Hastings confided that it had made his fingers sore. Round two to Hastings.

When the formidable Spilsbury was in the witness box, everyone expected a clash. Instead, Hastings cunningly avoided a confrontation by asking simply if it wouldn't have been better to have determined the trajectory of the bullet by a postmortem examination. Puzzled, Spilsbury had to agree. Then Hastings abruptly sat down. He had accomplished his aim. Spilsbury had said nothing which contradicted the defence's accident theory; he had not because he hadn't heard it. The jury acquitted and Mrs Barney was free to resume her life of sex and alcohol, dying a few years later in a Paris hotel.

Since then there have been many notable murder trials involving ballistics evidence, both in this country and others, but the truth is that ballistics, although an important forensic aid, plays a very minor role in criminal investigation in Britain simply because firearms are so little used by our criminals. Ballistics has played a vital role in Northern Ireland, where it has been possible to prove that a certain Armalite rifle has been used in twenty-seven murders, for example, but generally speaking ballistics is a low-priority science in forensic laboratories. The sheer knowledge that a bullet can be matched to a particular gun has had a positive deterrent effect.

Professional criminals tend to use shotguns, which leave less evidence for ballistics to examine, or if they use handguns, they are destroyed immediately afterwards.

The arrival on the scene of the comparison microscope had much to do with the growth of ballistics in modern forensic laboratories. In 1934 the first police forensic science laboratory was opened at Hendon. New techniques came into use, including the use of the periphery camera, which could photograph the whole curved side of a bullet to make comparison easier, and the dermal nitrate test, which was based on the principle that residues from the cartridge are driven backwards on to the hand of the person who pulls the trigger. The suspect's hand was coated in paraffin wax, which was then tested for nitrates. The dermal nitrate test became obsolete when it was realised that many commercial fertilisers contain nitrates, which could lead to misleading results. In 1974 six Irishmen were convicted of the Birmingham pub bombings because of the dermal nitrate test, but in their appeal they argued that the playing cards they had been handling immediately prior to their arrest had been coated with nitrate. Although they lost their appeal in 1988, the court accepted that the test was unreliable and flawed. Fortunately, in 1991 their second appeal was allowed and their conviction quashed.

Despite the great strides made in ballistics, it is still limited by human fallibility. The police have the task of collecting forensic evidence and forwarding it to the laboratory; if they fail to do this, there is nothing for the scientist to examine. If they do it badly, much of the evidence becomes flawed or is missed entirely.

This was illustrated graphically in the 'Bambi' case, when five members of the Bamber family were found shot dead in their Essex farmhouse on the evening of 6 August 1985. Police had been alerted by Jeremy Bamber, the twenty-seven-year-old adopted son of Neville and June Bamber, two of the victims. He said that he had received a telephone call from his father to say that his sister Sheila had gone berserk with a rifle – and then the line had gone dead. Sheila 'Bambi' Cafell, a former model, lay dead in the farmhouse, as did her two sons, Daniel and Nicholas. The murder weapon, a .22 automatic rifle, was in one of Sheila's hands, while a Bible lay in the other. Police assumed that because of Sheila's history of mental instability, she had shot her family dead and then committed suicide. Jeremy Bamber stood to inherit the family fortune of over half a million pounds. Thinking it was an open-and-shut case, the police destroyed forensic evidence, burning blood-soaked carpets from the house.

But five weeks later Jeremy Bamber's girl friend, twenty-one-year-old Julie Mugford, went to the police to tell them that Jeremy had boasted to her of being responsible for the murders, saying he had hired a 'hitman' to commit them. Bamber was arrested in London and questioned at Chelmsford police station for eighteen hours. He denied having anything to do with the murders, but admitted having burgled his father's office and taken money. He was bailed on the theft charge.

Now Essex Police had to face the embarrassing fact that what they had assumed to be the work of a mentally deranged suicide had been a clever plot by a cunning killer. The evidence itself proved that Sheila could not have committed the killings. The rifle had had to be reloaded twice, yet her fingernail polish was unchipped and her nightgown showed no oil residue from the cartridges. Neville Bamber, a big man, had put up a fight for his life and had his eyes blacked – the frail Sheila could hardly have attacked him in so violent a fashion.

Relatives had searched the house after the police had been and gone, and found a hidden-away silencer with blood on it. The police had missed this vital clue. With the silencer fitted to the end of the rifle, the weapon became so long that it was physically impossible for Sheila to have held the weapon on her own neck and pulled the trigger – twice. A policewoman of similar size demonstrated this; no matter how she wriggled, she could not point the weapon at herself.

Most important of all, if Jeremy Bamber's telephone had gone dead, meaning that his line was still connected to the farmhouse, how had he been able to telephone the police?

At his trial the evidence came out. How Bamber had talked of his plans to kill his family for weeks before the murders, and had drugged rats with marijuana and strangled them with his bare hands to see if he had the 'nerve to kill'. He had originally planned to set fire to the farmhouse but abandoned this idea when he discovered that the insurance was too small. Bamber had in fact left the farmhouse by a window, after setting the 'suicide' scene, leaving the doors front and back locked to make it seem a 'locked room' case. His motive was greed; he was paid a salary of twenty thousand pounds a year from the farm, but considered it wasn't enough.

The jury found Bamber guilty on 28 October 1986, and the judge sentenced him to life imprisonment, after describing him as 'evil beyond belief'. From prison Bamber still protests his innocence. It was a case which demonstrated incredible police ineptitude. 'Blunders' the press called them, and blunders they were – even if justice triumphed in the end.

In Great Britain we have strict regulations under the Firearms Act as to who can own weapons, and a special permit is required, which in effect limits the use of handguns to members of shooting clubs. But it was a member of such a club, Michael Ryan, who stunned the world on 19 August 1987 when he stalked the streets of Hungerford, in Berkshire, shooting at random with his Kalashnikov AK–47 rifle and Beretta pistol. He shot dead sixteen people, wounding fourteen more, before finally shooting himself when cornered by the police.

Ryan, who was twenty-seven, had no previous record of violence. He lived with his widowed mother, whom he shot, then set fire to the family house. He seems to have literally 'blown his top' that day, when an attempt to rape a woman in Savernake Forest was frustrated and he had to shoot her dead when she attempted to flee. Perhaps feeling that he had nothing left to lose, Ryan went on his murder stalk around his home town, bent on exacting some kind of mad revenge. He talked to police lucidly for ninety minutes, saying it had been 'like a bad dream', before finally blowing his own brains out. The government acted swiftly to ban all semi-automatic weapons.

There have been 'copy-cat' killings since, but guns are not really a problem in Great Britain. America, land of Samuel Colt's 'Equaliser' faces an epidemic of murder by shooting. Over sixty million handguns are owned by citizens who have the right under the Constitution to 'bear arms'. In 1975 there were 21,000 murders in the USA, of which 16,000 – over half – were by shooting, compared to 500 murders in Great Britain. Truly, with drug gangs in the USA using machine-guns routinely, the figures are staggering and can only get worse.

America *needs* a good ballistics system; thankfully we do not. The message for the rest of the world is that strict gun-control laws lead to fewer murders.

It is perhaps relevant to mention here the importance of gunshot wounds, which can tell an experienced ballistics expert almost as much as the bullet or cartridge case itself. Once the body has been photographed *in situ* and the position of bullet holes carefully measured to determine trajectory, and the scenes-of-crime officer has finished his examination and mapping of the scene, the body is removed to the mortuary for the postmortem examination. The clothing is examined for bullet holes or powder traces, then the wounds themselves are examined to determine the entry and exit points, and if the victim was known to have been standing when shot, the height of the killer can be estimated.

The entry wound will be small; a neat round hole. The skin, being elastic, closes up around the bullet as it enters the body and actually wipes it clean. Therefore around the entry wound there will be a bruise and possibly a ring of grease from the bullet.

If the bullet strikes at an angle, the entry wound will be oval rather than round. If the bullet was fired at point-blank range then the wound will be gross, with a clear imprint of the gun muzzle in the form of a bruise, and scorching around the entry wound or clothing. Particles of lead stripped from the bullet and partially burned powder will be found on the skin or clothing, sometimes driven into the skin like a tattoo. There will be pin-point haemorrhaging due to the unburned powder and metal shavings being driven into the victim's flesh, creating a stippled effect around the wound.

When a high-velocity bullet hits the body, a bow wave of air pressure causes the flesh at the entry wound to balloon out, and if there happens to be bone beneath the flesh at the entry site, instead of the neat round hole there will be extensive damage which can easily be mistaken for a bludgeoning wound. A bullet from a high-velocity rifle hitting a skull – or even a .22 fired at point-blank range – generates so much energy in the form of pressure waves that the brain is pulped.

Shotgun wounds present little problem, since the spread pattern can be determined and it is relatively easy to calculate how far away the killer was when he pulled the trigger. It is police practice never to wash gunshot wounds because of the danger of destroying evidence. Powder grains under the skin can be examined under the microscope to determine the manufacturer and even the type of cartridge used in the shooting.

Exit wounds do not always exhibit the massive damage attributed to them in thrillers. Providing the bullet does not hit bone in its passage through the body, the exit wound can be small. Much depends on the behaviour of the bullet in flight. If it tumbles it will cause great damage, less so if it waggles in flight, even less if it remains true and spinning.

But however the bullet hits you, you can be sure of one thing: it isn't *your* name on the bullet but, thanks to ballistics, it is the name of your killer . . .

Sir Bernard Spilsbury in his laboratory (MAGAZINE DESIGN)

Cable confirming Dr. Crippen's arrest (The Crippen Case, 1910) – the first use of wireless telegraphy to arrest a murderer (MAGAZINE DESIGN)

Items in the FBI's firearms' collection (MAGAZINE DESIGN)

Bullets from Frederick Guy Browne's Mark IV revolver, used in the murder of PC George William Gutteridge – the first British case in which ballistics evidence played a central role
(MAGAZINE DESIGN)

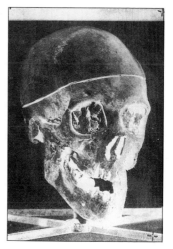

(Left) Mrs. Isabella Ruxton (The Ruxton Case, 1935) (Magazine Design)
(Right) The skull of one of the bodies found in the River Linn
(Magazine Design)

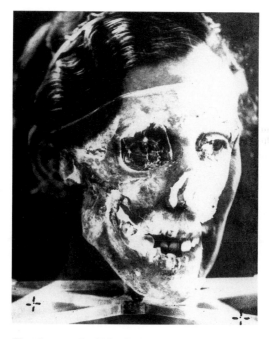

The photograph of Mrs. Isabella Ruxton with the
photograph of the skull superimposed
(Magazine Design)

Donald Neilson, The Black Panther
(SYNDICATION INTERNATIONAL)

Identikit picture and artist's impression of the Black Panther, issued by the
police (SYNDICATION INTERNATIONAL)

The mass of incriminating evidence found in Donald Neilson's Bradford home
(SYNDICATION INTERNATIONAL)

(Left) PC Chris Whiddon with the .22 rifle and silencer used by Jeremy
Bamber to kill five members of his family in August 1985
(SYNDICATION INTERNATIONAL)
(Right) Jeremy Bamber at the family funeral (SYNDICATION INTERNATIONAL)

(Right) Sex killer
David Evans escorted
by French police after
his arrest in 1988
(POPPERFOTO)

(Above) Mass murderer Dennis
Nilsen was a former chef with the 1st
Battalion Royal Fusiliers
(SYNDICATION INTERNATIONAL)
(Right) Nilsen used this and ties like
this to strangle his victims
(SYNDICATION INTERNATIONAL)

(Left) Peter Sutcliffe, the Yorkshire Ripper, being led away after the court hearing (SYNDICATION INTERNATIONAL)

(Above) Serial killer Ted Bundy. Bite marks on victims were matched to Bundy's teeth impressions (MAGAZINE DESIGN)
(Left) John Duffy, convicted in 1988 for the 'Railway Murders' (PRESS ASSOCIATION)

6

FINGERPRINTS: A QUESTION OF IDENTITY

We have examined the principal methods of murder in which forensic science plays a major role in the detection process: murder by poisoning or shooting – both of which leave indelible clues to the method employed. The other, more primitive methods, such as strangulation, bludgeoning, stabbing, burning or drowning, do not yield such ready clues, but the forensic scientists can still offer much expertise, although such cases are usually the province of the pathologist alone. Even so, he will often submit samples to the forensic laboratory for microbiological tests and the like.

In a case of strangulation – which technically is asphyxia, lack of oxygen – the pathologist will determine whether it was done with the hands (manual strangulation) or with a ligature (throttling). In both cases he will expect to find cyanosis: blue lips and ears, and frothing or bloodstaining around the mouth, with the tongue protruding. There will be tiny haemorrhages called 'petechiae' on the face and, particularly evident, in the whites of the eyes. If it is a case of manual strangulation, the delicate hyoid bone in the throat will invariably be broken – a classic indication of strangulation. There will also be extensive bruising to the throat. In the case of strangulation by ligature, the cord will usually be present, and if not leaves a distinctive groove. When found, the ligature is always carefully preserved and photographed, since the type of knot employed is a clue to the *modus operandi*. Albert DeSalvo, the Boston Strangler, always used a distinctive butterfly knot to finish off his ligatures: a dainty and artistic flourish to sign his brutal work.

With bludgeoning, the crudest and oldest of all forms of murder, there will usually be a lot of blood at the scene, with defensive wounds on the arms of the victim. Typically, the 'blunt instrument' of the detective novel is a hammer or poker, although every type of heavy object has been used, including a brick in a stocking – or even a heavy hook! The pathologist can often tell from the pattern of the wound what instrument was used. The Yorkshire Ripper, Peter Sutcliffe, used an engineer's ball-peen hammer, the rounded head of which left golf-ball type indentations in the skulls of his victims. And the sadist Neville Heath was trapped by the distinctive weave of the riding crop he used to thrash his victims.

With stabbing, the pathologist will be able to tell if a single-edged or double-edged knife was used, and the length of the blade. He will also determine which of the wounds was fatal. There will again be defensive wounds on the hands.

In cases of murder by burning – which are rare – the victim is characterised by a stiff, drawn-up pugilistic posture with fists clenched, caused by contraction of the muscles. If there is soot or carbon monoxide in the lungs, then the victim was alive when burning began.

Murder by drowning was the trademark of George Joseph Smith of the 'Brides in the Bath' murders. He married women for their pitifully small amounts of money and then, having insured them, arranged for them to have 'accidents' in the bath, murdering three wives in this way between 1912 and 1914. He was hanged at Maidstone in August 1915. The signs of drowning are froth at the mouth and distention of the lungs by water.

Botanists play a crucial role in drowning cases, in determining whether the victim was dead when he or she entered the water, or was put in the water after death. Many killers dispose of the bodies of their victims in water, hoping they will be washed out to sea. Microscopic algae called 'diatoms' are common in both fresh and salt water. If the victim's heart was still beating when submersed in the water, the circulation system will carry diatoms to such distant tissues as the kidneys, liver and bone marrow. If diatoms are present, then the victim was alive; if not, he or she was already dead. But there are differences between diatoms, and botanists can even detect *where* the victim died because of the local variety of the diatoms. In one case they were able to establish that a body washed up on the Belgian coast had gone in the water from a yacht off the Isle of Wight, proved by the diatoms recovered at the postmortem.

To detect whether the victim drowned in fresh or sea water – a cunning killer might drown his victim in a swimming pool, then dump the body in the sea – the chloride concentration of the blood is tested. In a drowning at sea the victim takes salt water into the lungs, which increases the chloride concentration in the blood. Since sea water has a higher osmotic pressure than blood, the blood remains undiluted. Fresh water, however, has a lower osmotic pressure than blood and is quickly drawn through the lungs and into the blood system, diluting it and reducing the chloride level. The presence of weeds or silt in the lungs can also help identify the place where the body entered the water. The cadaveric spasm is often seen in drowning cases – as in burning cases – and the dead person's hand might well be clutching a button torn from the jacket of the killer.

The recent case of thirty-one-year-old sex killer David

Evans is a text-book example of the various branches of forensic science combining to trap a killer – and it has its own 'water' element too.

Fifteen-year-old schoolgirl Anna Humphries was abducted while walking home from school in Penley, Clwyd, in North Wales. It was the afternoon of 8 November 1988. Police were soon on the track of a suspect, a local man living at Knowles Lane, Bettisfield, who had fled the area. David Evans had a long record for sex offences, having been jailed for five years in July 1978. Released early on parole, he raped again within five months of release and was then jailed for ten years on 13 January 1981, the trial judge telling him: 'I would be justified in giving you a life sentence.' Evans was again released early from prison on parole – but this time had killed within five months of release. It was a terrible *pattern* which had repeated itself, and the basis of all detection is the ability to spot patterns.

Evans had fled to France, but at the early stage there was nothing to link him to Anna's abduction – at this point her body had not yet been recovered. However, Evans had left his green Allegro car behind, and police sent this to the Home Office forensic science laboratory at Chorley, where it underwent a meticulous examination. Brilliant scientific deductions trapped Evans.

It was evident that the windscreen of the car had been recently replaced. Police traced the old shattered screen to a local garage and submitted it for analysis. Scientists at Chorley determined that it had been smashed from *within*, proof that a violent incident had taken place inside the vehicle. One of the shoes Anna had been wearing was found a mile or so from the spot where she vanished. The sole was cut and sliced, and glass fragments were found embedded in it. Chemical and microscopic analysis showed that the sole was made of a plastic which matched slivers of plastic found in the smashed screen, and the glass fragments in the shoe matched the glass in the screen. This was proof that Anna had been in Evans's car and that her feet had been in violent contact with the screen. Glass fragments from that screen were found on a sweater taken from Evans's home – proof that he had been in the car during or after the smashing of the screen; and bloodstains in the car indicated that an assault had taken place.

When Evans was arrested in France, British detectives went over to interview him. He told of having dumped Anna's body in the River Severn in Shropshire at Hampton Loade, hoping it would be washed out to sea. Police divers found the body almost where Evans had left it – it had been snagged on the branches of a submerged tree. Now even Anna's body could testify against him. A button found in Evans's car was matched to buttons on Anna's clothing, and that same clothing revealed paint fragments which under the microscope proved to be identical to the paint on Evans's car, linking him indisputably to the dead girl.

Had Evans pleaded not guilty, this mass of evidence would have convicted him; in the event, he pleaded guilty – and on Wednesday, 5 July 1989 he was sentenced to life imprisonment, the judge recommending that he should serve a minimum of thirty years.

Bodies which remain in the water for any length of time become water-sodden, the skin wrinkling and loosening, and even separating from the body on occasion. In the Australian 'Hand In Glove' case, a detached piece of skin from the victim's hand was found in the river near Wagga Wagga in December 1933. It resembled nothing more than a glove made of human skin. Scientists were able to fingerprint it and thus establish the identity of the victim, leading eventually to the conviction of the killer.

And thus we come to the heart of the problem. The age-old question facing any detective has always been how to identify the victim, or the killer, and various methods were tried before the advent of photography. The oldest system was what might be termed the 'needle in a haystack' method. The body or head of the victim would be displayed in public in the hope that someone might recognise it. Sometimes it worked.

On 2 March 1725 a human head was found lying on the foreshore of the Thames at Westminster. Local magistrates ordered the head to be placed on a pole in St Margaret's churchyard, and parish officers were ordered to stay in the vicinity and arrest anyone 'who might discover signs of guilt on the sight of it'. Neighbours of Catherine Hayes who lived in Tyburn Road (now Oxford Street) became convinced that it was the head of her husband, although she denied this, saying her husband John had been forced to flee abroad after killing a man in a quarrel. The local magistrate was informed and issued a warrant for the arrest of Catherine Hayes, who was found in bed with one of her lodgers. Upon being shown the head of her husband, now in a jar, she cried: 'Oh, it is my dear husband's head!' and proceeded to kiss the jar. She certainly 'discovered no signs of guilt'.

The magistrate was not impressed. Inquiries revealed that Mrs Hayes was sharing her body with two lodgers, Thomas Billings and Thomas Wood. Wood confessed to the crime, telling how Mrs Hayes had got her husband drunk, then persuaded the two lodgers to kill and dismember him. She had wanted to boil the head to make it unrecognisable, but the two men were too squeamish for this and simply threw it on the foreshore of the Thames. Mrs Hayes was tried for 'petty treason' in that she had rebelled against her husband, her lord and master. She was burned alive, while Billings was hanged. Wood had died in prison of fever. The execution of Catherine Hayes was a grim affair -- she tried to kick the burning faggots away with her feet, and took a long time to die. The chronicles record that it took three hours for her body to be reduced to ashes. How she must have wished she had boiled that head!

Another example of the 'needle in a haystack' method was demonstrated by Bow Street Runner Henry Goddard in 1853. He was employed to track down a man called John Todd who had fled to America with ten thousand pounds of his creditors' money.

Goddard took ship for America, and on arrival spent two days looking through hotel registers in New York, without result. Now Goddard made the mental effort which is the mark of any great detective: he tried to *think* like his quarry. He decided to head West, assuming that Todd would have made the same decision. He took a river boat which took him from Buffalo to Detroit, then on to Chicago and Milwaukee, making enquiries at each place at banks and land agents. In Milwaukee he asked for the name of the nearest large town and was told it was Janesville. He went there and stopped at the town's hotel, casually opening the register. There was the signature of John Todd. . . . He had found his quarry by luck and deliberate reasoning. Unfortunately he was unable to bring Todd back to justice, since America did not extradite for bankruptcy offences.

But such methods of identifying the victim or killer depended largely on luck more than anything else. What was needed was a *scientific* method of establishing identity. Once the identity of a victim had been established, tracking down the killer would be made that much easier by the advent of the railways in the 1840s and by Samuel Morse's remarkable invention, the telegraph. In 1845 John Tawell earned the dubious distinction of being the first murderer to be arrested by use of this new invention.

Photography was in its early stages and proved to be of little real use, since it required the subject to sit still for at least fifteen minutes, and even then, a collection of poor photographs showing men with beards and moustaches was of little help, when the suspect would probably shave off his beard after committing the crime. Another problem lay in the fact that photographs simply couldn't be *classified*. Even so, police in Marseilles began to use photographs, and the Sûreté built up its own collection of some eighty thousand portraits.

An early and rare example of the success of detection by photograph came in 1876, when a woman's head and other parts of her body were found floating in the Seine. Paris police decided to publish a photograph of the head and actually sell it in tobacconist's and corner shops. The morbid public bought hundreds of copies of the photograph – thus paying for its production – and then someone finally recognised the head. It belonged to the wife of an old soldier called Billoir. When questioned in his lodgings in the rue des Trois Frères, he insisted that his wife had left him, but detectives found traces indicating that a body had been dismembered in his room.

Billoir then confessed, saying he had kicked his wife during a quarrel and she had collapsed and died as a result. It was a pure accident, he claimed, but, frightened of being accused of murder, he had panicked and disposed of his wife by dismembering her and throwing the pieces in the Seine. Medical evidence proved him to be a liar. There was no sign of a bruise from a kick on her body, and the blood in the remains indicated that the victim had been alive when Billoir started to dismember her. She had been unconscious, not dead. Billoir went to the guillotine in 1876, remarking: 'The doctors have done for me.' He might just as well have said forensic science . . .

However, the main problem for the police remained the identification of habitual criminals. A man arrested in one city might be wanted in two or three more under different names, but there was no way of confirming this or of keeping track of criminals' movements. Criminals always gave false names when arrested in the hope of being punished as 'first offenders'. Charles Peace, the notorious Victorian burglar and murderer, often resorted to aliases to escape punishment, and even served prison terms under different names.

Photography had been a start, but there was more to come. Some of the intellectual foundations were being laid by men like Lambert Quételet, a Belgian astronomer who became fascinated by 'the frightening regularity of the recurrence of suicides'. He published his book *On Man* in 1835, and *Anthropometry, or The Measurement of Different Faculties in Man* in 1871. Quételet attempted to apply statistics to the problem of criminality – he also wrote that 'Society contains within itself the seeds of all future crimes.'

His books were devoured enthusiastically by Louis-Adolphe Bertillon, a young medical student who, together with his father-in-law, founded the science of anthropology, and later demography – the study of regional groups and races. Bertillon's second son was Alphonse, a genius who found himself stuck behind a desk in the clerical office of the Prefecture of Police, tediously copying out forms by hand. He was twenty-six years of age.

As a relief to the boredom, he decided to try and apply statistics to the study of physical characteristics, and began attempting to develop an early form of the 'Photofit' pictures by slicing up photographs and making different arrangements of noses, chins, mouths and eyes. He was like a child playing with a jigsaw – except that his intentions were deadly serious.

He had perhaps been influenced by the Italian criminologist Cesare Lombroso, whose book *Criminal Man* had caused a controversy by suggesting that criminals are simply throwbacks to primitive types, and could be recognised by their 'degenerate characteristics' – receding chins, weak mouths, sloping foreheads and the like. Lombroso was on the wrong track – many detectives look much more like this than do criminals, and some killers have had choirboy looks – but at least it was a definite scientific approach to the problem, and served to inspire Bertillon.

Bertillon came to the conclusion that no two human beings have exactly the same measurements, and that by measuring each prisoner by length and width of hand, length of fingers and forearms, he could devise a filing system, a classification of criminals by physical attributes. It was a complicated system, involving many measurements and cross-references. For example, a man whose head was 210 millimetres wide would be filed under 210. When a prisoner came in size 210, the 210 file would be consulted, with his other measurements leading to other files, and so on.

The young Bertillon put his ideas forward to his chief. The Prefect rejected them as being absurd, accusing Bertillon of playing a practical joke. Bertillon's father then used his influence with the chief, pointing out that if his son could prove that every human being is unique, he would be making the scientific discovery of the century. The Prefect gave in. In November 1882 Bertillon was given three months to try his system. If in that time he succeeded in identifying one habitual criminal, the experiment would continue. Bertillon set feverishly to work, with the aid of two clerks assigned to him.

The method he had decided upon was to take eleven basic measurements of the body, having established that the chances of any two men having all eleven identical were more than four million to one. He also included two photographs, one full-face, the other in profile, and then added what he called a *portrait parlé* – a spoken portrait, which mentioned any distinguishing marks such as moles, scars or tattoos.

Every prisoner who came into the prefecture was

measured and photographed, the resulting data being stored on cards in filing cabinets with 81 drawers. Since Bertillon could hardly have four million drawers, he settled on four basic measurements which offered odds of 276 to one, subdivided into seven other measurements. The basic flaw in the system was apparent at the start: it depended on every clerk being meticulous in his measurements, and in the nature of things clerks tend to get bored and sloppy.

For three months Bertillon worked away non-stop, building up his collection of files, while other officers sneered at the waste of time and money. Just as Bertillon was beginning to despair, a criminal was brought in named Dupont. Bertillon had six Duponts in his files, but this one had a mole near his left eyebrow. Bertillon took his measurements and then went to his files. He pulled out the cards and found that Dupont's real name was Martin, and he had previously been arrested on 15 December 1882. When faced with his real identity Martin confessed.

The system worked, and many more arrests followed as a result. The word *bertillonage* passed into the French language as the fame of the method spread. Bertillon solved a case when he identified a man dragged from the river. The identity of the corpse led to the killer. By 1888 a new Department of Judicial Identity had been founded at the prefecture, with Bertillon as its chief.

In 1892 he was instrumental in solving the Ravachol case. Ravachol was an anarchist, one who believed in Bakunin's phrase that 'the act of destruction is a creative act', and who imagined that society could be changed for the better by bombs and assassinations. Anarchist bombs were going off all around the world in the 1880s, with Tsar Alexander II of Russia falling victim to one, along with French and American politicians. They were even active in London. One, who attempted to blow up the Greenwich Observatory but was killed by his own bomb, inspired Conrad's novel *The Secret Agent.*

In 1892 the home of the judge who had sentenced two anarchists to imprisonment in France was blown up. An informer named a teacher called Chaumartin as the instigator of the plot. When arrested he admitted planning the attack, but said the actual bombing had been carried out by a fanatic named Léger, and inquiries revealed that Léger was actually a wanted anarchist called Ravachol, a muscular, sallow man in his twenties, with a prominent facial scar. His real name was François Koenigstein, and he was known to have been implicated in at least four murders involving robbery.

On the evening of the explosion Ravachol had sat in a local café talking to a waiter about the explosion, expressing his admiration and satisfaction at the act. The waiter noticed the scar on his face, which had been circulated in police descriptions, and when Ravachol called again two days later, the waiter notified the police. Ravachol was arrested after a fierce struggle and taken to the prefecture. Bertillon took his measurements and photographs and was able to establish that Léger was Ravachol/Koenigstein. Without this scientific proof of his real identity, Ravachol could not have been convicted. As it was, he eventually went to the guillotine crying out: 'Long live anarchy!' The café where he had been arrested was later blown up with an anarchist's bomb, but the case made Bertillon famous throughout Europe.

But even as he celebrated, elsewhere work was underway which would make bertillonage obsolete. It had been known for centuries that fingerprints were unique, the ancient Chinese having used thumb impressions to seal documents, and a seventeenth-century anatomist had described the ridges of fingerprints in a book. By the 1820s a professor of anatomy named Johann Purkinje had suggested a crude method of classification, and in India in 1858 a civil servant, William Herschel, asked a contractor to sign an agreement with the print of his hand.

In 1860 Herschel, now a magistrate in Calcutta, found that Indian pensioners were cheating by turning up to collect their pensions twice. To prevent this, Herschel hit on the idea of having these illiterate men dip their finger in ink and place their fingerprint on the receipt. It stopped the cheating overnight.

In 1877 Herschel wrote to the Inspector-General of Bengal Prisons outlining his ideas on fingerprints, but his ideas were rejected as being wildly impracticable. At the same time a Scottish doctor living in Tokyo, Henry Faulds, was working out his own theories about fingerprints, and had actually had some success in identifying a burglar by this means. In October 1880 Faulds wrote to the scientific journal *Nature* about his theories. Herschel, now in retirement in England, wrote to *Nature* claiming to have first used fingerprinting in 1858. This caused a fierce controversy, with the irascible Faulds claiming that Herschel was trying to steal the credit for his discovery. He set off for England determined to put the matter straight, and once there tried vainly to interest Scotland Yard in his ideas. He found no police officer willing to listen to him.

Then an eminent scientist, Sir Francis Galton, who had been impressed by the article in *Nature*, wrote to the editor of the journal, asking for the address of the discoverer of finger-printing. They gave him Herschel's address. When he visited Herschel and announced his interest, Herschel generously handed over all his material.

It took Galton three years just to ensure that fingerprints were indeed unique. Next came a method of classifying them. Since most fingerprints centre around a triangular shape, Galton called it the delta – the Greek sign for delta being a triangle. He then identified arches, whorls and loops, but got stuck there, finding no simple method of classification. In 1891 he published a paper on fingerprints in *Nature*, acknowledging his debt to Herschel – further infuriating Faulds, who wrote him an angry letter. The following year Galton published his book called simply *Fingerprints*.

The Home Secretary, Asquith, had been on the verge of introducing bertillonage into England, Scotland Yard's identification system being very poor, but then he came across Galton's book and had second thoughts. Bertillonage was just too complicated; if fingerprinting actually worked, it would be much easier to operate. He appointed a committee to examine the merits of fingerprinting. Headed by Charles Troup, a Home Office civil servant, the committee's other two members were Major Arthur Griffiths, and Sir Melville Macnaghten, the Assistant Commissioner of Police after the Ripper murders of 1888. The committee was impressed with the simplicity of fingerprinting, but troubled by the fact that no practical system of classification had yet been devised. Typically, the Troup Committee dithered.

They also had to face the fact that bertillonage had been enthusiastically accepted and introduced throughout most of Europe; even Hans Gross, 'the father of criminology', urged its introduction in his book *Criminal Investigation*. In 1898 this came about in Austria. It was in use in Germany, and was introduced in Argentina in 1891. Head of the Statistical Bureau of La Plata Police was a man called Juan Vucetich. He had read about Galton's work on fingerprinting in a journal, and when he realised that the problem of classification had not been solved, he took it up as a personal challenge.

Like Galton, he accepted the delta as the chief point of identification, and soon realised that there were four basic types: those with no triangle, those with a triangle on the right, those with a triangle on the left, and those with two triangles. It was simple to number these 1, 2,

3, 4, using A, B, C, D, for the thumbs. Although not the complete solution to the problem, it was at least a simple if crude form of classification, easy to arrange in a filing cabinet. Vucetich was a cop, and he knew that what a cop wanted was not a complicated theory, but a quick and simple process.

In July 1892 he was able to solve a murder with his method of classification. A woman living in a shack in a small coastal town near Buenos Aires told police that she had found her two children lying dead in their bed, their skulls smashed in. As she went to open the door of the shack, a man called Velasquez had rushed out. He had been pestering the twenty-six-year-old unmarried mother to marry him. The woman Francisca Rojas, was adamant that she had not touched the bloodied bodies of her six-year-old boy and four-year-old daughter.

Velasquez was arrested and brutally questioned for a week by Police Chief Alvarez, but still he protested his innocence. Finally Alvarez went to the shack where the murders had taken place and examined the scene. On the door he found a clear fingerprint in blood. He had the wood sawn out and took it back to the station. Now he took the mother's fingerprints: they were a perfect match. When shown the evidence of her guilt – how could her bloody fingerprint be on the door if she had not touched the bodies? – the mother broke down and confessed. It was a clear vindication of Vucetich's system.

Now the quest for the ultimate classification system swung back to India, where a British civil servant, Edward Richard Henry, became interested in fingerprinting because he found the bertillonage system he was using in the Nepal Police too complicated. It only needed a bored clerk to be a millimetre off in his measurements for the system to fail. As soon as he was back in England on leave, he lost no time in contacting

Galton, who placed his material at his disposal – the mark of a true scientist.

Back in Calcutta, Henry brooded over Galton's many photographs of fingerprints, and it was during a long railway journey that he suddenly saw the answer to the problem of fingerprint classification. The answer lay in the delta, as Galton had foreseen; Henry accepted the loops, arches and whorls, although he added tented arches, and divided loops into two types. Henry wrote: 'The deltas may be formed by either (a) the bifurcation of a single ridge, or (b) the abrupt divergence of two ridges which have hitherto run side by side.' Basically, all Henry had to do was to establish the limits of the delta – from what he called the 'inner terminus' to the 'outer terminus' – and then draw a line between the termini and count the number of papillary lines that intersect it. (The papillary lines are those fine lines you can see running parallel across your fingertips, which turn into various types of eddies and whirlpools towards the centre. For 'eddies and whirlpools' read loops, arches and whorls.)

This in essence is the basis of the Henry system of fingerprint classification, now standard through the world. Faced with an unknown fingerprint, the detective has to decide which of the five basic types it belongs to: two types of arches, two types of loops, and whorls, and then count the number of lines. Since the vast majority of fingerprints belong to the simple loop-and-delta system, identification is quick and simple. Most great ideas are simple and elegant, which makes it all the more surprising that a great scientist like Galton had not grasped this obvious solution immediately.

Henry managed to persuade the Governor-General of India of the value of his discovery, and in July 1897 it was adopted in that country as the sole means of identifying criminals. By August 1897 Henry had solved a number of murder cases with his system, and in 1900 he published his fingerprint-classification system. It was greeted with such acclaim that on 31 May 1901 Henry was appointed Assistant Commissioner at Scotland Yard and had set up the Central Fingerprint Branch by July of the same year.

One side effect of Henry's success was that he was able to prove with statistics that the Henry system of fingerprinting was three times as efficient as bertillonage. It came as a blow to Bertillon, who had to face the bitter knowledge that his lifetime's work had been superseded by a better system. Within weeks of his death, for example, fingerprinting had been adopted as the standard method of criminal identification throughout Europe.

However, Bertillon had been quick to see the advantages of fingerprinting, even if he spoilt the effect by insisting on adding it to his system of bertillonage, which made it even more cumbersome. But Bertillon has one claim to fame: in October 1902 he became the first man in Europe to solve a murder by means of fingerprints. On 17 October 1902 Bertillon was asked by an examining magistrate to inspect the scene of the crime: a luxurious apartment in the rue Faubourg Saint-Honoré. The apartment had been burgled and a valet strangled. On a shard of glass from a broken cabinet door, Bertillon found a perfect set of fingerprints, which he photographed. But since fingerprints were not classified in the bertillonage system, but merely added to the file cards, it meant examining hundreds of thousands of cards with a magnifying glass. It took him three days to find a match: the killer was a swindler called Henri-Léon Scheffer.

The Scheffer case should have convinced Bertillon of the need to scrap bertillonage and adopt the Henry system of fingerprint classification. But it did not; to admit that bertillonage was obsolete would have meant admitting failure. But obsolete it was.

The first British murder to be solved by fingerprints came in 1905 in Deptford, south-east London. On 27 March a shopkeeper called Farrow was discovered lying dead in the back parlour of his premises, while his wife lay upstairs in a bloodstained bed, alive but unconscious. Scotland Yard detectives were quickly on the scene. The motive had clearly been robbery, since the couple were known to have hoarded money on the premises. Witnesses had seen two men leaving the shop at the time of the murder. The only clue was a bloody thumbprint found on the lid of a rifled cash box, discovered by Sir Melville Macnaghten himself. He then had the prints of the attacked couple taken for elimination purposes – it was the first time the prints of a corpse had been taken in England. A search among the eighty thousand or so prints on file at the Yard failed to find a match to the cash-box print.

Two brothers, Alfred and Edward Stratton, became suspects in the case. They had long criminal records and had vanished from their usual haunts just after the murder. They were tracked down by traditional detective methods and arrested. When fingerprinted, Albert Stratton's thumbprint was found to match that on the cash box. At the subsequent trial at the Old Bailey on 5 May 1905, Inspector Collins was the fingerprint expert for the prosecution, and by an ironic coincidence, the fingerprint expert for the defence was Henry Faulds, the embittered Scot who claimed to have invented fingerprinting. The forensic truth prevailed, and both brothers were convicted and hanged.

By 1910 the Henry system of fingerprint classification had been adopted throughout Europe, including Russia, save for France, where they clung to the outmoded bertillonage. Bertillon was disgraced when his evidence helped convict Captain Dreyfus, later proved to be innocent, and this disgrace was further compounded when the *Mona Lisa* was stolen from the Louvre on 21 August

1911. The thief left his fingerprints on the glass covering the painting, but Bertillon could not identify the prints. They were excellent prints, plainly visible to the naked eye. Fingerprints are made by sweat secretions from the skin, which include fatty substances from the sweat pores along the papillary lines. Latent – or invisible – prints can be made visible by dusting with fine powder such as aluminium. On white surfaces, such as china, a black powder is used.

When the man who had stolen the *Mona Lisa* – Vincenzo Perrugia – was arrested two years later, Bertillon found he had his card on file as a petty thief with several convictions. The man's prints were also filed, yet Bertillon had failed to identify him, It exposed the basic flaw in the system of bertillonage in brutal fashion, and Bertillon died on 13 February 1914 in the knowledge that his work had been in vain. He had been a scientific pioneer, but a failed one.

The most eminent criminologist in France was Professor Alexandre Lacassagne, who achieved sudden fame in 1889 through his involvement in the Gouffé case. Lacassagne was Professor of Forensic Medicine at Lyons, and his assistant was a remarkable young man called Edmond Locard, who was soon to outstrip his master. His book *Traité de Criminalistique*, published in 1912, made his name. In that book Locard says: 'To write the history of identification is to write the history of criminology.' Locard was obsessed with the problem of identification, which is why he seized on the new science of fingerprinting, determined to make his own contribution. What Locard did was to make a refinement to the Henry method. He realised that the pores in the fingertips are as individual and unique as fingerprints, and so developed the science of poroscopy. He first used his system in 1912 in Lyons to convict a burglar named Boudet. He made a photographic enlargement of the prints Boudet had left at the scene of the crime, and counted for the jury the number of pores in the area he had selected: 955 of them. He then showed them the same area of Boudet's fingerprint, and again counted the pores: 955 of them. The jury was impressed and convicted. In his book Locard mentions seven cases solved by this method in 1912 alone.

But poroscopy rarely comes into fingerprinting; the Henry system is good enough on its own. To recapitulate: the Henry system is based on four groups of ridge patterns: arches, loops, whorls and composites. Arches are divided into plain or tented. Loops are either ulnar if they slant towards the little finger, or radial if they slant towards the thumb. Since loops account for sixty-five per cent of all fingerprint patterns, they are subdivided according to the core and delta of the pattern, the core being the centre, the delta the division of a ridge. The Henry system made possible over a million groupings, since each finger is given a numerical value. A minimum of sixteen matching characteristics is required to secure a conviction in this country, twelve in the USA.

By a strange coincidence, proving that life imitates art, just as the detective was invented in fiction before he existed in fact, so fingerprinting was first mentioned in fiction long before any police force knew of its existence. In his book *Life on the Mississippi* (1883), Mark Twain has an anecdote told by a dying man of how he tracked down the killers of his wife and child by means of a bloodstained thumbprint. The dying man explains that he was told as a youth: '. . . there is one thing about a person which never changes from the cradle to the grave – the lines in the ball of the thumb . . . those lines are never exactly alike in the thumbs of any two human beings.'

As well as detecting criminals, the adoption of fingerprinting was to prevent many cases of mistaken identity occurring, although it did not help fifty-five-

176

year-old Adolf Beck, accused in December 1895 of swindling jewellery from a lady. He was positively identified by the victim. Furthermore, the *modus operandi* fitted a swindler who had operated as John Smith and been sent to prison in 1887 for similar swindling offences against women. A sample of Smith's handwriting was examined by an expert, who concluded that it was identical with Beck's. Since his crimes as 'Smith' were also taken into account, Beck was sentenced to seven years' hard labour.

Over and over he protested his innocence from prison, claiming that he had a 'double' who was committing crimes for which he was being blamed. Even when his lawyer was able to prove that Smith had been a Jew and was circumcised, and Beck was not, it did not help. There existed as yet no Court of Appeal.

Beck's troubles were not over. Released on parole in 1901, three years later the same circumstance happened; a girl stopped him in a London street and accused him of swindling her out of her jewellery. Beck ran away in panic but was arrested by a constable. After three months in custody and facing another trial, the *real* John Smith was arrested. Beck was freed and given five thousand pounds compensation. It was a remarkable case, and the handwriting of both men was indeed indistinguishable. The case proved beyond doubt the need for a positive system of identification.

Similar cases of mistaken identity were still to occur – and do occur to this day. George Ince was tried for the 'Barn Murders'. The jury failed to agree. At a retrial he was acquitted. The police felt certain they were watching a guilty man walk free – yet a couple of months later the real killer was arrested, still in possession of the gun used in the killings. The George Edalji case had led to the setting-up of the Court of Criminal Appeal in England in 1907. And in 1908 in Scotland, Oscar Slater was tried for the murder of Marion Gilchrist, found battered to death in her Glasgow apartment. Miss Gilchrist's maid identified Slater as the man she had seen running away from the flat. He was found guilty and sentenced to death, but because of the lurking uncertainty in the case, the sentence was commuted to one of life imprisonment.

Conan Doyle, creator of Sherlock Holmes, became involved in the case after Slater had served five years in jail. He read all the evidence and was convinced of Slater's innocence. Due to his efforts, a retrial was ordered, but once again Slater was found guilty. After Slater had served eighteen years, the maid, now living in America, confessed that she had identified the wrong man because of police pressure, and another witness told a similar story. As a result of a new inquiry, Slater was freed, his sentence quashed and compensation paid to him. Yet the police had found a bloody handprint on a chair at the murder scene, and had they known anything about fingerprinting they could have cleared Slater there and then.

Fingerprinting took time to establish itself in the USA, and it was not until 1928 that New York decreed all offenders should be fingerprinted. And this was despite some early successes by a brilliant New York policeman, Inspector Joseph A. Faurot. In 1904 he had gone to London to study fingerprinting under Inspector Collins of the Yard, and had returned to the USA full of enthusiasm for the Henry method of classification. He soon caught a hotel thief by fingerprints, and in 1908 solved a murder. But the case which grabbed the headlines was a fairly simple burglary case. Faurot testified in court that he had found the fingerprints of Caesar Cella on the window of a burgled shop. The judge was not convinced – after all, fingerprinting was just a new fad. The judge invited Faurot to give a demonstration in court, sending him outside while several members of the public made impressions of their index fingers on a window in the courtroom. The judge then asked one of them to also place his fingerprint on the top of a glass table. He then invited Faurot to identify which fingerprints on both window and table were identical. It took Faurot just four minutes to accomplish this, and the case reached the headlines, making America aware of the importance of fingerprints.

The Bureau of Investigation was established by Congress in 1908 to act as an investigative arm for the Department of Justice, but the Bureau was kept chronically short of money and personnel, and it was not until 1924, when J. Edgar Hoover was appointed Director, that any improvements were made. Progress under Hoover was rapid. He persuaded Congress to grant money for a Fingerprint Bureau, and he quickly built up its nucleus of 800,000 fingerprints – it now has over 200 million in its collection. By 1932 nearly 5,000 law-enforcement agencies around the country were cooperating with the Bureau, which became the Federal Bureau of Investigation in 1935.

In 1967 the FBI set up the National Crime Information Centre (NCIC) in Washington, with a computer which could be reached by terminals in every police department in every state. Fingerprints and photographs can be checked within minutes.

Today the FBI deals with thirty thousand fingerprint enquiries every day, using laser equipment to scan eighty fingerprints per second to find a match. The FBI has also made advances in fingerprint identification, using laser illumination to make latent fingerprints on flesh or paper fluoresce and become visible under iodine fumes. Special X-ray techniques can also 'visualise' prints on human skin, and the very latest technique is the use of Kromekote cards, which are similar to photographic paper but with a very high gloss. To transfer a latent print from human flesh, the card is placed over the skin and held with a firm pressure for three seconds. The card is then removed and dusted with ordinary black fingerprint powder. Any print successfully retrieved by this method will be a mirror image of the normal print and must be reversed in the photographer's darkroom. The survival time of latent prints on flesh depends on a number of factors, including the state of the skin and atmospheric conditions, but latent prints have survived on flesh for up to ninety minutes.

By comparison with the FBI's collection, the Police National Computer at Hendon, installed in 1976, has two and a half million prints on file, stored in a retrieval system known as Videofile, which can be displayed on VDU terminals around the country for speed of identification. Henry could never have dreamed that his system would become so sophisticated.

But in the early days the basic Henry system of indexing all the fingers and thumbs of a convicted felon meant a long delay in finding a match. What was badly needed was a *single* fingerprint collection. In England this was achieved by Superintendent Harry Batley, who devised the Single Fingerprint System in 1930, and almost as an afterthought decided to collect palm prints as well.

The first murder conviction by palm print took place in 1942, when a seventy-four-year-old pawnbroker, Leonard Moules, was attacked and killed by two men robbing his shop. DCS Fred Cherrill of the Yard, who had been Harry Batley's assistant, found one single palm print on the inside of the safe door. When two suspects were arrested, Cherrill matched the palmprint of one of them to that found at the murder scene. Both men were convicted and hanged at Pentonville Prison.

Criminals were becoming aware of the danger of fingerprints, and in the USA gangsters like John Dillinger and Alvin 'Creepy' Karpis attempted to alter their fingerprints by surgery. Dillinger had his burned off with acid; Karpis had his finger pads sliced off. In both cases the original fingerprints reappeared as the finger-tips healed. Nothing will destroy fingerprints. Even in drowning cases where the skin becomes sodden and wrinkled, scientists have devised a method of taking the prints by injected water under the skin so that the finger pad fills out, enabling a print to be taken.

The first major post-war case involving fingerprinting came in 1948, when three-year-old June Devaney was snatched from her hospital cot on 14 May, only to be found dead in the hospital grounds, sexually assaulted and with her skull smashed in. The killer had swung her by her heels against the stone wall surrounding the hospital. The killer had left his fingerprint on a bottle at the side of the murdered child's bed.

Detective Inspector Colin Campbell, head of the Lancashire Fingerprint Bureau, recovered the print but unfortunately it was not on file at Scotland Yard. The killer had no previous criminal record. DCI John Capstick of the Yard's Murder Squad was in charge of the investigation, and he decided that desperate measures were needed: he made the decision to fingerprint every male in Blackburn in the relevant age bracket – some 50,000 of them. The Mayor of Blackburn was the first to have his prints taken. Five hundred sets of prints a day were being examined, officers working overtime.

Two months after the murder the killer's prints had still not been matched, although over forty thousand males in Blackburn had been fingerprinted. On 11 July 1948 a policeman called at 31 Birley Street, to take the prints of twenty-two-year-old Peter Griffiths, a former guardsman. His prints were set number 46,253. The following afternoon an exhausted fingerprint officer cried out: 'It's him!' Griffiths was arrested and made a confession to the murder, saying he had lost his temper 'because she wouldn't stop crying'. He added: 'I hope I get what I deserve.' He did. The defence pleaded diminished responsibility, but the jury found him guilty of deliberate murder. Griffiths was hanged on 19 November, just seven months after the murder.

There have been many fingerprint successes since, and great advances have been made in the science of dactyloscopy. Prints are now 'lifted' by a piece of transparent tape and fixed to a card. Latent prints on porous surfaces like paper and cloth can be developed by using iodine fumes or ninhydrin spray. Even lip prints can be classified, and in one case in the USA involving a hit-and-run driver, the lip prints of the victim were found on the front bumper of the suspect's vehicle.

Fingerprints can now be transmitted by wireless telegraphy – or faxed – and many police cars in the USA are now fitted with VDU screens for instant comparison. When this system was first introduced in San Francisco in 1984, there was a dramatic upsurge in the number of crimes solved. The French, too, have learned valuable lessons. They developed an application of the light-sensitive qualities of silver nitrate, used in photography, for developing latent prints on wood. Since fingerprints are made essentially by sweat, they contain a certain amount of salt, and when sprayed with silver nitrate the salt develops like a photograph when exposed to light.

But in truth fingerprinting plays a very small role in crime-solving in Britain today. Only two per cent of all crimes are solved by fingerprints. Although the Great Train Robbers of 1963 conveniently left most of their fingerprints at their hideout at Leatherslade Farm, in practice even the pettiest of criminals has learned to wear gloves. Still, fingerprints have been developed from *inside* gloves before now. . . . The fact that fingerprints can be identified acts as a deterrent.

Before leaving the subject it is important to emphasise that fingerprinting still has a vital role in crime-fighting, and the importance of the single fingerprint was demonstrated in the case of twenty-five-year-old John Cannan,

who was convicted of the abduction and murder of
Shirley Banks on 8 October 1987. When Cannan was
first arrested, the body of newly wed Mrs Banks had
not been found. Cannan was in possession of the car
she had been driving, but claimed to have bought it at
auction. He insisted that he had never met Shirley
Banks, and police had nothing to link him to the missing
woman.

They had conclusive evidence of rape and assaults;
in the rape case a genetic-fingerprint test on semen left
in the victim's underclothes was matched against his
blood sample. It showed that he was the rapist, with
the odds of error being a staggering *260 million to one.*

A careful examination was made of items recovered
from Cannan's flat in Bristol. On the cover of a report
from a private detective whom Cannan had hired, police
found one single thumbprint. Mr Paul Jobbins, a senior
fingerprint officer with the police, was able to 'lift' Mrs
Bank's prints from items at her home, her parents' home
and the office where she worked, and was able to match
her thumbprint against the impression on the document
found in Cannan's flat. This was crucial evidence, since
the private detective had not handed in his report until
28 September – some twenty days *after* Mrs Banks
disappeared. It proved that Mrs Banks had been in
Cannan's flat – held captive there for some time –
despite his denials that he had ever met her.

Shirley Banks, although dead – her body was discovered lying in a remote stream on 3 April 1988 –
was able to testify against her murderer by that single
thumbprint.

On 28 April 1989 the jury found Cannan guilty on
all the charges of rape, abduction and murder, and after
sentencing him to three life terms of imprisonment and
other jail terms totalling thirty-four years, Mr Justice
Drake told him: 'I would add the recommendation in
this case that the period you serve in prison shall be the

period of your life. You should never again be at liberty outside prison walls.'

And so Cannan, believed by some police officers also to have been responsible for the mysterious disappearance of estate agent Miss Lamplugh from central London in July 1986, and certainly one of the most dangerous killers of recent times, was trapped by a single thumbprint. The success in detecting Cannan belongs to Bristol Police, but the triumph is that of Edward Richard Henry, the pioneer of modern fingerprinting.

7

THE BODY IN QUESTION . . .

Fingerprints can help identify a body, but what happens when the body is so mutilated, badly decomposed or burnt that no fingerprints remain? What if only a *part* of the body is recovered – say, a headless torso without limbs? What if there is no body at all, only a strong suspicion of murder?

Identifying a body is often the most difficult aspect of a murder investigation, and this problem was recognised by Edmond Locard, who published his two-volume *Proofs of Identity* in 1932. (Incidentally, in the course of that work he declared Anastasia to have been a fraud.)

For the murderer the immediate task is the disposal of the body of his victim. The typical murderer leaves the body where it falls, which is obvious when one realises that over half of all killers commit suicide immediately after the act, or telephone the police to tell them what they have done. But there remains that small core of cold and calculating killers who plan to get away with their deed. They try to hide the corpse, either by secret burial or putting it into water, weighted down – although bodies have a nasty habit of surfacing . . . Or they might try to disguise or destroy the body by dismembering, boiling, burning, or dissolving in acid.

John George Haigh dissolved his victims in acid; James Camb shoved a corpse out of a porthole of an ocean liner into shark-infested seas; Brian Donald

Hume dropped the dismembered body of Stanley Setty into the sea from an aeroplane; Dennis Nilsen cut up some of his sixteen victims and flushed them down the toilet; others he burned on a garden bonfire.

The reason for hiding or disposing of the body is that the killer is only too aware that the identification of the corpse often leads to the unmasking of the killer. But the human body is surprisingly difficult to destroy entirely, as we shall see. Let us examine a typical modern case.

On Sunday, 31 August, 1986, the dismembered parts of a body were found by a motorist at a lay-by on the busy A22 road at Ashdown Forest, Sussex, between Nutley and Wych Cross. It was the revolting smell which had attracted the motorist's attention. The remains lay in two shallow graves about five feet apart, covered with a thin layer of earth and bracken. One grave contained the torso, minus head and arms. The legs had been sawn off at the knees. The amazing feature was that the torso had been expertly skinned like a rabbit to disguise the victim's identity. The torso was wrapped in blue floral-patterned curtains. The other grave contained further remains wrapped in two nightdresses. But the head and hands – the two vital parts of the body for identification purposes – remained missing.

That in itself was a clue: the killer felt it necessary so gruesomely to hide the identity of his victim. But in general the case was the kind of clueless situation which only a sadistic thriller writer could have invented, and it was always going to be a headache for the police.

An autopsy was carried out by Dr Michael Heath, forensic pathologist at the London Hospital, and his initial findings were that the remains were those of a white woman aged between twenty and forty. Cause of death could not be established.

The pathologist conducted more exhaustive tests over the next few days and discovered more medical clues.

The woman was about thirty, and had probably been butchered about eleven days before she was found, which meant she had been murdered over the August holiday weekend. The victim had given birth at least once, and had a prominent left rib and a vaginal scar. The pathologist was also able to tell police that the killer had removed all the internal organs from the torso, apart from the heart and lungs. Finally, the victim had been about five feet three inches in height.

It seemed an impossible case to solve, but good detective work and the skills of forensic scientists rose to meet the challenge. Simple deductive reasoning told detectives that the killer had gone to such lengths to disguise the body in order to hide his own identity. The case was featured on the BBC TV *Crimewatch* programme, with dummies wearing the nightclothes found in the graves, and the distinctive curtains forming a backcloth. A viewer recognised the curtains: she had sold them at a car-boot sale opposite Crawley railway station. This pointed to Crawley as being the home town of the victim. The nightdress had come from a Tesco store and had not been on sale until late 1985.

The press were calling it 'the Case of the Body with No Name', but the police were making progress. Detective Superintendent Bryan Grove of Sussex CID, a senior investigator with thirty years' experience, had never before in his career encountered a case where a body could not be identified; but without fingerprints, skin, possible tattoos or scars, teeth or skull, he seemed powerless. When asked if this could be the 'perfect murder' he replied gruffly: 'There is no such thing. We know quite a bit about the victim already.' Tests were being carried out on the bones as he spoke, and the cause of death had been established, although the police did not release this information to the press. Oddly enough, it was the killer who gave himself away. He panicked.

Kassem Lachaal was a Moroccan living in a council house at Greenwich Close, Broadfield, Crawley. In his mid-forties, he had a reputation of being a ladies' man. Under Moslem law he lived with two wives, but under that same law he had to sleep with each wife on alternate nights.

Lachaal went to his solicitor in Crawley, asking him to get in touch with the police to inform them that his younger wife, twenty-five-year-old Latifa Lazaar, was missing from home. He said he feared the body found in Ashdown Forest might be her and the blame might be put on him. This turned the spotlight on him, and police began probing into his background. They discovered that Lachaal was a man who preyed on women, and had had dozens of affairs among the large tightly knit Moroccan community. Furthermore he was already on police files, having served an eighteen month jail term for drugs smuggling. He had been released from prison in August 1986, just a few days before the murder.

Forensic examination of the bath in the missing woman's house indicated that a body had been dismembered in it, although Lachaal and his relations claimed the woman had gone back to Morocco for a holiday, as she had been homesick.

Lachaal and his second wife were arrested, and before their trial the head of the missing woman was found. Teeth identification proved that it belonged to the missing woman, and forensic tests established that the head belonged to the skinned torso. It was the end result of a long and intensive police investigation in which 800 people had been questioned and more than 130 missing wives and daughters checked out.

To prove that the skinned torso was that of Latifa Lazaar, officers from the murder squad flew to Morocco to take statements and blood samples from Latifa's relatives there. The genetic fingerprint test could prove whether the body was a close family relative – or 'consanguinity'.

The trial of the husband and wife accused of murder began on 29 February 1988 at Lewes Crown Court. The prosecution told how the victim's throat had been cut with a knife, and that husband and wife had conspired together to effect and conceal the murder. Forensic scientist David Northcott told the court that a total of 140 bloodstains had been found on the wooden floor of the bathroom where Latifa had been dismembered. The bloodstains were of Latifa's blood group and could not have belonged to either of the accused. On 24 March 1988 the jury took six hours and forty-six minutes to find Kassem Lachaal guilty of murder. They cleared the wife of murder but found her guilty of concealing the crime. Kassem Lachaal was jailed for life, his wife for eighteen months. It was a case where guilt was written in the victim's blood.

We have seen how in previous centuries attempts at identification were made by putting the body on show, as in the case of Catherine Hayes; we have also seen cases of miscarriages of justice brought about by mistaken identity. The unreliability of eyewitnesses has been scientifically demonstrated in tests. The case of the Tichborne claimant is an intriguing example of how easily people are *willing* to be deceived about identity.

Lady Félicité Tichborne was distraught when her beloved son Roger was lost at sea in 1854. Imagine her delight when twelve years later she received a badly spelled letter from her 'son' in Wagga Wagga, Australia, asking her to send him money so he could come home. He had not drowned in the accident off Brazil, he explained, but had managed to swim to shore. Lady Tichborne sent the money, and in due course was invited to meet her son in a Paris hotel. Lying in a darkened room was a vast bulk of a man weighing twenty-six stone, his face turned to the wall. When she had last seen him, Roger had been exceedingly thin . . .

The credulous mother accepted the man as her son, Sir Roger, and gave him an allowance of a thousand pounds a year until he could legally establish his claim to his father's estate. The fraud might have gone on working, but Lady Tichborne died and 'Sir Roger' was chief mourner at her funeral. He borrowed large sums of money to fight his claim to inherit the Tichborne fortune through the courts, on the understanding that the lenders would be richly rewarded once he came into his rightful fortune. The case dragged on for almost a year, involving some two hundred thousand pounds in legal costs. A commission of inquiry visited Australia and discovered that 'Sir Roger' was in fact a local butcher called Arthur Orton. A revealing note found in his pocket book read: 'Some men has plenty money and no brains, and some men has plenty brains and no money. Surely men with plenty money and no brains was made for men with plenty brains and no money.' It is the creed of the swindler. He was tried for perjury and the jury lost no time in finding 'Sir Roger' guilty and his real identity to be Arthur Orton. He was sentenced to fourteen years imprisonment. Of course, the fraud was only made possible because of the unwillingness of the half-blind Lady Tichborne to accept that her son was dead.

The next four murder cases demonstrate the lengths to which killers are willing to go to dispose of their victims' bodies.

Frederick and Maria Manning were a husband-and-wife team who turned to murder for profit. They lived at Minver Place, Bermondsey, and twenty-eight-year-old Maria frequently had an Irishman of fifty called Patrick O'Connor visiting her. She had known him before she married Frederick, who was the same age as herself. O'Connor worked on the docks and also had a business as a moneylender. When the Mannings found themselves in financial difficulties they sent O'Connor a note inviting him to dine on 8 August 1847. He was never seen alive again after that date.

His disappearance caused some concern, and all his acquaintances were questioned. Maria Manning was very cool to police officers, saying she had no idea where O'Connor was. When police visited the house again to question her further, they found the house had been vacated in a hurry. Police searched the house, and after prising up flagstones in the kitchen they found the body of O'Connor buried in quicklime. He had been shot in the head and also bludgeoned. The fugitive Mannings were traced and arrested, Maria in Edinburgh and Frederick in the Channel Islands. Tried at the Old Bailey, Frederick said that Maria had shot O'Connor in the head, and he had finished him off with a crowbar. The Mannings were hanged in November 1847 before a crowd of fifty thousand at Horsemonger Lane Gaol. Since Maria chose to wear black satin for her execution, it made the material immediately unfashionable. China statuettes of the couple were sold to the public and have today become collector's items.

Murderers do find it extraordinarily difficult to dispose of the bodies of their victims – even educated murderers. John White Webster was a professor of chemistry and mineralogy at Massachusetts Medical College, and had borrowed money from a Dr George Parkman, who was something of a miser. When he failed to repay the debt, Dr Parkman went to Webster's college rooms and angrily demanded his money back, threatening to expose Webster to the college authorities. Webster did not have the money, but he did have some firewood in his grate. He hit Parkman over the head with a piece of kindling and, after dismembering the body, burned it in his assay oven. Parkman's sudden disappearance led to a reward being offered for his whereabouts, and a college janitor remembered having seen Parkman go into Webster's rooms. The janitor discovered that the wall behind the assay oven was very hot, and that night he took some bricks out of the wall and saw part of Dr Parkman's leg. The really incriminating evidence which police found in the debris was Parkman's teeth, still perfectly preserved. Webster tried to commit suicide before his trial in Boston on 19 March 1850. Found guilty of murder, he was hanged on 30 August.

Henry Wainewright was a London businessman who had a shop in the East End. He also had a mistress named Harriet Louisa Lane, a twenty-year-old milliner's apprentice. He set her up in a love nest at Mile End. Wainewright found he could not afford to keep two homes – he was being driven to bankruptcy. The solution was obvious: Harriet had to go. He murdered her and cut up her body, wrapping it in American cloth in two large parcels and storing it at his shop at 215 Whitechapel Road. However, the problem came when he was forced to give up the shop and had to get rid of the incriminating evidence. He asked a former employee to give him a hand carrying the heavy parcels, which had a very unpleasant smell. After staggering along for a while, Wainewright told his assistant to wait while he fetched a cab. While he was away the assistant looked in one parcel and saw to his horror a severed arm and decomposing hand. After Wainewright had returned with a cab and taken the two parcels away, the former employee decided to track him on foot and followed the cab to a house near London Bridge. He managed to alert a constable, who arrested Wainewright in the act of taking the parcels into his brother Thomas's house. The brothers were tried at the Old Bailey in November 1875. Thomas was sentenced to seven years for helping to conceal the crime, but Henry was sentenced to death. Hanged at Newgate on 21 December

1875, he shouted at the crowd: 'Come to see a man die, have you, you curs!'

Thirty-eight-year-old Frederick Bayley Deeming was arrested in Australia in 1892 after his wife's corpse was found cemented under his hearth-stone, her skull having been fractured by a blunt instrument. The smell had alerted neighbours at his Melbourne home. Since Deeming had arrived in Australia from Liverpool in 1891, under the alias Albert O. Wills, the Melbourne press used its London correspondents to trace him to a house he had rented in Rainhill, Liverpool. Cemented under the kitchen hearth Liverpool Police found his first wife, Maria Deeming, and her four children. Deeming seemed to favour hearth-stones, but they brought him no luck and failed to conceal his handiwork. He was hanged on 23 May 1892. There was no obvious motive for his crimes – he got no profit from them – and some criminologists have suggested that he may have been the elusive Jack the Ripper.

What this quartet of cases proves is that bodies are very difficult things to hide, and invariably come to light. 'Murder will out', as Congreve so accurately wrote.

But when a body is finally discovered – perhaps years later – badly decomposed or even in skeleton form, how can the police identify the body? It was in 1889 that Lacassagne turned his attention to this problem, and transformed the identification of corpses into an exact science. Lacassagne was the kind of man who was intensely interested in facts and collected them.

In 1885 he had been called to a curious death scene. An old man was found dead in a locked hotel bedroom. He had been shot through the head, and since he was still clutching a revolver in his hand, it seemed that suicide was the obvious solution. Save for one thing: the bedclothes were drawn up under the old man's chin. How could he have shot himself and then drawn the bedclothes up? Lacassagne found other suspicious facts. There were no powder burns on the skin. As for the revolver, that could have been placed in the old man's hand after death. Lacassagne had experimented with corpses and found that this was possible: the dead could be made to clutch objects. Lacassagne was convinced it was a case of murder, and when the old man's son was questioned he confessed to the crime.

It was a classic example of Lacassagne's brilliance, his obsession with *facts* which led to detection. Gradually, over the years and case by case, he began solving the problem of identity.

His greatest moment came in 1889 when he was forty-five years old. That November a canvas sack was discovered in bushes at a riverside at Millery, some ten miles from Lyons. It was found to contain the naked body of a dark-haired man in a bad state of decomposition. The man appeared to have been strangled, and a further piece of evidence came to light: the remains of a trunk which seemed to have originally contained the sack, since it stank of rotting flesh. A label on the trunk revealed that it had been sent from Paris to Lyons on 27 July.

That was the date on which Paris police were notified of the disappearance of a man named Gouffé, a middle-aged widower who had an office in the rue Montmartre. A porter had seen a stranger hurrying away from the office on Friday, 27 July – the last time Gouffé was ever seen alive. Police delving into the missing man's background discovered that he had a very full and complicated sex life with many ladies whom he visited regularly. Any one of them – or their husbands – might have had a motive for murdering him. Gouffé's brother-in-law went to Lyons but refused to identify the body as that of Gouffé, since Gouffé had chestnut hair and the corpse's was black. The body was duly buried as an 'unknown'.

However, a policeman called Goron washed a sample of the hair; when the mud and blood was removed the original colour was revealed: chestnut. The body was exhumed and finally arrived at Lacassagne's laboratory at Lyons University in a state of advanced decay. Lacassagne could do nothing but remove the rotting flesh, and he was left with the skeleton and hair with which to work. The skeleton told him a lot. The victim had walked with a limp in his right leg – as Gouffé had done. The teeth showed his age to be around fifty – Gouffé was forty-nine. Hair from Gouffé's hairbrush was compared under the microscope with that from the corpse – it was identical. When Goron came to his laboratory Lacassagne told him: 'I present you with Monsieur Gouffé.'

Once the corpse had been identified it was a fairly routine matter to track down the killer, a man called Michel Eyraud, who duly went to the guillotine.

In England in 1903 another failed attempt to dispose of a body was revealed in the sensational 'Moat Farm' murder. Samuel Herbert Dougal was a man who had devoted his life to preying on women. Two wives had died mysteriously while he was serving in the army. His discharge was arranged when it was discovered that he was forging cheques on a General's account, and he was jailed for a year. On his release he went to stay at a London boarding house, where he met Miss Camille Holland, a very refined spinster who was completely taken in by the smooth-tongued but rough-edged Dougal.

He persuaded her to elope with him and she bought Moat House Farm in Essex in 1899 as both a love nest and an investment. Dougal had promised to work hard to make the farm pay; in fact he spent most of his time seducing housemaids, until Miss Holland had had enough of it and ordered him to leave. Shortly afterwards she vanished. Dougal told neighbours that she had gone off on a holiday, and for the next four years he continued to live at the farm, forging Miss Holland's signatures on her cheques.

In March 1904 as a result of 'information received', police called at the farm to enquire about Miss Holland's whereabouts. Dougal gave an unconvincing explanation and later fled, being arrested in a London bank trying to pass another cheque. He was charged with forgery.

The police spent many days digging up the farm in search of Miss Holland's body, and finally located it, very badly decomposed. It was laid on a door supported on two chairs in the greenhouse, where the inquest took place. Her skull had been shattered by a bullet wound. Dougal was named as her murderer. At his trial, evidence was given about the remains of the middle-aged woman who had been shot below the ear. How could they prove it was Miss Holland? the defence challenged. The answer lay in her boots, which she was still wearing when unearthed. The cobbler who had made them for her had placed his initials in the heels in brass tacks. Dougal went to the gallows, confessing to the murder seconds before the trap fell.

The English equivalent of Lacassagne was Bernard Spilsbury, who had decided as a young medical student to specialise in the narrow field of pathology. In 1910, when he was thirty-three, his name became famous throughout England because of his involvement in the Crippen case.

Dr Hawley Harvey Crippen was an American, born in Michigan in 1862. In 1900 Crippen came to England, where he worked for a London firm selling patent medicines. His medical diploma was unorthodox, obtained from a college of homeopathy. He moved to 39 Hilldrop Crescent, where his wife took in lodgers to make ends meet. Belle Crippen was a dominant woman, and Crippen a little mild-mannered man – that is, until he took a mistress who put fire into his veins. Ethel LeNeve (real name Neave) was also a dominant woman but much younger, only seventeen when Crippen first met her. When the firm which employed him went bankrupt, Crippen bought some of the stock and set up in business for himself, with Ethel as his book-keeper and typist.

Meanwhile the real Mrs Crippen was making something of a success on the London music halls under the name Belle Elmore; she was a vivacious and outgoing type, even if she did indulge in bouts of screaming abuse at Crippen. (Crippen appears to have been an emotional masochist who was drawn to dominant women.)

Crippen and Ethel were far better suited; Crippen was basically a conman or petty swindler, and Ethel was a pathological liar. Ethel refused to have sex with Crippen until they were legally married, and kept pressing him to divorce Belle. When Crippen discovered his wife in bed with a lodger, Ethel took this as sufficient proof that his marriage was over, and surrendered her virginity to him in a hotel room on 6 December 1906, seven years after they had first met. The situation did not improve for the couple. For a time Crippen became a dentist, with Ethel as his assistant, but sex was still an illicit act performed in cheap hotels. As in all classic 'eternal triangle' situations, there was only one solution: Belle had to go.

On 17 January 1910, Crippen bought seventeen grains of hyoscine from a medical supplies shop, and in the early morning of 1 February he poisoned his wife. That night Ethel slept at Hilldrop Crescent. After dismembering his wife and burying her, Crippen pawned her jewellery and told anxious friends who enquired about her that his wife had gone to America.

Friends made enquiries of the shipping line and in New York: nobody of her name had sailed on that line nor was anything known of her whereabouts in the USA. The police were informed and Chief Inspector

Walter Dew of Scotland Yard visited Crippen at Hill-drop Crescent to ask: 'Where is your wife?' Crippen said she had left him to go and live with a man in Chicago. The house was thoroughly searched but nothing was found to indicate foul play.

Crippen might have got away with it if he hadn't panicked and fled, sailing on board the SS *Montrose* as 'Mr Robinson and son' – Ethel was dressed as a boy. Meanwhile Drew, alerted by Crippen's flight, had returned to Hilldrop Crescent with a team of officers, and under the cellar floor, covered in quicklime, he found human remains. The *Daily Mail* carried the story of the wanted 'cellar murderer', and the captain of the SS *Montrose* recognised Crippen from the photograph. He radioed London to report that he suspected he was carrying Crippen aboard as a passenger, and Drew took a faster ship and arrested Crippen as the ship reached landfall. Crippen thus became the first murderer to be arrested by means of Marconi's wireless telegraphy.

It fell to Spilsbury to assist at the autopsy on what was presumed to be the remains of Mrs Crippen: the head, skeleton and limbs were never found, and all he had to work with was a pile of flesh and internal organs. Essentially the case revolved around the issue of identification; the prosecution had to *prove* to the satisfaction of the jury that the remains were those of Belle Crippen. First it was established that the remains contained traces of hyoscine. Then the next most important clue was a piece of flesh from the abdomen which bore an operation scar – as had Mrs Crippen. Defence experts claimed it was a piece of flesh from the thigh, and the 'scar' was just a fold in the skin. Spilsbury, in his calm and patient manner, showed that it came from the abdomen, pointing out that part of the rectus muscle of the abdominal wall was still attached to the specimen in question. He had shamed his elders with superior knowledge.

There was other damning evidence, particularly the fact that the remains had been wrapped in Crippen's own pyjama jacket. He insisted he had bought the pyjamas in 1905; the prosecution proved they had been bought in 1909, catching him out in a direct lie. This blatant untruth influenced the jury to convict as much as anything else, and they took less than half an hour to find Crippen guilty. He was hanged on 23 November 1910. Ethel LeNeve was tried separately and was acquitted. She died in 1967 at the ripe old age of eighty-four.

Spilsbury went on to become the 'expert's expert', but he had an early lesson in how a brilliant barrister could overcome the most convincing scientific evidence. When fifty-year-old Frederick Henry Seddon, together with his wife, poisoned their lodger, Miss Eliza Barrow, in September 1911, the motive was plain greed. Seddon, an insurance agent, had persuaded his victim to sign all her assets over to him; once that was accomplished she became a liability to be disposed of. However, a suspicious relative went to the police and Miss Barrow was exhumed. Spilsbury was asked to examine the body and he concluded that death was not due to heart failure as certified on the death certificate, but was more likely a case of poisoning.

Dr William Willcox had the task of establishing which poison had been used, and precisely how much. Willcox was the foremost toxicologist of his day. It was he who had proved that hyoscine had been the murder agent employed in the Crippen case by dropping an extract into a cat's eye and seeing it contract. Detecting arsenic in Miss Barrow's remains was easy; now Willcox set to work carrying out a series of Marsh tests to decide how much arsenic had been used. He assumed that the poison had been evenly distributed in the stomach and selected a piece of stomach weighing one two-hundredth of the total stomach weight. He got a result for arsenic and multiplied that by two hundred. He came up with a total of just over two grains, the fatal dose being two to three grains.

When he gave his testimony, Edward Marshall Hall cross-examined him. Did he not realise that although Miss Barrow had originally weighed ten stone, when exhumed natural evaporation had led to her being less than half that weight? Had Dr Willcox used his multiplication system properly, he would have found just one grain – less than the fatal dose. Dr Willcox was forced to concede the point. Marshall Hall came close to getting Seddon acquitted, but Seddon himself sealed his own doom by his performance in the witness box, which revealed him to be an obsessive miser who lusted after every penny. He was duly convicted and hanged.

Spilsbury was seen at his best in the Crumbles murder of thirty-four-year-old Emily Beilby Kaye. The killer was her lover, Patrick Mahon, a conman and very successful philanderer – the two seem to go hand in hand. In 1923 he met and seduced Emily, who became pregnant as a result. They decided to live together in a lovenest at a rented bungalow called The Crumbles, which stands on the Sussex coast between Eastbourne and Pevensey Bay. On the weekend beginning 12 April 1924 Mahon went by railway to the bungalow, taking with him a saw and a knife. He killed the mistress who had become a nuisance and dismembered her body.

Meanwhile Mahon's wife had become suspicious of his absences and searched his clothing. In a pocket she found a cloakroom ticket from Waterloo Station and asked a friend to investigate. When he presented the ticket at the left-luggage office he was handed a Gladstone bag filled with bloodstained female clothing. The police were alerted and they put the cloakroom under observation, arresting Mahon when he tried to claim the bag. He claimed the blood on the clothing was from dog meat, but tests showed it to be human. The

Crumbles address was found on him and police visited the bungalow, discovering boiled human flesh in a saucepan and chunks of human flesh in various containers, and ashes in the fireplace, which contained bone fragments.

Spilsbury had the remains taken to St Bartholomew's Hospital and set about reassembling hundreds of fragments of a human body. The head and right leg were missing – Mahon later admitted throwing pieces from a moving railway carriage – and that head was important, since Mahon claimed to have hit his mistress over the head with a bucket during a quarrel, although the bucket was undented. There was no other apparent cause of death. Could Mahon have burned Emily's head in the fireplace? Spilsbury carried out an experiment with a sheep's head, burning it in the kitchen hearth and reducing it to ashes within four hours. And since Mahon – who had pleaded not guilty to murder, claiming the death had been accidental – had bought the knife and saw *before* Emily Kaye was murdered, it indicated premeditation. The jury convicted him of murder and he was hanged on 9 September 1924.

Spilsbury's fame had been established. He was involved in the Brides in the Bath murder case, the Brighton Trunk Murder, and the Rouse 'burning car' murder case among others. He had become a star, every word and utterance faithfully recorded as if it were divine wisdom. In fact, his reputation aroused concern among legal circles, since it was felt that a jury's faith in him could result in a miscarriage of justice. He had been knighted in 1923, and a letter to a newspaper summed up the criticism against him by saying: 'For some reason or other, Sir Bernard Spilsbury has now arrived at a position where his utterances in the witness box commonly receive unquestioning acceptance. . . . But a reputation for infallibility is quite out of place in medical and surgical matters.'

The next major case of a murder involving the disposal of a body was the Brighton Trunk Murder. On 17 June 1934 the Brighton railway station cloakroom attendant became aware that a trunk in his department was beginning to smell. When opened by the police it was found to contain the torso of a woman wrapped in brown paper. A name written on the paper had been partly obliterated by blood, but the second half of the word was 'ford'.

Cloakroom attendants all over the country were asked to check their parcels for suspicious smells – after all, the rest of the body had to be somewhere – and as a result the legs of the victim were found in a suitcase at King's Cross. Both trunk and parcel had been deposited on 6 June.

Spilsbury found that the legs and torso were from the same body, a woman in her mid-twenties who had been five months pregnant. Her general condition suggested that she was a woman of good income, since her hands and feet were well manicured and her armpits shaved. Despite the police tracing the trunk to the shop in Brighton where it had been sold, the trail went dead from then on, and it remains one of the few unsolved murders.

Spilsbury was also involved in the case of Alfred Arthur Rouse. On Bonfire Night 1930, Rouse picked up a hitchhiking tramp, and after knocking his passenger unconscious, doused him with petrol and set him alight, hoping that the charred corpse would be taken for his own. It was Spilsbury who examined the charred remains and found a petrol-smelling rag between the victim's legs. He also discovered that the victim had been alive when the fire started, because of smoke in the lungs. Rouse's story of a fire started by accident was destroyed by Spilsbury's testimony, and Rouse was duly hanged.

The Buck Ruxton case established the reputation of

another pathologist, Professor John Glaister of the University of Glasgow, who performed a remarkable feat of forensic restoration. On 29 September 1935 four parcels containing human remains were discovered on the banks of a Scottish river, the Linn, close to the Edinburgh-Carlisle Road. Police recovered two human heads, an armless torso, two upper arms and mounds of flesh. The killer had taken great pains to disguise the identity of his victims, removing teeth, slicing off the fingers, noses, lips, ears and even gouging out the eyes. The dissection had been carried out with some surgical skill. A vital clue lay in the fact that a piece of newspaper had been used to wrap part of the remains: the *Sunday Graphic* for 15 September 1935. This helped pin-point the time when the bodies had been dumped, and was ultimately to lead to the killer. Professor Glaister had the task of examining the maggot-ridden remains, and had them removed to the Anatomy Department of the University of Edinburgh. Together with Dr Miller, an anatomist, Glaister set about reconstructing the seventy-odd pieces of human remains.

First he had to decide which pieces belonged to which bodies. At the start, Glaister thought the bodies were those of a man and a woman, one skull being very masculine. Later he established that they were two females. By examining the skull sutures – those hairline cracks in the skull which do not completely seal until about the age of forty – Glaister was able to establish that one woman had been forty, the other under thirty. X-rays of the wisdom teeth of the younger woman further reduced her age to twenty. Glaister had two tables labelled Body 1 and Body 2, and he and Dr Miller began laying out the pieces according to which body they fitted – rather like assembling a jigsaw.

It was relatively easy to see that one woman had been taller than the other. The sex, age and stature of a skeleton can be determined from measurements made from the long bones, the pelvis and the skull. The growing ends of the bones (epiphyses) are soft and cartilaginous during growth, but gradually harden into solid bone in adulthood. The head of the femur fuses between eighteen and twenty years, and part of the hip during the twenty-fourth year. After that age the skull and teeth are used to determine age. The height of a person can be determined by measuring the long bones, since there is a fixed relationship between the length of the limbs and the total length of the body. The Dapertuis and Hadden formula is the table pathologists use for this purpose. In this case, the older woman had been the taller of the two, by a clear six inches.

The skeleton of the taller woman was assembled almost completely, but the other body was minus a trunk. The taller woman had five stab wounds in the chest and several broken bones. The hyoid bone was also broken, indicating strangulation. The smaller and younger woman had been bludgeoned to death.

The police, meanwhile, had discovered that the pages from the *Sunday Graphic* had been part of a special 'slip' edition printed for the Morecambe and Lancaster editions only. And in Lancaster a Dr Buck Ruxton had reported his wife missing, saying she had run off with her maid . . .

Clothes in which the remains had been wrapped were identified by the maid's relatives. She was Mary Rogerson. The other victim was Mrs Ruxton – that bottom sheet matched the one remaining on Ruxton's bed. The clues piled up against Ruxton, an excitable and jealous Indian who believed his wife was being unfaithful to him. He had given away bloodstained carpets from his house and a bloodstained suit to a patient's husband. Professor Glaister had Ruxton's bath dismantled and sent to him: the victims had been dismembered in that.

Norman Birkett, the defence counsel, had only one line of defence open to him – to suggest that it had not been proved that the remains found were those of Isabella Ruxton and Mary Rogerson. It was a forlorn hope. The medical experts, Professors Glaister and Smith, and Dr Miller, established the identities beyond doubt. They had the brilliant and innovative idea of photographing a studio portrait of Mrs Ruxton and enlarging it to lifesize; then they photographed her skull and superimposed one image over the other: they matched exactly. It was a method which was copied later. Ruxton was unconvincing in the witness box, verbose and hysterical, and the jury took less than an hour to convict him. He was hanged at Strangeways Prison on 12 May 1936. Professor Glaister wrote a classic book about the affair: *Medico-Legal Aspects of the Ruxton Case* (1937).

In 1940 Sir Bernard Spilsbury suffered a stroke, but continued to perform over a thousand autopsies a year, taking a particular interest in carrying out postmortems on men who had been judicially hanged. In 1947 he committed suicide in his laboratory. His place as the 'star' expert witness was taken by Professor Cedric Keith Simpson of Guy's Medical School. He made his name during the war, when, on 17 January 1942, workmen in London demolishing a bombed church found a skeleton with shreds of flesh clinging to it, hidden under a slab. Simpson examined the remains in Southwark mortuary and concluded only that the victim was a woman who had been buried in the past year.

In his laboratory he could see clearly that it was a case of murder. The head and legs had been deliberately severed and quicklime had been used on the remains to speed decomposition. Skull sutures established the victim's age as between forty and fifty, a fibroid growth was visible in what remained of the womb, and the teeth and dental plate in the upper jaw should make identification easy, providing her dentist could be traced.

Police examined the lists of missing persons and noted that Rachel Dobkin, wife of a fire watcher at the church, had been missing since early 1941. Her husband, Harry Dobkin, had served several jail terms for failing to pay his estranged wife maintenance. He had the motive and opportunity. Mrs Dobkin's dentist was traced and identified his bridgework on her teeth, and her doctor testified that she had indeed suffered from a fibroid growth of the uterus. A tiny clot of blood in the larynx revealed the cause of death to be strangulation. To clinch matters further, Simpson superimposed a photograph of Mrs Dobkin over the skull – the technique first used in the Ruxton case – and got an exact match. Dobkin was sentenced to death, and hanged at Wandsworth Prison on 27 January 1943.

Simpson was also involved in the 'Wigwam' murder case of 1942, when Joan Pearl Wolfe, a teenager living rough, was found murdered on Hankley Common, Godalming, on 7 October. She had been sharing a crude wig-wam on the common with a man. She had been stabbed with an army jack-knife which had a hooked tip. A thirty-year-old Canadian soldier, August Sangret, who was part Red Indian, was arrested for the murder and was duly convicted and hanged.

The John George Haigh case of 1944 was a classic example of a man who imagined that because he had disposed of the body, murder could not be proved against him. In fact, the body is only one aspect of the *corpus delecti*, which literally translates as the body of the crime. Other elements include proof that a death has occurred, proof of the identity of that person, and proof that the killing resulted from unlawful violence. It is also helpful to be able to prove the classic trio of elements in a murder: motive, method and opportunity.

Haigh, at thirty-nine, was a businessman who rented premises in Crawley. He was also a swindler. A permanent guest at the Onslow Court Hotel in South Kensington, Haigh made a practice of inviting wealthy fellow guests to invest in his projects. Once they handed over their money, he murdered them. He disposed of several people in a drum of acid at his works, but was arrested and tried for the murder of sixty-nine-year-old Mrs Olive Durand-Deacon. She was just a pile of sludge at the bottom of a forty-gallon drum of sulphuric acid. A supremely confident Haigh told the police: 'Mrs Durand-Deacon no longer exists . . . I have destroyed her with acid. How can you prove murder if there is no body?'

How indeed . . . At his trial Haigh claimed to be a vampire with an insatiable lust for blood. The prosecution presented Professor Simpson. He had examined the sludge at Crawley and had found human gallstones. He also found the victim's acrylic dentures, which were proof enough of identity. There was also eighteen fragments of human bone and twenty-eight pounds of human fat. Haigh was hanged at Wandsworth Prison on 6 August 1949.

Most killers tend to dispose of their victims at the scene of the crime. John Reginald Halliday Christie, repulsive sex murderer and necrophiliac, hid six victims in his house at 10 Rillington Place in London's Notting Hill district. The case attracted enormous headlines, and a macabre joke of the time was: 'Poor Christie – six women in the house and nobody to make him a cup of tea.' He was hanged on 9 March 1950.

In 1949 thirty-nine-year-old Brian Donald Hume hit on an original idea. He dismembered his victim's body and from a hired light aircraft dumped the parcels containing the remains over the Essex marshes. However, the remains were washed up on a mud flat. At his trial Hume claimed not to have murdered Stanley Setty, but to have disposed of the remains for an underworld figure. Found not guilty of murder, he was convicted of being an accessory and was jailed for twelve years. On his release in 1958 Hume confessed to Setty's murder in a Sunday newspaper for a substantial sum of money. He subsequently fled to Switzerland after robbing English banks, and killed a taxi driver in a botched bank raid. Jailed for life by the Swiss, in August 1976 he was returned to Britain in chains, and now resides in Broadmoor.

Many killers have displayed a leaning towards water. In the first of only three murder convictions without a body in England this century, James Camb, a ship's steward, was found guilty of shoving the body of Eileen Isabella 'Gay' Gibson out of a porthole on the liner *Durban Castle* off the coast of West Africa. Camb was sentenced to death on 22 March 1948, but was subsequently reprieved.

On 19 October 1976 airline pilot Peter Hogg, then fifty-seven, strangled his wife in their bedroom following a row about her promiscuity. He drove nine hundred miles with her body in the boot of his car and dumped her weighted corpse in the middle of Britain's biggest lake, in Cumbria. Seven years later, divers looking for a missing French student found the body, well preserved in the icy water. The wedding ring on her finger bore an inscription of the date of the wedding, together with the couple's initials. Hogg was sentenced to four years for manslaughter on 8 March 1985.

Thirty-two-year-old Kevin Owlett of Wetherby failed to learn from Hogg's mistake and committed a copycat murder of his wife between May and June 1988, dumping her body in Crummock Water in the Lake District. Her body was found by divers; on 14 April 1989 Owlett was sentenced to life imprisonment.

Other killers have thought they have committed the 'perfect murder', only for justice to catch up with them years later. On 12 December 1962 a little boy, Stephen Jennings, aged three, vanished from the family home at Gomersal in West Yorkshire. It was a bitter winter and the little boy could not have walked far. The whole village, together with hundreds of police officers, joined the search for the toddler, which went on for three months without success. From the first, police suspected that the father, twenty-five-year-old William Jennings, knew something about his son's disappearance, but had no clues to link him to any crime. Later he was jailed for ill-treating his other children. When he came out of prison he got divorced, moved away and remarried, starting a new life.

Twenty-five years later, a man out walking his dog in Gomersal found the tiny skeleton of Stephen Jennings lying beside a stone wall, less than half a mile from the Jennings' former home. It was on 7 April 1988 that the remains were found and police reopened the case. Archaeologists were called in to help exhume the remains. Dr John Hutton led a team from Bradford University to examine the shallow grave. He had offered to help in the search for the graves of the Moors Murders victims and was working on a new concept of forensic archaeology, a science used in the USA for the past ten years but virtually unknown in Britain. The theory behind this concept is that when a body is buried, the soil layer is disturbed and is often replaced in the wrong order. Small insignificant clues such as minor undulations in the ground can become vital clues.

The remains were examined by pathologists skilled in paediatrics, two orthopaedic surgeons and an ondontologist. They estimated that the remains were those of a boy aged between three and four years, and broken bones suggested that severe violence had been the cause of death. After keeping his grim secret for a quarter of a century, William Jennings was arrested in the Midlands and brought back to Yorkshire for questioning. He confessed to the killing, saying it had been an accident. At his trial in Leeds in May 1989, medical experts testified that only extreme and prolonged violence could have produced the fractured bones examined. Jennings' account of an 'accident' did not fit the medical evidence, and on 19 May a jury found him guilty of murder and he was jailed for life.

Sometimes the mere finding of human remains can result in a confession. In 1963 the wife of Peter Reyn-Bardt vanished from the family home in Cheshire. The husband was suspected of her murder but nothing could be proved – there was no body, and he didn't crack under questioning. Then in 1983 workmen uncovered a woman's skull in a nearby peat bog. When shown the skull by the police, Reyn-Bardt immediately confessed to the murder and was jailed for life. Yet he had confessed to the wrong skull! Radio-carbon dating showed the skull to have belonged to a woman who had died in AD 210. A year later 'Pete Marsh' or Lindow Man was found in the same bog.

In 1981 a Japanese student in Paris hit on a novel way of disposing of the body of his victim – he ate her. Issei Sagawa, who was thirty-three had a genius-level IQ; he also had a taste for human flesh. His girl friend was a fellow student, Renee Hartewelt, a twenty-five-year-old girl from a wealthy family, studying French literature. She vanished on 12 June 1981 and was later found in two large suitcases. The lips, breasts and large parts of the thighs and buttocks were missing, as was the tip of her nose. The small Japanese man had been seen carrying the suitcases and was traced – it was Sagawa. In a refrigerator in his room police found one of the victim's lips, her left breast, part of her thigh and both buttocks. Asked what he had done with the rest, Sagawa said he had eaten it. Cooked? he was asked. No, raw and thinly sliced, he replied. He had truly possessed in the most complete way the object of his affections. He had tape-recorded and photographed the killing of his girl friend. Found unfit to plead by reason of insanity, he was eventually returned to Japan and incarcerated in a mental hospital. While there he wrote a best-selling book called *In the Fog*, which recounted his appetite for white female flesh. There was uproar in France when Sagawa was declared cured in September 1985 and was released from hospital as a free man.

Dr Katunayakage Samson Perera, aged forty-two, was a lecturer at Leeds University's Dental School. A native of Sri Lanka, Dr Perera lived at a luxury home in Wakefield. He and his wife had adopted a girl from their native land, but she did not adapt to English customs and was homesick. Then she vanished. Detective Inspector Tom Hodgson was on the verge of retiring – this was to be his last case. He investigated the case as a routine missing-person inquiry, following information from a concerned neighbour, but the doctor's replies to his questions were evasive. He said the girl, thirteen-year-old Nilanthie, had returned home to Sri Lanka. He gave the name of the travel agency and airline used. Hodgson, a veteran cop, checked it out. There hadn't been any flight to Sri Lanka on the day specified, and on no flight had the girl's name appeared. A search of Dr Perera's home revealed bits of rotting human flesh in flower pots, including a complete vertebra curled up to fit. Asked to explain this, the doctor said it was leftover pork from a meal, saying: 'It is a basic fact of biology that meat is an excellent nutrient . . .'

In his laboratory at Leeds University, police found human remains in flower pots, coffee jars, and in margarine containers immersed in dissolving fluid. The prosecution's expert witness was Professor Alan Usher, head of forensic pathology at Sheffield University and a Home Office pathologist in the great tradition of Spilsbury, Simpson and Francis Camps. Using a demonstration skeleton in court, he pointed out to the jury the differences between a male and female skeleton. The bones he had examined were those of a young girl around the age of puberty. At the end of an eleven-day

211

trial, Perera was found guilty of murder and was jailed for life.

Haigh believed he could not be convicted of murder without a body, but in this country we have had three cases of such convictions. The first was that of Camb, the second was that of the Hosein brothers, jailed for life for the kidnap and murder of Mrs Muriel McKay in 1970. It was believed they had fed her body to pigs on the farm they owned. Then, as we have seen in the chapter on blood, Ian Simms was convicted as the result of a genetic fingerprint 'by proxy' of the murder of Helen McCourt, and sentenced to life imprisonment in early 1989.

It is a brave murderer who thinks he can outwit the forensic scientist by trying to hide or disguise the corpse of his victim. A wide variety of scientific disciplines can help in the process of identification. A veterinary surgeon will distinguish between animal and human bones; an anatomist can determine the sex, age, height and often the race of the skeleton. A serologist can test any blood or bone marrow for grouping. The forensic ondontologist – or teeth expert – can determine the age and race of the victim; teeth of Asian origin have 'mongoloid pits' on the inner surfaces of the concave incisor teeth. And dentists helped identify one of Christie's victims, Ruth Fuerst, because of the Central European fillings in her teeth.

Forensic dentistry is of great value when it comes to identifying victims from their dental records in such mass disasters as the Bradford City Football Club fire, for example, or air crashes. The history of forensic dentistry – or ondontology – could fill a chapter in itself. It has a long history – evidence has been discovered on Ancient Egyptian mummies of root-canal work! And the Romans used to identify the dead by examining their teeth. But it was left to Dr Oscar Amödo, a professor of dentistry in Paris, to publish the definitive medico-legal textbook on identification by teeth in 1898. It remains the standard textbook on the subject, ranking with Glaister's *Medical Jurisprudence* for pathology students.

Russian pathologists conducted an autopsy on badly burnt remains found in a shell crater near the Berlin bunker in 1945 and determined from dental records that they were indeed the remains of the Führer. Teeth are always convincing. Harry Dobkin was trapped by his victim's teeth, as was Haigh; and in the USA handsome serial killer Ted Bundy, who slaughtered young women, pleaded not guilty at his nationally televised trial. Evidence against him was circumstantial – except for one thing. Bite marks on the buttocks of one of his victims were matched conclusively by an ondontologist to Bundy's teeth impressions. It convinced the jury that Bundy was lying through his teeth, and he subsequently died in the electric chair.

Arthur Hutchinson, brutal killer of the Laitner family in Sheffield, was placed firmly at the murder scene by teeth marks on a piece of cheese he had carelessly nibbled.

Teeth can tell a scientist a lot – particularly the age of the victim. But teeth can also convict a killer . . .

Archaeologists and palae-pathologists can determine how long ago a person died. The use of X-rays can help establish the age of the victim by the degree of ossification of the bones, a lifelong process which acts as a kind of 'skeletal calendar' to the forensic expert. Sometimes bodies can be identified by scars or tattoos, and if the skull has ever previously been X-rayed, the frontal sinuses will provide a forensic match which will establish identity beyond doubt by comparing the radiological outline.

A new method of establishing the identity of a body was demonstrated at an inquest in Essex on 7 July 1989. The skeleton of a man who had disappeared in March 1988 was found in secluded woodland near Braintree.

213

Police used a new technique pioneered in Israel. Dr Peter Vanezis, a forensic pathologist at the London Hospital, used a video camera to superimpose the skull of the skeleton on to a photograph of the missing man. It was a perfect match and identified the remains as being those of thirty-four-year-old John Silvey. Detective Superintendent Peter Whent told the coroner that no identification was found on the body, the missing man had no dental records, and it was impossible to carry out genetic-fingerprint testing because of the lack of material to test. The new video system was the only way in which an identification could be made, and saved hours of police time. Of course, it is only a sophisticated refinement of the method pioneered in the Ruxton case, but it will have great value in difficult identification cases, such as those resulting from the King's Cross fire.

Science is developing rapidly all the time, and very soon it may well be impossible for there ever to be a 'body without a name'.

However mutilated or decomposed, forensic science will supply the name of the body in question . . .

8

THE MICROSCOPE:
THE ALL-SEEING EYE

It will have become obvious to the reader by now that the cases so far examined reveal that the most valuable tool in crime detection – apart from the human brain – is the microscope. It can detect clues invisible to the naked eye, and it is often the 'invisible' clues which trap a killer.

As long ago as 1910 the great Edmond Locard formulated his 'exchange principle', which means in essence that the criminal always leaves something at the scene of the crime – or takes something away. He may leave samples of his skin under the fingernails of his victim; footprints, fingerprints or fibres from his clothing. And he may take away, on the soles of his shoes, samples of the soil peculiar to the area, or hair and blood from the victim.

The exchange principle – which today we call 'contact traces' – is very important. Indeed, it is the very basis of forensic science. It states firmly that when a crime is committed, things are altered irrevocably. These changes can lead to the detection of the criminal.

Contact traces can include tyremarks from a vehicle, marks of tools used to force windows or doors, drag marks across ground, ink, paint, oil, blood picked up at the murder scene or left behind, fragments of clothing, fibres, stains – blood, sweat, saliva or semen – and hair, vegetation or pollen. In fact, almost everything can constitute a clue, in every type of crime. A forged signature on a document can be compared under the comparison microscope with a genuine signature. Even typewriters have their own characteristics, depending not only on the different manufacturers, but on the fact that moving parts wear and impart that degree of wear on to the paper, and examination under the microscope can tell if a suspect's typewriter typed a particular ransom note. A notable success was in the case of Leopold and Loeb, the two brilliant students with genius-level IQs who kidnapped a millionaire's son and sent a ransom note long after they had killed the boy. Brilliant or not, they were still in possession of the typewriter when arrested.

Forensic laboratories keep exhaustive files on all makes of typewriters, inks, tyres and treads, vehicle paints and household paints, plus a whole range of carpet and fabric fibres which might feature in a case. All these have to be examined through the microscope, with synthetic fibres being identified by their refractive index and various staining tests. None of this would have been possible without the microscope, that most basic tool of the scientist.

The telescope was invented around 1607 in Holland by Zacharias Janssen, although the magnification properties of lenses had been known for centuries prior to that, spectacles being invented about 1290. It was another Dutchman, Antonie Van Leeuwenhoek, who invented the microscope in 1670. It was a crude affair, and modifications and refinements took place over the following centuries until it took its present form.

The first recorded use of the microscope in a murder case occurred in France in 1847, in what was to become known as the Praslin Affair. Duke Choiseul-Praslin murdered his wife Fanny because she objected to an affair he was having with a servant, Henriette De Luzy.

However, fearful of losing his children and his position – his wife was threatening divorce – he murdered her in such a way as to make it look as if she had been killed by a burglar she had disturbed.

Police called to the scene found that her throat had been cut and there was blood everywhere. Under a sofa they found a bloodstained pistol. The Duke said it was his, explaining that he had heard his wife's cries for help and rushed into her bedroom brandishing his pistol, but when he saw how badly injured his wife was he dropped the weapon, the better to cradle her to him. This accounted for the blood on his clothing. But when the police searched the Duke's own bedroom they discovered a bloodstained handkerchief and dagger.

This put a different complexion on things, and the police became suspicious. The wife had been bludgeoned before having her throat cut, and so the police handed the bloodstained pistol over to a pathologist with the questions: Was it dropped in the Duchess's blood, as the Duke maintained – or had it been used to bludgeon her to death? The pathologist, Tardieu, studied the pistol under the microscope and noticed a hair close to the butt, skin tissue on the trigger guard, and other samples of human hair and flesh. The microscope had convicted the Duke of his wife's murder, but before he could be taken to prison he managed to poison himself and died in lingering agony, still refusing to admit his guilt.

The microscope began to claim for itself a separate place in forensic medicine, when several cases were solved by the detection of human hairs. The study of hairs alone could fill a volume. Under the microscope the difference between animal and human hair can be detected, and the differences between head hair, pubic hair, armpit hair and facial hair was known long ago. Not only that, but it was quickly realised that hair was different from person to person, and from race to race.

Negroid hair is very distinctive, for example. The first treatise on hair appeared in 1857, and by the turn of the century many scientists of the calibre of Locard and Victor Balthazard had turned their attention to the subject, making it a science in itself. In 1910 Balthazard, the Paris Medical Examiner and the man who had solved the Guillotin case, published his treatise on human and animal hair, and in 1931 Professor John Glaister published his *Hairs of Mammalia From the Medicolegal Aspect*. It remains a standard textbook on the subject.

Hair plays an important part in a murder investigation. Because of its absorbent qualities it shows traces of poison, and analysis of the hair can reveal what poison has been used and in what dosage. When the hair of Napoleon was analysed in the 1960s, some hundred and fifty years after his death, it was found to contain over thirteen times the normal quantity of arsenic. And hairs tend to get left on the clothing of victims.

Hair, which is composed mainly of the substance keratin, is extremely difficult to destroy – except by fire – and will remain in the grave long after the body has rotted away. Microscopic examination can reveal whether the hair fell out or was pulled out forcibly, the race of the owner, what part of the body it came from – women's pubic hair is shorter and coarser than males', for example – and whether it has been cut recently.

A human hair consists of a central core, called the medulla, surrounded by the cortex, which contains pigment and so gives hair its colour, and finally there is the outer layer, or cuticle. Forensic laboratories keep recognition charts which enable hairs to be quickly identified as being either animal or human. Today hair is examined by neutron-activation analysis. This makes the sample hair radioactive so that its emissions can be analysed to determine the various elements and amounts present.

In 1893 Hans Gross published his *Handbook for Magistrates*, published in England as *Criminal Investigation (1907)*. It became an instant classic text, recounting cases solved by fingerprints, footprints and, most importantly, by the microscope.

Edmond Bayle had succeeded Bertillon as head of the Paris forensic science department, and his most brilliant case came in 1924. On 8 June the body of a man wrapped in a sheet was found in the Bois de Boulogne. He was identified as Louis Boulay aged seventy, and had been killed by blows to the head. The corpse was removed to the Laboratory of Judicial Police in Paris, where the director, Dr Bayle, took charge of it. All that was known was that nine days previously, the victim had left the office where he worked to post letters, and had not been seen since. The motive for his murder appeared to be robbery, since his wallet and gold watch were missing. The body was very dirty, and had obviously been stored somewhere before being dumped in the Bois de Boulogne that Sunday morning.

Bayle spent a lot of time examining the corpse. He found sand and sawdust in the clothing, the sawdust being a mixture of oak and pine wood, while the shirt bore traces of anthracite. Yeast and mould were also found. When cultivated in the laboratory, the yeast was found to be wine yeast. In the trouser turn-ups were fragments of varnish containing the dye rhodamine.

Since the body had lost a lot of blood – yet no blood was found in the vicinity of the body – it was a reasonable assumption that he had been killed elsewhere, and his body then dumped where it was found. And for those days when he had been missing, it was also a logical assumption that he had been kept in a cellar of some kind.

Meanwhile the police were conducting the usual

investigation into the murdered man's background, trying to trace his friends and associates. Chief Inspector Riboulet toured cafés and bars, showing people a photograph of Boulay, hoping someone might recognise him and be able to fill out the details of his secret life. The Inspector found that Boulay acted as a bookie's runner, and would therefore have carried cash around with him. Then a clerk from Boulay's office remembered that he had once had a letter opened by mistake by a man of the same name in an upstairs office. Boulay had received the opened letter with the comment: 'Oh, it's only from Tessier.' He went on to say that he was changing his custom from Tessier to another bookie, because he didn't like the cellar from which Tessier worked. The clerk could even remember the address Boulay had mentioned, the rue Mogador.

Lazare Tessier, the concierge at 30 rue Mogador and an illegal bookie, was brought in for questioning, and in his absence his cellar was searched. Bayle collected bags of samples from the cellar, which he took back to his laboratory. The floor of the cellar had been covered in sand and sawdust, with wine casks and pieces of wood coated in varnish. The varnish contained the dye-stuff rhodamine. Traces of human blood were found on a piece of wood, despite attempts to wash it off. The most telling clues were a green jersey belonging to Tessier, fibres from which had been found on Boulay's clothing, and a torn Metro ticket dated 30 May 1924 – the day Boulay had vanished.

Tessier refused to plead guilty to the crime, but the mass of forensic evidence convicted him; however, the jury must have felt uneasy at having to convict on the evidence of just the microscope and found Tessier guilty of manslaughter. He was jailed for ten years. Three years later the brilliant Dr Bayle was himself murdered – such are the quirks of fate.

The entire case of the murder of Boulay had been

solved in Bayle's laboratory, and it is instructive to see just how many branches of science were employed. *Botanical* examination of the wood; *biological* examination of the yeast; *microchemical* detection of the dyestuff; *biochemical* identification of human blood.

Today the picture is even more complex, with every branch of science contributing to the forensic laboratory. The condition of the lower bowel of the victim might tell scientists as much as a signed confession from the murderer. Chemical analysis will reveal not only the type of ink used in a forged document, but its age too. A single strand of hair might be linked to a killer.

In the Sacco and Vanzetti case the medical examiner for Boston, Dr George Burgess McGrath, offered to prove conclusively that hairs found in a cap at the scene of the murders had come from the head of one of the defendants. The prosecution refused his offer, fearing that they might be laughed out of court. It remains a pity that the offer was not accepted, for it *could* have stilled the controversy about their guilt which rages to this day.

It was through microscopic comparison that the legendary pathologist Sir Bernard Spilsbury solved the 1930 Messiter case. Vivian Messiter was killed by a hammer blow from William Henry Podmore. On the face of the murder weapon Spilsbury found two eyebrow hairs from the victim. While this simply confirmed that this was indeed the hammer which had struck the fatal blow, the press headlined the case: 'Two Hairs Hanged This Man'.

Lacassagne took pain to impress on his pupils at the Lyons Institute of Forensic Medicine the importance of the microscope, and it was not surprising that one of his best students, Emile Villebrun, should in 1883 write his thesis on the medicolegal aspects of fingernails. Villebrun made a special study of the scratches left by fingernails and the significance of the dirt and material to be found under them. Villebrun, in analysing various murders, noted that the fingernail makes a distinctive groove when it tears skin, depending on the shape of the nail. Several murders had been solved by microscopic analysis of scratches made by the fingernails of the victims.

In 1910 Edmond Locard, frustrated by the limitations of bertillonage, set about attempting to transform forensic medicine into an exact science. He set up his own laboratory in two attic rooms in the Palais de Justice and set about convincing the police of his value to their investigations. An early success involved a gang of coiners whom the Paris Police had been trying to smash for a long time. They arrested three men but found no evidence to link them to any counterfeiting. Locard, who had heard of the case, asked the Inspector in charge if he could examine the clothing of the suspects. The Inspector was dubious and reluctant, but handed over the clothes of one man. After brushing dust from the clothing, Locard examined it under the microscope and detected metal fragments; when chemically tested they proved to be tin, antimony and lead in exactly the same proportions as that found in the counterfeit coins. The Inspector handed over the clothing of the other two men. The results were the same and as a consequence all three men were convicted; the police were suitably impressed.

Locard went on to solve many more cases, establishing his reputation not only with the Lyons Police but throughout the Continent. He published a book in 1922: *Detectives in Novels and Detectives in the Laboratory*, in which he described in racy terms many of the cases of murder, rape and robbery which he had solved. Locard did not believe in hiding his light under a bushel.

If Locard had made France and Europe aware of the importance of the microscope, then an Australian,

Charles Anthony Taylor, did the same for his half of the globe. An industrial chemist, he became a Government food analyst, and in 1921 was involved in a murder case. On 31 December in an area of Melbourne notorious for its prostitutes, the naked body of a young girl was found in a narrow street called Gun Alley. The pathologist of the Victoria State Government examined the victim and found that she was barely an adolescent, her breasts just beginning to bud. Blood smeared between her thighs indicated that it was a sex murder, and a vaginal swab proved this to be the case. She had been strangled and bludgeoned. She was identified as Alma Tirtsche, a schoolgirl of thirteen, missing from home since the previous day. Detectives questioned prostitutes in the area and ascertained that the body had been dumped after 1 a.m.; she had been killed elsewhere, then carried in a blanket of some kind and left in the alley. Logic indicated that the killer had to be someone who lived locally. One curious fact was that the girl's body had been carefully washed.

Police began to suspect a local shopkeeper, Colin Ross. When questioned, as all locals were, he admitted having seen the girl on the day in question, just loitering about. He hadn't given her any thought. But he gave a very accurate description of the girl, down to the slightest detail of what she had been wearing. Far too accurate a description for a casual observer. Other eyewitnesses placed Ross in Gun Alley at about the time the body had been dumped, one person even having seen him carrying a blanket-wrapped bundle.

Ross was arrested and questioned further. Two blankets from his shop were sent to Charles Taylor for analysis. The first revealed nothing under a magnifying glass, but the second had a red-gold hair, and careful examination disclosed another twenty-one, which Taylor mounted on a strip of card. The longer hairs – some over twelve inches, which in those days indicated a female – had been pulled out by the roots; the shorter ones had been broken off. Microscopic analysis showed the hair to be of human origin, and the degree of pigmentation proved it to be of someone thirteen years or over but under thirty, when colouring begins to decline. The short hairs had come from the nape of the neck of a redhead. The victim was a redhead . . .

At Ross's trial the defence argued that the witnesses who placed Ross in the vicinity of Gun Alley were either prostitutes or criminals and therefore unreliable. However, the evidence of the hair counteracted that and Ross was found guilty, and hanged at Melbourne Gaol on 24 April 1922 – the first man in Australia ever to be convicted purely on forensic evidence.

America's equivalent of Locard or Taylor was a chemist named Edward Oscar Heinrich, who was dubbed by the press 'the Edison of crime detection'. He became Professor of Chemistry at the University of California. He solved many cases, but perhaps his most remarkable feat of detection concerned the case of an inventor named Charles Henry Schwartz, who owned a small factory called the Pacific Cellulose Plant in California where he worked in the laboratory. Schwartz was trying to invent an artificial silk and told friends that he had succeeded. Aged thirty and happily married, he seemed to have everything going for him.

But on 25 July 1925 his laboratory was rocked by a huge explosion. When the flames were finally doused, a charred body was found in the building – which Mrs Schwartz identified as being that of her husband. Since the lab had been blown up deliberately it seemed a clear case of murder – perhaps by competitors.

Heinrich was asked to examine the scene of the crime, and the charred corpse was sent to his laboratory for X-rays. He observed that a molar was missing from the upper jaw of the dead man; Schwartz's dentist confirmed that he had pulled that tooth recently. Heinrich's most important discovery was that the victim had been dead even before the explosion occurred, having been killed with a blunt instrument. Which was puzzling, to say the least . . .

Then a few days later Mrs Schwartz telephoned the police to say that a burglar had broken into her house and stolen nothing but every single photograph of her husband. Heinrich managed to trace a photographer in Oakland who had a negative of a studio portrait of Schwartz. Heinrich ordered a print.

When he compared the photograph to the corpse, Heinrich knew immediately that he was not looking at the body of Charles Schwartz. An ear had escaped burning, and the lobe was quite different from the one in the photograph. (It is interesting to see how some of Bertillon's conclusions were correct.) The molar had been removed quite violently just before or after death, the eyes had been gouged out, and an attempt had been made to destroy the fingerprints with acid. Conclusions: someone wanted the police and all concerned to believe that the corpse was that of Charles Schwartz. Who had the motive? Charles Schwartz, who had insured himself for $185,000. His business had been failing and he was in financial trouble. What he had done was to get a man who looked remarkably like him – in this case a travelling missionary called Warren Barbe – and use him as his 'double'. Barbe had blue eyes while Schwartz's were brown, hence the need to gouge them out. Charles Schwartz was eventually tracked down to a room in a boarding house, but shot himself in the head before police could arrest him.

Between the wars, the case which captured the public attention was the Lindbergh kidnapping in the USA, and it is instructive to examine this case in detail to see how forensic science was utilised in the hunt for the culprit.

On 1 March 1932 the famous aviator Charles Lindbergh was at his home in Hopewell, New Jersey, with his wife and child. At 10 p.m. a frantic nurse discovered that the child, Charles Jnr, aged nineteenth months, was missing from his cot. And so the nightmare began . . .

There were few clues for the police to follow up. On the window sill of the baby's room a ransom note was found demanding fifty thousand for the return of the child. There were smudged footprints in the earth below the window, while nearby lay a crude home-made ladder in three sections. There were no fingerprints.

Police concentrated on the ransom note. It was written in block capitals by a poor speller – 'anything' was written as 'anyding'. Handwriting experts concluded that it had been written by a man of German origin and poor education. The note bore a distinctive signature: two interlocking rings, one red, one blue. The case caused a sensation throughout the nation and the world.

A week after the kidnapping a well-wisher named Dr John F. Condon sent a letter to his local newspaper in the Bronx offering one thousand dollars of his own money for the return of the child. He got back a letter with two identical interlocking circles, asking him to act as a go-between in the ransom negotiations, and to place an ad in the personal columns reading 'Money is Redy' (sic) when he was in a position to hand it over.

Lindbergh asked Condon to go ahead and place the ad. That evening a man with a deep voice telephoned Condon, saying his gang would soon be in touch. A rendezvous was arranged at a cemetery at night. At the gates a man disguising his face with a handkerchief asked Condon if he had brought the money. Condon said it was not yet ready. When the man took fright and ran away, Condon chased and caught him, assuring him he could trust him. The man identified himself as 'John' and suddenly asked: 'Would I burn if the baby is dead?' Condon asked: 'Is the baby dead?' The man said the child was alive and on a boad (boat). As a token of good faith he promised to send the baby's sleeping suit. It arrived next day; Lindbergh identified it as that of his son.

On 2 April 1932 Lindbergh accompanied Condon when he went to hand over the ransom money; he clearly heard the kidnapper's voice as he shouted: 'Hey doctor!' The money was handed over but the baby was never returned. On 12 May its decomposing body was found in a shallow grave in woods near Lindbergh's home. The baby had been killed by a blow to the head on the very night of the kidnapping.

The police were clueless, unable to prevent Lindbergh paying the ransom. They did suspect one of Lindbergh's maids, Betty Gow, of being an accomplice to the kidnapping; another maid, Violet Sharpe, committed suicide by poisoning after she had been questioned. Ordinary detectives were getting nowhere, but the forensic detectives were making progress.

Wood technologist Arthur Koehler examined the ladder used in the crime. Three rails were made of North Carolina yellow pine, four of Douglas fir, and ten of Ponderosa pine. The yellow pine rails contained nail holes indicating that they had been taken from elsewhere, and 'rail 16' had square nail holes and was different in that it had been planed down from a larger piece of wood. He declared the ladder to be of 'poor workmanship'. Because of tiny grooves in the wood caused by a defective planer, Koehler knew he could trace it to a particular lumber mill. Out of 1,598 mills which handled yellow pine, he eventually found the correct mill at the Dorn Lumber Company in South Carolina.

Police had been able to secretly mark the ransom bills without Lindbergh's knowledge. All banks were asked to look out for these bills, which included 'gold certificates'. They began to turn up in New York and Chicago. In early September 1934 the gold certificates started to appear in northern New York and the Bronx.

On 15 September 1934 a man driving a dark blue Dodge sedan drove into a garage in upper Manhattan and paid for his fuel with a ten-dollar gold certificate. Because these had ceased to be legal tender, the pump attendant noted the car registration on the back of the certificate. Four days later a bank teller found it was part of the Lindbergh ransom and notified the police. They traced car registration 4U–13–41–NY to Richard Bruno Hauptmann, a carpenter living at 1279 East 222nd Street in the Bronx. Police surrounded the house, and when Hauptmann left the next morning, they quickly arrested him. He was a tall, lean man in his mid-thirties. In his wallet police found twenty-dollar bills from the ransom money, and concealed in his garage was a further cache of the ransom money, including $860 and a gun. The evidence seemed overwhelming against Hauptmann.

Hauptmann told police that the money from the Lindbergh ransom had been left in his house by a friend, Isidor Fisch, who returned to Germany in December 1933 owing Hauptmann seven thousand dollars from a business deal. Hauptmann said that Fisch was a petty confidence trickster, and when he heard that Fisch had died of TB in March 1934, he took the shoe box which Fisch had left in his safekeeping and examined it. It had been lying on a shelf and had been soaked from a leaking roof, but it contained $14,600 in money and gold certificates. Hauptmann dried it out and started spending it . . .

Hauptmann was tried for murder and kidnapping in Flemington, New Jersey, on 2 January 1935. Rail 16 had been traced to Hauptmann's own attic. Detective Bornmann had noticed a missing board and found what remained of it with a 'rung' sawn out of it. And Condon's phone number was found panelled on the back of a closet door in Hauptmann's house. Witnesses had seen Hauptmann hanging around the Lindbergh home; Lindbergh himself identified Hauptmann as the 'John' whose voice he had heard in the cemetery. On 13 February 1935 Hauptmann was convicted and sentenced to death.

In the 1980s Ludovic Kennedy interviewed all the surviving witnesses and examined the evidence in the case, subsequently writing a book: *The Airman and the Carpenter* (1986) claiming that Hauptmann had been 'framed' by his friend Fisch. Kennedy points out that Hauptmann was comfortably off and had no motive; furthermore, as a skilled carpenter he would have made a better job of the ladder. As for the handwriting, found on the ransom note and identified as being that of Hauptmann, Kennedy dismisses that as evidence fabricated by the handwriting experts. As for 'rail 16' – why should Hauptmann have taken up one of his own attic floorboards when he had plenty of other wood? Kennedy maintains that rail 16 was 'planted' on Hauptmann by Detective Bornmann.

Kennedy manages to be both plausible and unconvincing. A careful study of the evidence leads to the conclusion that, despite some police bungling, they got the right man. Graphologists had concluded from the ransom note that the writer was German – *before* Hauptmann's arrest. And Judge Trenchard admitted forensic evidence relating to saw marks on wood and wood-graining, proving that the ladder found at Lindbergh's home had been made in Hauptmann's attic. I can hardly think of more damning evidence in any case. Hauptmann went to the electric chair on 3 April 1936.

One result of the Lindbergh case was the passing of the 'Lindbergh law' enabling the FBI to enter a case if the victim had been taken across a state line, and the death penalty to be enacted for the crime of kidnap. Alvin 'Creepy' Karpis, a bank robber, was arrested by

J. Edgar Hoover for kidnapping in 1936 and spent the next thirty-three years in jail, in the latter stages being a friend and mentor to Charles Manson. Lives intermingle . . .

The spectroscope was invented by Bunsen in 1859. It worked on the principle that the spectrum of every element has its own individual signature, revealed in the series of dark lines called absorption lines. It was the spectroscope which first told us what elements the stars and planets are composed of, since it analyses the light they emit; but it can also tell us exactly what traces of dye, mud, snuff, tobacco, coal dust, etc., there are on the body of a murder victim. When a spectroscope is used together with a related instrument called a spectrophotometer, which measures the intensities of light of different wavelengths, all kinds of interesting results can be obtained. The spectrophotometer began to assume importance in the years following World War II. A fibre can be analysed by passing a beam of light through it and looking at its spectrum. The absorption lines reveal its chemical composition. However, some substances *absorb* the light which lies beyond visible light – at either end of the spectrum: infra-red and ultra-violet. Salt, which is invisible to infra-red rays, can be used as a kind of scientific detective.

A sample being prepared for infra-red spectrophotometry is mixed with salt. When the light emerges from the sample it is *minus* the rays which have been absorbed by the salt, and the spectrum of this light will reveal what is *missing*. This technique, and its offshoot, omission spectroscopy – vaporising a sample between two electrodes and analysing the spectrum of its light – is often used in hit-and-run cases where the vehicle can leave traces of paint on the victim.

Thomas McMahon, an IRA terrorist, was convicted of the murder of Lord Louis Mountbatten because paint on his boots was matched by spectroscopic examination to the paint used on *Shadow V* the Earl's yacht; sand on his boots was identical to that of the slipway where the yacht had been berthed, and chemical analysis of his clothing showed traces of nitroglycerine, used to blow up the yacht. McMahon was jailed for life in November 1979.

In America car manufacturers routinely send samples of the paint used on their vehicles to 171 crime laboratories around the nation.

A murder case from Florida demonstrates the application of the full range of forensic techniques available to police officers. Sharon Zellers, aged nineteen, disappeared as she drove home from work at Disney World on the evening of 30 December 1978. Her parents quickly notified the police, and an air search of central Florida was made, for her car.

On 3 January 1979 her Ford Falcoln car was found abandoned in an orange grove, some three hundred feet from a nearby motel. Bloodstains were visible in the interior of the car on the driver's side, together with a purse. Detailed photographs were taken of the vehicle and immediate area. A dusty shoe print was found on the interior of the car's windscreen on the passenger side, with a second matching shoe print on the inside of the passenger door window. The prints were from military-type boots. The fact that the vehicle had been exposed to the elements for three days had destroyed any latent fingerprints.

The car was taken to the evidence section at police headquarters and meticulously examined. A single strand of hair was found at the base of the seat-belt attachment on the passenger side. A further search revealed several more matching hairs. The car interior was carefully vacuumed and samples collected. The shoe prints were lifted onto cards for evidence. A red fibre was also found.

The body of Sharon Zellers was found a couple of

days later in a well about fifty feet from where her car had been left. She had been battered to death. The effects of water on the victim made fingerprint identification impossible. Dr Thomas Ford, a nationally renowned forensic ondontologist, was able to make a positive identification from the victim's dental record.

Routine detective work revealed that on the night Sharon was murdered, a guest at the nearby motel had sent for an ambulance. He had been bleeding profusely from the mouth, and claimed he had cut his tongue during a fight at the local skating rink, when he received an upper cut and bit his tongue. A small amount of blood was recovered from the room he had occupied, and his name was established from the motel register.

The hospital doctor who attended to the man said the patient had lost about three-quarters of an inch from the front of his tongue, which had been bitten off. Security guards at the skating rink were adamant that there had been no fight on the night in question. A nurse at the hospital, who had treated the man's wound, said he could not have bitten off his own tongue – *the curve was in reverse to his bite*. The conclusion was that the victim had bitten it off . . .

Meanwhile the suspect, Robert C. Cox, had returned to his military unit in Georgia and was effectively out of police hands. But the detective in charge of the case was not to be deterred. He examined the man's service record and discovered that he had a history of attacking women. Cox was questioned but denied ever having seen Sharon Zellers, and had to be released. However, the police got court permission to take hair and blood samples from him for possible DNA testing – then in its infancy in the USA.

When the detective wanted to contact Cox again, in mid-1986, he discovered that Cox was in prison, serving nine years for attacking two women in one month in separate incidents eighty miles apart.

In January 1988 the car blood residues were delivered to the Cell Mark Diagnostic Laboratory in Maryland, which was carrying out DNA testing. The result was disappointing. The lab reported that there had not been sufficient DNA material to make a test. But the McCrone Associates Inc. Laboratory in Chicago had had more luck with the hair samples, and were able positively to match the hairs found in the victim's car to the suspect's head.

On 27 June 1988 Cox stood trial in Orange County Court for the murder of Sharon Zellers. The prosecution presented its evidence, and when it came to mentioning the missing piece of Cox's tongue which had been bitten off, the prosecutor said that only Sharon could have done that, adding: 'She marked him, God bless her, she marked him.' On 2 July 1988, almost ten years after the murder, the jury found Cox guilty of the murder and he was sentenced to death. He now resides on Florida's death row. The result was a tribute to dedicated detective work, and the forensic scientists involved.

Handwriting is another area providing clues which forensic science can use to solve crimes – especially in fraud cases. But it is the murder cases which attract attention. Graphologists claim to be able to pin-point handwriting to a specific individual – even if he has printed in block capitals or otherwise attempted to disguise his writing style. However, it takes years of training to become that expert. In the Dreyfus affair, in France, it was that same Bertillon, then a junior records clerk in the Sûreté, who helped convict an innocent man.

Captain Alfred Dreyfus, of Jewish origin, served on the French General Staff as an officer. French security experts were alarmed at the flood of military secrets that were finding their way to the German embassy. A woman cleaner at the embassy – in the pay of the

French – discovered a torn-up handwritten letter in the wastepaper basket there. The letter referred to the sale of military secrets, so the hunt was on to find the 'mole'. The General Staff was anti-semitic, and so Dreyfus made a good scapegoat. He was asked to write a specimen letter – which Bertillon subsequently claimed was identical to the original. Dreyfus, charged in 1894 with treason, was sentenced to life imprisonment.

He was to serve twelve years on the notorious Devil's Island in French Guiana. In January 1898 the famous novelist Émile Zola published his *J'accuse* letter, condemning the court martial of Dreyfus as illegal. It was to be a long battle to clear the name of Dreyfus, but the real traitor was eventually identified, and in 1906 the Court of Appeal cleared Dreyfus. Restored to the army, he was promoted to Major. He died in 1935.

All forensic laboratories have a specialist document examiner who uses a whole variety of scientific aids to analyse questioned documents, including infra-red photography and chromatographic analysis. The specialist will have detailed knowledge of all inks, papers, watermarks, various types of handwriting and different makes of typewriters.

In the 1970 kidnapping of Mrs Muriel McKay, the Hosein brothers, who believed their victim to be the wife of the owner of the *News of the World*, sent a ransom letter to the newspaper demanding a million pounds, with instructions about the delivery of the money. At their trial the brothers pleaded not guilty. A handwriting expert produced a photographic enlargement of the ransom note, which had been written in block capitals in a lined page torn from an exercise book. When this was superimposed as a transparency over pages from an exercise book found at the Hoseins' farm, there was a perfect match with the indentations of the writing of the ransom note, even to staple marks and torn edges of the letter received by the newspaper and recovered by the police. Two other notes were given in evidence, written by Arthur Hosein in a disguised hand, one of them bearing his fingerprints. This conclusive evidence, discovered by the microscope, served to convict both brothers of murder, kidnapping and blackmail, and they were jailed for life.

Handwriting is as unique as fingerprints, especially when it comes to signatures, which become repetitive, formalised and distinctive over the years. In the case of the only solicitor to have been hanged – Major Herbert Rowse Armstrong, for the poisoning of his wife with arsenic – it was also established that he had forged her signature to her will.

Graphologists use what is known as the metrical analysis method, which measures the height of individual letters, expressed as a graph.

Typewriters offer the criminal no safety either, since from the moment they are first used they begin to deteriorate, with individual characters becoming worn or broken. One handwriting expert puts typewriters in the same category as ballistics and fingerprints, estimating the odds of two typewriters performing identically to be in the region of 1 in 3,000,000,000,000. And as has been noted, it was an Underwood portable typewriter which helped convict Nathan Leopold and Richard Loeb for the kidnap-murder of fourteen-year-old Bobby Franks, in 1924.

A more serious matter is the recent scandal involving officers of the West Midlands Serious Crimes Squad. In July 1989 the Chief Constable, Mr Geoffrey Dear, was forced to move fifty-three of his officers out of the CID and into desk jobs, following allegations that senior detectives had fabricated evidence against suspects and had 'invented' verbal admissions and confessions. This was proved when the notebooks of detectives – said to have been written up at the time of interviewing the suspect – were examined by forensic scientists using a method called electrostatic deposition analysis (ESDA). In several cases the test showed that officers had altered documents, inserting other material weeks and even months after the initial entries in the log books. As a result of the success of the ESDA tests, there followed a rash of original case papers being 'lost' by detectives fearing exposure, and two officers were suspended after papers went missing. The Chief Constable immediately ordered that all documents in disputed cases should be kept locked in safes awaiting investigations by inquiry teams. It will be interesting to see if any of the men convicted by these forged documents and now serving long prison terms will be cleared and granted pardons.

We trust the police, and it is they who use the latest scientific tests on our behalf to detect crime. It is fitting, therefore, that in the rare cases where corruption is found or suspected, those same tests should be used against the police.

In Britain we have eight major Home Office forensic science laboratories, with Scotland Yard having its own Metropolitan Police Forensic Laboratory. In the USA the FBI has a crime laboratory at its headquarters in Washington, and every major police force has its own crime laboratories. All of them use the microscope as the basic tool in crime-fighting.

The weak link between the crime and the microscope is the detective on the spot. He examines the undisturbed crime scene and chooses which evidence to submit to the laboratory. Evidence may be overlooked – as in the 'Bambi' case – mislaid, or badly handled and corrupted before it even reaches the safe hands of the forensic scientist. The quality of scene-of-crime examination in both the USA and this country leaves something to be desired, with estimates showing that only between three and ten per cent of potential evidence at a crime scene is actually collected. In some American states the use of scene-of-crime officers has been discontinued, and instead a mobile laboratory is driven to the site, equipped with every type of test to deal with whatever evidence exists.

A method of improving the means by which evidence samples are collected and delivered to the forensic laboratories must be found quickly, otherwise we are cheating the all-seeing eye of the microscope and depriving ourselves of justice.

Meanwhile, on 5 September 1989 special British postage stamps were issued marking the 150th anniversary of the Royal Microscopical Society. They depict a snowflake, blue fly, blood cells and a microchip under the microscope, honouring an instrument which has given us sterling service ever since its invention in 1670.

9

THE SEX KILLERS

While the microscope, with its great versatility, can look into the heart of the atom, it cannot look into the souls of men. Neither can we, using our ordinary common experiences and sense. Even skilled psychiatrists have only limited access to the mind of the sex killer. That mind, that vision of the world it encompasses, cannot be entered merely by an act of will, a powerful projection of empathy. The mind of the sex killer is as complex and convoluted as a painting by Richard Dadd; a weird and alien landscape of private devils and cruel lusts.

The sex killer has a complete lack of normal moral scruples or inhibitions. To him the world is his private chicken coop and he the fox, free to strike where and when the mood takes him. The very randomness of his acts, the absence of any link between him and his victim, has made the problem of detecting his type by scientific means apparently insoluble; but even in this field progress has been made.

The old records contain very few details of sex crimes. Men raped, of course, but since a woman could be had for a few pence, it would have seemed absurd to any individual to devote his life to the pursuit of sex to the point of murder. *The Newgate Calendar* has little on the subject, and it can truly be said that the sexual serial killer is a relatively modern phenomenon.

An early case was that of Fanny Adams, aged eight,

who was raped and murdered by Frederick Baker on 24 August 1867 at Alton, Hampshire. The main evidence against him lay in his diary entry for that day, which read: 'Killed a young girl today. It was fine and hot.' Baker was hanged for the crime. At the time of the murder, which caused an enormous sensation, the Royal Navy was introducing tinned meat to the sailors, who didn't think much of it and suggested it was the remains of 'Sweet Fanny Adams' – which is the derivation of our modern expression: 'Sweet FA'.

But even the Jack the Ripper murders of 1888 were not recognised at the time as being the work of a sex killer, but rather as the acts of a man who was morally insane. The unknown 'Jack', who murdered five prostitutes in the Whitechapel area of London in the autumn of 1888, was never caught, and speculation as to his identity continues to this day.

It was with the turn of the century that the problem of the sex killer really began. 1894 had seen a French 'Ripper', Joseph Vacher, begin his series of gruesome murders, which included raping and sodomising girls and boys, with castration and disembowelling often featuring in his crimes. In the space of three years he had committed eleven murders when caught. Lacassagne spent five months examining Vacher and came to the conclusion that he was shamming insanity. Vacher went to the guillotine on 31 December 1898.

On 9 February 1929 a German sex killer began his series of infamous crimes which led to him being dubbed the 'Monster of Düsseldorf'. He began with arson and attacks on animals; after that he graduated to murder. Some nine victims later – ranging in age from an eight-month-old girl to middle-aged men and women – on 24 August 1929 there was a double murder of two girls, one aged fourteen, the other five. Both had been strangled and had their throats cut. Then came four more attacks, followed by a murder in September, another in October and two more attempted murders that month, with the murder of a five-year-old child in November.

Düsseldorf had been subjected to a reign of terror, but the killer had come to the end of his tether. It seems that he suffered some inner moral collapse. He persuaded his wife to turn him in to the police for the large reward on offer.

We know more about Peter Kürten than most killers of his type, simply because he was examined by a psychiatrist, Dr Berg, for many months, and described freely and fully his early experiences, motives and methods. The result was Dr Berg's classic book on Kürten: *The Sadist*. It makes terrifying reading. Kürten had suffered from excessive sexual excitement from the age of thirteen onwards and had practised bestiality with sheep, pigs and goats – quite apart from attempted incest with his sisters. Then on one occasion he stabbed a sheep while having intercourse with it and so enjoyed the result that this incident seems to have triggered off his mania. While serving a long prison sentence for burglary, Kürten used to deliberately get himself put in solitary confinement so that he could fantasise about getting his revenge on society, of blowing up the city with dynamite. On his release he was delighted to see a blood-red sky over Düsseldorf – and so began his reign as the 'Monster'.

Kürten got sexual satisfaction from arson, stabbing people at random or hitting them over the head with a hammer, and once decapitated a swan in a park lake and drank the blood which spurted from the stump of its neck. Some of his crimes contained elements of sodomy and necrophilia. He often masturbated over the secret grave of one of his victims.

At his trial, which began on 13 April 1931, Dr Berg described Kürten as being 'the king of sexual perverts'. Sentenced to death by decapitation, Kürten told Dr Berg that the greatest thrill he could imagine would be to hear his own blood running into the basket. He was executed on 2 July 1931, after eating a huge last meal. Yet Kürten, a revolting creature, was actually a perfectly normal man in outward appearance and apparently happily married . . .

And there is the nub of the problem. How can we hope to detect the monsters among us? Most serial killers – the serial killer murders more than once and on separate occasions; the mass murderer kills many people on one occasion – are perfectly normal in appearance and outward behaviour. Usually of above average intelligence, they are often attractive individuals. Peter Sutcliffe, Ted Bundy, Albert DeSalvo, Dennis Nilsen – all were considered ordinary decent people, hardworking and honest, by those around them.

And why should sex crimes have become so prevalent *now*? That they have can be seen from the statistics. In England in 1938 there were 5,018 sex crimes reported. By 1951 the figure had increased to 14,633. In 1955 it was 17,078 and by 1961 it was over twenty thousand. Since then it has appeared to double every year, an increase far greater than the growth of population.

There are many theories to explain the *why*. Most experts believe that the problem lies in our overcrowded cities and point to experiments which show that when rats are deliberately forced to live in overcrowded conditions in the laboratory they begin raping and killing one another. I have my own theory. Sex is mainly a *mental* activity, and the justly maligned media have encouraged a kind of mental sex hunger by placing an undue emphasis on sex. Young men are led to expect far more than reality can deliver, and they kill out of a sense of frustration.

In 1824 Thomas De Quincey published his celebrated essay *Murder Considered as One of the Fine Arts*. Supposedly a paper which was to be read to the 'Society for the Encouragement of Murder', it has often been misunderstood as gallows humour. But De Quincey was using irony to point out psychological truths. Let us suppose that such a society existed. How would we go about encouraging sex murder? *By doing exactly what we do now*: exploiting and packaging sex as a commercial product. By 'doing dirt' on sex, as D. H. Lawrence said. It may be that the page-three girls have done more to incite sex crimes and contributed to the current twenty-nine per cent increase in rape cases than any other single factor. As a professional writing about murder for a living, I am often struck by the fact that many sex killers, when arrested, are found to be in possession of an extensive library of pornographic magazines and video films. Ian Brady, the Moors Murderer, had the works of the Marquis de Sade. The result is that our young – with more leisure time than any other generation – walk our streets full of resentment against an abstract 'society' and feeling sexually underprivileged.

Throughout the twentieth century each decade has been marked by monstrous sex crimes which stun the imagination. In February 1926 the 'Gorilla Murderer' began his series of murders in the USA. He usually raped and killed landladies – twenty-two of them – and his victims ranged in age from a baby to a sixty-year-old woman. Earle Leonard Nelson was arrested in Canada in June 1927, after crossing the border to kill. He was executed on 13 January 1928.

In 1931 Sylvestre Matuska planted bombs on railway lines in Austria, causing trains to crash. One crash on 12 September saw twenty-one people killed and dozens more injured. Matuska ejaculated as he watched the train crash, so intense was his pleasure. Tried in Vienna in June 1932, he was sentenced to life imprisonment.

That same year a sex murder occurred in the USA which aroused enormous revulsion. It was solved as a result of dogged detective work and forensic science, and deserves to be examined at length.

On 28 May 1928 an old man knocked on the door of a basement apartment at 406 West 15th Street in the Chelsea district of Manhattan. He said he was looking for the man who had advertised for a job in the *New York World Telegram*. Giving his name as Frank Howard, the old man explained that he owned a farm at Farmingdale, Long Island, and would be willing to pay fifteen dollars a week for a good worker.

The man who had advertised was Albert Budd, who was finding it hard to support his wife and four children on a doorman's wage. The family were delighted with the job offer, but the mild-looking old man said he would return a week later for a firm decision. He failed to keep the appointment but sent a telegram apologising for having been unavoidably delayed. In fact he arrived the next day, bearing a gift for Mrs Budd – a pail of pot cheese – expensively dressed and with a wallet stuffed with dollar bills. He had dinner with the family, then gave the eldest children money to go to the cinema. After talking expansively for a while, the old man kindly offered to take the ten-year-old daughter, Grace, to a birthday party at the house of his married sister at 137th Street in Columbus. The parents gave their permission without hesitation and Grace went off trustingly holding the old man's hand. She was never seen alive again.

When she failed to return home by next morning, the parents went to the police, who were able to tell them that there was no such address as that given by the old man: Columbus only went as far as 109th. Further checking revealed that there was no 'Frank Howard' who owned a farm in Long Island, and neither was there any clue to his identity, since he had taken back the telegram he had sent to the Budd family.

Detective Will King of the Missing Person's Bureau took on the case as a personal challenge, and the first thing he did was to trace the original telegraph form. It took two clerks thirteen hours to find it among thousands of forms. It had been sent from the East Harlem office of Western Union, but since it would have been impossible to search every house in that district for the missing child, King set out instead to trace where the pail of pot cheese had been sold. Every store in Harlem was traced and eliminated before King found the street hawker who had sold it. He gave an accurate description of the old man, but that was of little help.

There was intense newspaper and radio publicity about the abducted child, which resulted in hundreds of crank letters but no real clues. After a few months the police were forced to abandon the search as hopeless. The trail had gone cold. But Detective King refused to give up and devoted his career to finding the child – or her killer.

The years went by. Then, on 11 November 1934, Grace Budd's mother received a macabre letter; naturally, it was anonymous. The writer said that a friend of his, a Captain Davis, had acquired a taste for human flesh while in China, where children were being eaten during a famine. On returning to New York, Davis had kidnapped two small boys and beaten them 'to make the flesh good and tender', then killed and eaten them. The writer went on to say that he had decided to try it for himself and so had abducted Grace, taking her to a house in Westchester, where he stripped himself naked, strangled the child, then cut her into small pieces and took her back to his own home to eat her. 'How sweet and tender her little ass was, roasted in the oven. It took me nine days to eat her entire body. I did not fuck her tho I could of had I wished. She died a virgin.' It might have been a letter from De Sade himself . . .

The father took the letter to the police. Detective Will King had declined to retire two years earlier, still determined to track down the killer of Grace Budd.

Now he had his second clue – the first had been the telegram signed 'Howard'. A comparison of the hand-writing of the two items showed them to have been written by the same man.

The flap of the envelope which had contained the letter carried a design partly blacked out with ink. Under the spectroscope it proved to be the letters N.Y.P.C.B.A. King deduced that the letters stood for the New York Private Chauffeurs Benevolent Association, which had its address at 627 Lexington Avenue. King spent several hours at the association's office comparing the handwriting of every employee with that on the letter, but found none of the four hundred-odd samples matched. King then addressed the assembled employees. Had any of them taken the Association's stationery for personal use? One man, a chauffeur called Lee Siscoski, admitted that he had, saying he had left some envelopes in his room at 622 Lexington. King hurried to that address, but found no envelopes there. Then Siscoski recalled that he had previously rented a room at 200 East 52nd Street. He might have left them there . . . This was a boarding house, and when Detective King described 'Howard' to the landlady she nodded in rec-ognition. 'That sounds like the man in number seven – Albert Fish,' she said.

The signature of Albert Fish in the register matched the handwriting of the man who had written both the telegram and the letter; naturally Detective King was anxious to talk to the man. The landlady said that Fish had moved, but he would be back sometime to collect the monthly cheque sent to him by one of his sons. Another officer might have asked the landlady to phone the police the next time Fish showed up, but Detective King rented a room in the boarding house and sat down to wait.

It was three weeks before Albert Fish arrived on the scene. King arrested him without fuss, but on the way to the police station the old man turned nasty, lunging at King with an open razor in each hand. King grabbed his wrists, banging them against a wall to make him drop the razors, and then handcuffed him. When he searched his prisoner he found his pockets to be full of knives and razors.

Fish confessed to the murder of Grace Budd immediately, and described in detail cutting off her head and drinking some of her blood. It had made him vomit. He had dissected the body at the waist with a knife. Police took Fish back to his house, Wisteria Cottage, in Worthington Woods, and under the floorboards found the bones of Grace Budd.

Back at headquarters, Fish at first denied having committed any other murders, but finally told his story of four hundred child murders committed between 1910, when he was forty, and 1934. This figure was never verified, but it is certain that Fish killed dozens of children in twenty-four years.

Psychiatrist Frederick Wertham was asked to examine Fish in jail, and Fish came to like and trust him. Later, Wertham was to devote a chapter in his book *The Show of Violence* to Albert Fish. He said that although Fish looked meek and inoffensive, he was 'the most complex example of the polymorphous pervert I have ever encountered'. Fish practised every known form of sexual deviation from sodomy and sadism to eating human excrement and driving needles into his scrotum. Under X-ray, several needles years old were discovered in his body. Fish even enjoyed inserting cotton wool soaked in alcohol into his anus and setting it alight. Wertham was convinced that Fish was insane, but the jury took a different view and sentenced Fish to death. Fish told reporters: 'Going to the electric chair will be the supreme thrill of my life' – although his last words in the execution chamber were: 'I don't know why I'm here'. The needles caused problems with his electrocution, shorting-out and causing extensive burning.

Sex killers continued to plague us in the decades to follow. William Heirens – the 'Lipstick Killer' – was a student aged eighteen at the University of Chicago who began his criminal career as a burglar, but found himself stealing women's underwear and eventually having an orgasm by simply entering a window. Then he graduated to murder, breaking into the apartment of widow Josephine Ross and stabbing her in the throat as she lay in bed, afterwards knotting her nightdress around her neck. On 1 October 1945 he was interrupted while breaking into a nurse's apartment; he fractured the woman's head with an iron bar and tied her to a chair. On 10 December 1945 he broke into the apartment of ex-Wave Frances Brown and murdered and mutilated her, scrawling in lipstick on the wall behind her bed: 'For Heaven's sake catch me before I kill more. I cannot control myself.' Later he killed a six-year-old girl, raping her and then dismembering her body. He was caught when a caretaker heard suspicious noises from an empty apartment, and was subdued only after a fierce struggle with police. A search of Heirens' room at the university revealed dozens of women's panties. Heirens was subsequently sentenced to life imprisonment.

Wartime London had been terrorised in the blackout by a ferocious killer who murdered four women in four days. Gordon Frederick Cummins was a young trainee pilot who would have gone on to become a modern-day Jack the Ripper if he had not been caught. On 9 February 1942 he strangled forty-year-old Evelyn Hamilton. On the tenth Mrs Evelyn Oately, aged thirty-five, was found dead in her flat. Her throat had been cut and the lower part of her body mutilated with a tin-opener, on which fingerprints of the killer were found. On the eleventh Margaret Lowe, forty-three years old, was strangled with a stocking and then mutilated with a razor blade. Doris Jouannet was strangled and mutilated on the twelfth. Cummins was caught because he left his gas-mask case behind at the scene of a fifth attempted murder, and his service serial number was stamped inside. Twenty-eight-year-old Cummins, was sentenced to death following an Old Bailey trial and hanged on 25 June 1942. Sir Bernard Spilsbury carried out the postmortem on him – as he had on one of the victims.

In January 1947 came the case of twenty-two-year old waitress Elizabeth Short, known as the 'Black Dahlia' because of her fondness for black underwear. Her body was found on a vacant lot in Los Angeles, severed at the waist. She had been suspended upside down and tortured. The murder was never solved, although the case attracted dozens of crank confessions.

John Reginald Halliday Christie killed at least six women in his house at 10 Rillington Place, London W11, between 1942 and 1953, displaying necrophiliac traits in that his victims had to be dead or unconscious – gassed by him – before intercourse took place. He also kept a collection of pubic hairs from his victims in an old tobacco tin. He too seems to have undergone some kind of inner moral collapse and was wandering around London like a vagrant when arrested. In his confession he told of looking down at the body of Muriel Eady, adding: 'Once again I felt that small, quiet thrill. I had no regrets.' Tried for the murder of his wife, he was sentenced to death in June 1953 and was subsequently hanged.

Ian Brady and Myra Hindley – the 'Moors Murderers' – were a classic example of *folie à deux* in action: a couple who supported one another's fantasies and delusions, sharing the same madness. Brady was a Nazi fan who read De Sade avidly and infected Myra Hindley with his mix of sex and sadism. They turned to murder almost as a natural progression: it was 'murder for kicks'. Their first victim was sixteen-year-old Pauline Reade, murdered on 12 July 1963 as the Beatles were beginning their reign in the pop charts and preaching that love is all you need. It wasn't enough for Brady and Hindley. Keith Bennet, aged twelve, went into a moorland grave on 16 June 1964. All the victims were taken from the Manchester area and buried on Saddleworth Moor. Brady and Hindley had their photographs taken gloating over the graves. John Kilbride and Lesley Ann Downey were very young victims. The deadly couple took obscene photographs of the girl and tape-recorded her screams for mercy. Their final victim was teenager Edward Evans. They were caught because Brady tried to induct his brother-in-law into his murder schemes, but he promptly went to the police. During their trial at Chester Crown Court the air of superiority which the couple shared came across strongly. Both the accused had come to feel that other people were simply insects, morons, maggots, cabbages. They *deserved* to be killed . . . The couple were jailed for life on 6 May 1966 and remain in prison still.

The same kind of motiveless hatred of society – or at least contempt for its conventions – was seen in the Charles Manson 'Family' murders in the USA in the early 1970s. There was a *casual* quality about the murders of Sharon Tate and others, as if all human life was basically meaningless. In fact, from the 1960s onwards there has been a steady rise in what newspapers termed 'motiveless murders'. There is simply no such thing as a motiveless murder. The motive might be obscure, even non-existent to the normal person, but every killer has his own reasons. The Moors Murderers and the Manson 'Family' killed to demonstrate their superiority over the rest of mankind, a Nietzschean motive.

It could be argued, of course, that Dr Neil Cream murdered without cause or motive when he killed four prostitutes in London in 1891–2 by giving them 'med-icinal pills' which in fact contained strychnine and which they took in the privacy of their own homes, so that Cream did not even observe their death throes. But it is obvious that Cream derived some kind of morbid pleasure from the act, or the *imagining* of the murder-to-be.

Not for nothing had F. Tennyson Jesse categorised the six motives for murder in her book *Murder and Its Motives* (1924). She listed them as: elimination, gain, revenge, jealousy, lust and conviction. It remains pretty comprehensive to this day. Even the Manson killings can be listed under conviction, since they were con-vinced of the need for 'Helter Skelter' – the killing of what they termed the 'Pigs'.

Locard included a chapter devoted to 'Crime Without Cause' in the seventh edition of his *Treatise On Crimi-nalistics* (1940), writing: 'Crime is a physical phenom-enon conditioned by psychological fact. Neither in physics nor in psychology is there an effect without a cause. In vain do modern novelists do their utmost to depict such acts which, in the minds of their authors, are purely gratuitous manifestations of "play", expressions of a consciousness which wants to be free of the Kantian axiom and, moreover, all law. All pun-ishable acts – in fact all acts – have their cause.'

By 'modern novelists' Locard was no doubt referring to André Gide, who had postulated the idea of the *acte gratuit* in his novel *The Vatican Cellars* (1914), in which a young man decides to push a fellow traveller out of the door of a moving train for no particular reason other than a desire for sensation.

On 4 July 1975 Peter Sutcliffe, the Yorkshire Ripper, attacked his first victim, beginning his five-year reign of terror of the north-west of England, during which he was to kill thirteen women and seriously injure many more. His method was to attack his victims from behind, hitting them over the head with a hammer, before plunging a Phillip's screwdriver into their lower abdomen. Yet five years previously, in August 1969, Sutcliffe came to police attention when he hit a prosti- tute over the head with a brick in a sock. He felt she had cheated him. Sutcliffe was let off with a caution.

Had the police been able to check all men who had attacked by striking over the head when the 'Ripper' killings began in the Bradford area, the name Sutcliffe would have come immediately to their attention. They could not carry out such a check because the massive five-year inquiry, which cost over three million pounds was never put on computer; the facts from the massive inquiry – the most expensive in British criminal history – were recorded by hand on a card-index system which made cross-reference virtually impossible. The police were further led astray by hoax letters and a tape from a Geordie, which led them to look at Sunderland when they should have been concentrating on Bradford, where Sutcliffe actually lived and killed. There can be no denying that the police made a series of inexplicable blunders.

Some of Sutcliffe's victims were prostitutes; others were schoolgirls or housewives. Sutcliffe was to attempt to justify his activities by telling his brother that he was 'just keeping the streets clean'. That was a lie. The truth was that Sutcliffe enjoyed the feeling of power that striking and mutilating his victims gave him.

When Sutcliffe was caught it was by accident. He had gone to Sheffield to seek out a prostitute to kill, but was spotted by a vice-squad patrol car. They noted that he had false number plates fixed to his car and arrested him. Even then, had he wished, he could have denied being the Ripper; there was no evidence against him and his conviction was as a result of his own confessions. He was a lorry-driver by profession, and in the cab of his truck police found a hand-lettered card reading: 'In this truck is a man whose latent genius, if unleashed, would rock the nation, whose dynamic energy would over-power those around him. Better let him sleep?'

Straightaway the problem can be seen, the curious paradox. How could any man consider that the cow-ardly murders of thirteen defenceless women consti-tuted genius? Sutcliffe was an example of the frantic ego assertion which characterises so many of today's sex killers.

Dennis Nilsen was a job centre executive officer who was also a deadly scavenger. In his fifty prison note-books, which he handed to author Brian Masters so that he could write his incisive book on the case: *Killing For Company* (1985), Nilsen attempts to analyse his own motives. Highly intelligent and articulate, he is all the more frightening for that. Over a period of some four-and-a-half years in the heart of London, he lured sixteen young men to their deaths and – with two excep-tions – *nobody missed them*. This was because he chose his victims from among the young and dispossessed, the poor, homeless and hopeless, the natural losers; young men who were homosexual or drug addicts, young men who were lonely, hungry, and who trusted the tall, slim man with the bushy brown hair and spectacles. After all, he was an ex-policeman . . .

Nilsen's crimes eclipse those of most other murderers not simply by numbers, but by the impassive, implac-ably cruel nature of his killings, the sheer arbitrary and irrational choices behind them all. On one level he was quite a nice man; on another level he was a killer of intense ferocity with dirty little motives which scabbed his soul. He masturbated over his victims and period-ically took them out from under the floorboards in order to fondle and have sex with them by placing his penis between their thighs. He sat them in the opposite armchair to watch TV with him or listen to music or simply join him in conversation. He kept one corpse in an armchair for a week because 'it was so nice to have someone to come home to'. Lonely, shy, friendless, Nilsen truly killed for company. At one period he had six bodies under the floorboards of his flat and was not alone any more. Yet at his subsequent trial evidence emerged about his feelings of superiority. The unemployed young vagrants and homosexuals he disposed of by burning or dismembering and flushing down the toilet – he was caught because the drains beneath his house became blocked with human remains – were 'scum': sixteen of them.

Handsome Ted Bundy was a student first at Seattle them at Salt Lake University, a young man brimming with self-confidence and style. The man with the looks of a Robert Redford and a charming, articulate manner to match, was a product of the American Dream. Success was his for the choosing. Instead, he elected to pursue a four-year orgy of destruction across the USA which left dozens of young women maimed or dead. Police believe Bundy killed twenty-one women, but the real figure may be as high as forty.

What makes killers like Bundy so different is that their murders are deliberate acts of ultimate evil. They make a conscious decision to be *out of control*. There are no excuses; no deprived background, poverty, or physical handicap. In the manner of his passing Bundy brought out all the worst aspects of the American character. New President George Bush had promised a 'more kindly America'. When Bundy went to the electric chair on 24 January 1989, after some ten years on death row, Americans celebrated by holding parties, wearing T-shirts bearing the legend: 'Burn, Bundy, Burn'. At the moment of his death thousands of spectators outside the prison roared their approval, hooting their horns gleefully. A nearby bar was serving Bundy 'fries' and Bundy 'toast'. Looking for a psychological motive for Bundy's murders is almost useless. There are some

253

minds which are unfathomable. Like killer sharks, they
lurk in the icy ocean depths, rarely showing their ugly
snouts. But those disgusting scenes at Bundy's execution
need no psychological explanation. They were a blot
on the character of a civilised nation and revealed the
American Nightmare at its worst.

Henry Lee Lucas was another American Gothic. It
was he who finally made America aware of the menace
of the serial killers in their midst. The FBI estimates
that serial killers slaughtered some 5,000 Americans in
1983. The epidemic seems peculiarly American. Around
the world, according to Interpol, no more than fifty
serial killers have been identified over the past twenty
years. Newspaper accounts of Lucas's claim to have
murdered 360 people from coast to coast by virtually
every known method: stabbing, shooting, strangulation,
mutilation, decapitation and even crucifixion, led to one
top police official admitting that there could be as many
as thirty-five such killers at large in America at any one
time, with the numbers constantly increasing.

In September 1984 one-eyed vagrant Henry Lee
Lucas led FBI officers on a gruesome nationwide tour,
showing sites where he had disposed of bodies. At that
time 144 of his serial slayings had been verified, and
Lucas, at forty-eight, was named the worst mass murderer in US history. Now under sentence of death in
Texas, he is wanted by law officers in a dozen other
states for questioning about unsolved murders.

All the cases of sex murder so far mentioned had one
thing in common: they were not solved by forensic
medicine or by clever detection. The killers were caught
in the main by *accident*. Since the killers struck at
random and left so few clues, there was very little scope
for forensic science. It had no role to play.

The turning point in the fight against the sexual criminal came with the Colin Pitchfork case, which we examined in detail in the chapter on blood typing. This case

marked the introduction of the DNA fingerprint into criminal investigation, and from now on every time a rapist or killer had intercourse with his victim he left his 'fingerprints' behind as surely as if he had signed his work.

Now forensic medicine had a positive role to play in this area, and perhaps equally as important in historical terms is the case of the 'Railway Murderer'. This investigation saw the introduction of 'psychological profiling', pioneered in the USA. Coupled with the use of the computer and the DNA fingerprint, it made all the difference. With these new tools detectives could hunt the sexual criminal with good chances of success.

It began in 1982, with five women being raped in that year by two men, one tall and one short. (The *folie à deux* situation is not as rare as might be imagined. One has only to think of Bonnie and Clyde, Leopold and Loeb, Snyder and Gray, Fernandez and Beck, and Hulten and Jones.)

By November 1984 the short rapist started to work alone. Police began to notice a disturbing pattern to these rapes, twenty-seven of them taking place in the London area. Nearly all the attacks occurred close to railway stations, those unmanned and isolated stations where women alighted almost into pitch darkness. It was felt that the rapist might be a railway worker, since he seemed to have a good knowledge of station and rail layouts. His *modus operandi* was unmistakable. He engaged his victims in conversation – which is comparatively rare, since most rapists prefer to perform in grim silence – he threatened his victims with a knife, then tied their hands with string and raped them. He seemed to derive a sadistic pleasure out of frightening his victims and inflicting unnecessary violence.

From studies of this type of rapist, police knew that there was an extreme likelihood that he would progress from rape to murder, and accordingly a team of detectives was set up specifically to catch him. This inquiry was code-named Operation Hart and was under the command of Detective Superintendent Ken Worker.

On 14 January 1986 the body of Alison Day, aged nineteen, was found in the River Lea in Hackney, east London. She had been tied up, strangled and probably raped. She had been missing ever since she failed to keep a date with her boyfriend on 29 December, and those seventeen days in the water had destroyed vital forensic evidence. However, she was wearing a sheepskin coat, the pockets of which had been weighted with stones from a nearby public car park, and on the coat were found fibres which might have come from her killer. The most vital clue lay in the method of strangulation: a form of tourniquet. A scarf around the throat had been used as a ligature, with a stick inserted which tightened it when turned. This garroting feature was to be noted in future cases.

On 17 April 1986 fifteen-year-old Maartje Tamboezer, whose father, an oil company executive, had not long been living in this country, set off to cycle beside a short stretch of railway track on the way to Horsley, in Surrey, to buy sweets. In the course of that journey she had to dismount. Someone had strung fishing line across the path, forcing her to detour across a field close to a copse of trees. There a man lying in ambush seized her, battered her unconscious and raped her. Afterwards he strangled her and then attempted to set fire to the body, thrusting paper tissues into her vagina with the obvious intention of destroying his sperm traces. Whoever the killer was, he appeared only too aware of the threat posed by forensic science . . .

Detective Superintendent John Hurst of Surrey CID took charge of this murder inquiry, which was to assume enormous proportions in terms of manpower. Hundreds of possible witnesses were questioned. Some had seen a smallish man rushing to catch the 6.07 train from East Horsley to London. That in turn led to two million tickets being examined in London, in the hope that one might be bloodstained or bear fingerprints. That search met with no luck.

However, the police did have some clues. Despite his care, the rapist had left semen traces in the clothing of his victim, which scientists could test for blood type. It was group A and the man was a secretor. An enzyme called PGM (phosphoglucomutase) enabled the scientists to narrow the sample down even further. Although a third of the population are group A, these special factors would eliminate four out of five suspects – if they could find any.

But there was another clue which led police to link this murder to that of Alison Day *and* all the rapes which Operation Hart was investigating. It lay in the peculiar manner in which the perpetrator had tied the hands of his victims in a 'praying' attitude. He had used brown string which was unusually wide. If they found that ball of string in the possession of a suspect it would be enough to convict him.

A month later – the period between attacks was getting shorter as the killer's mania grew – twenty-nine-year old Ann Lock, who worked for London Weekend Television, was murdered as she returned by rail from the studio to her home in Brookmans Park in Hertfordshire. It was Sunday, 18 May 1986. The victim, married for only four weeks, had just come back from her honeymoon in the Seychelles. When she failed to return home, her frantic husband telephoned the police to report her missing. Initially he was given a hard time by the police as a possible suspect – in police experience, murders are usually committed by the next of kin, with 'stranger-to-stranger' murders being rare – simply because his wife's body was not found until ten weeks later, in thick undergrowth near the Brookmans Park railway station. On the night she vanished, other passengers noticed that someone had moved the benches in that station to force passengers to make a detour. Ann Lock had not been able to collect her bicycle, which was still chained to railings at the station. Instead she had been seized by her killer, raped, allowed to suffocate, and set on fire. The blood group of sperm recovered and the PGM reading linked this killing to the previous two and to the railway rapes.

Detective Chief Superintendent Vincent McFadden was in charge of this inquiry. Since the rapes and murders were taking place over a wide area, several forces – including the Railway Police – had been drawn in and were duplicating each other's work, unaware that there was a common thread linking them all. That was, until McFadden decided that the man he was seeking was responsible for all the crimes. He got the various forces involved to link their computers to share information, and he put pressure on Operation Hart to get results quickly.

Operation Hart, in search of an elusive rapist, had started with a list of 4,900 sex offenders, and subsequent inquiries had whittled that number down to 1,999. At number 1,594 on that list was John Duffy. He had been charged with raping his ex-wife and beating up her boyfriend. More importantly, he was a former British Rail carpenter. On 17 May, the day before Ann Lock vanished, Duffy had been arrested on suspicion while loitering near a railway station, and was found to be in possession of a knife of such length that it constituted an 'offensive weapon'. Duffy explained that he used it in his martial arts class in Kilburn, where he was studying Zen Buddo. The explanation was accepted and he was released – but his arrest was logged in the computer. Unfortunately, this did not come to anyone's attention immediately.

Operation Hart officers continued work on their list of 1,999 names, taking blood samples from each person for elimination purposes, and in due course they called upon Duffy to supply a sample. On 17 July 1986 Duffy arrived at the police station with his solicitor and refused to give a blood sample – immediately drawing attention to himself. Detectives realised that the small man with the ginger hair and pockmarked face fitted the description given by victims. Moreover he had an unblinking stare – 'laser-eyes' one victim reported – which had been mentioned by several victims. Duffy was interviewed, was just that shade *too* helpful, and said nothing of any consequence. He had to be let go. When Superintendent Worker tried to interview Duffy again as being a likely suspect, he found that Duffy was in hospital, an inpatient at the Friern Barnet Hospital, apparently suffering from loss of memory.

A few hours after that first interview at which he had refused to give a blood sample, Duffy had staggered into Hampstead police station looking very battered. He complained that he had been mugged and had lost his memory, and officers had arranged for his removal to hospital. Now Superintendent Worker found that doctors refused to allow him to interview Duffy, claiming it might hinder his recovery. The Superintendent was content to allow Duffy to remain in hospital for the present. At least he knew where he was – or so he thought.

In fact Duffy was being treated as a part-time patient, and while absent from the hospital raped another schoolgirl. The description she gave did not lead police to consider Duffy as a 'possible'.

It was at this point that the police decided to enlist the help of a new technique, pioneered in the USA, which has incredible potential and acts as a kind of 'psychic detective', looking into the soul of the criminal. Psychological Offender Profiling (PROP) is a system of building up a portrait of the likely offender or killer from clues recovered at the murder site. By subjecting the evidence in the case to behavioural analysis, psychologists can produce remarkably accurate descriptions of the suspect, often indicating his home area, marital status, type of occupation, and even the car he drives.

The police asked Dr David Canter, a professor of psychology at the University of Surrey, to set up a team to review all the information on computer about the murders and rapes. Starting with the premise that the crimes were all the work of the same man, the professor was able to provide the police with a startling description of the man they were seeking.

By examining witness statements and visiting the scene of each crime, Dr Canter was able to deduce that the killer lived in the Kilburn/Cricklewood area of London, was married and probably childless, with his marriage going through a turbulent patch, was probably employed in a semi-skilled occupation which brought him into contact with the public, and had two close male friends. Duffy fitted all the criteria *exactly*.

Psychological Profiling, explains Dr Canter, involves sifting *all* the available evidence. 'We do not deduce anything from a single clue, but look for a system of patterns. We try to point the police in fruitful areas.' The FBI, which has been using psychological profiling for the past ten years, claims a success rate of forty per cent. The method has helped solve such cases as the Los Angeles 'Night Stalker' rapist and the Atlanta child murders.

Dr Canter listed 17 points about the killer, and when this analysis was matched against the 1,999 names on the computer, it instantly flashed up the name of John Duffy.

Duffy was immediately put under surveillance at his home in Barlow Road, Kilburn. But skilled as the undercover detectives were, Duffy soon realised that he was being followed and seemed to relish playing games with his 'tail', deliberately losing them to demonstrate his

superiority. Chief Superintendent John Hurst decided
that Duffy must be immediately arrested: there was too
much risk involved in letting him run free – he might
even kill again while under police observation.
Duffy was the most difficult suspect Chief Superintendent Hurst had ever had to question. The thirty-
year-old Irish-born man simply looked at him with his
disconcerting stare, eyes wide like lasers. He admitted
nothing. His attitude was that it was up to the police
to prove the charges against him. And he was well
aware that he could only be held for thirty-six hours
before being either charged or set free. The Chief Superintendent had to find his evidence within that time limit.

A search of Duffy's house revealed many knives, but
nothing to link him with rapes and murders. His ex-
wife was interviewed and said that Duffy had once told
her that he had raped a girl, saying it was her fault for
being frigid. Duffy liked to tie his wife's hands and rape
her, rather than have normal sex, and the more she
struggled the more aroused he became . . .

It was in the home of Duffy's parents that police
found what they were looking for; conclusive proof
of guilt. A ball of brown string was identified by the
manufacturers as having a unique fault which was
common to the string used to bind the victims. Even
when that piece of evidence was thrust before his eyes,
Duffy did not blink or reply.

Then a friend of Duffy's, martial arts enthusiast Ross
Mockeridge, went to the police to tell them that Duffy
had pressured him to punch him in the face and slash
his chest with a razor, explaining that he feared the
police were trying to 'frame' him on a rape charge.
Mockeridge had obliged reluctantly.

Five of Duffy's rape victims picked him out on an
identity parade, but Duffy just gazed at them with his
'laser-beam' stare, which several police officers admitted
they found intimidating. The string evidence linked

Duffy to the murder of Maartje Tamboezer, but there was no clinching evidence in the cases of Ann Lock and Alison Day. Then the forensic laboratory came up with what the police desperately needed. Seventy garments had been seized from Duffy's home. One by one they were examined, until finally thirteen fibres found on Alison Day's sheepskin coat were matched with fibres from a sweater with a certainty which made it as good as a fingerprint.

The two-man rapes of 1982–4 were never officially solved, although Duffy was one and the police believe they know the identity of the other man involved. In 1983 there had been no rapes because Duffy was trying hard to become a father – he had a low sperm count. He was sacked from British Rail in 1982 for bad time-keeping. His first solo rape was in November 1984, when he attacked a girl. at knife-point on Barnes Common. By now Duffy and his wife were becoming estranged, quarrelling frequently. His wife left him in June 1985 and two months later Duffy raped her, attacking and wounding her boyfriend.

At the trial of Duffy, four rape victims testified about Duffy tying their hands in a 'praying' position – just as the hands of the murder victims had been tied.

Duffy was convicted of two murders – those of Alison Day and Maartje Tamboezer. There was insufficient evidence to convict him of the murder of Ann Lock. He was also convicted of four rapes. In February 1988 the trial judge sentenced Duffy to serve a minimum of thirty years in prison.

Duffy, who must have considered himself a master criminal, a Moriarty of murder, at last gained some kind of recognition: he became the first sex killer in Britain to be caught by the computer and the psychologist.

10
FACETS OF MURDER–
THE WAY AHEAD

Forensic science has progressed far since the early days, and continues to do so. Just as we marvel today at the DNA fingerprint, so the introduction of fingerprinting appeared miraculous to the late Victorians – and we can expect many more exciting scientific developments in the future.

Murder is not only a reflection of society at a particular time, but it is also a closed universe of its own, obeying its own laws. The statement by Quételet that 'society contains within itself the germs of all future crimes', for example, takes us into another dimension in which human beings are regarded as little more than machines whose actions can be predicted.

The murder rate in England and Wales has, in fact, never varied more than between 3.2 and 3.9 people per million each year. By the use of statistics it can even be predicted with some accuracy how many people in Britain will get bitten by dogs next year. The police can and do use statistics to programme computers to predict how many people will be murdered in say, Brighton, next year. And that can further be refined to state how many by knife, by gun, by poison.

Put like that – that these murders are *bound* to happen – it seems as if the killer is merely a blunt instrument of fate who should not be judged too harshly. If he had not committed the particular murder, someone else would have had to do so. Although this appears a logical, scientific conclusion to be drawn from statistics, we cannot allow ourselves to think like that. Every individual must be deemed to be responsible for his own actions, otherwise organised society would perish, all laws become meaningless. It is in this sense that Dr Samuel Johnson wrote: 'If a madman were to come into this room with a stick in his hand, no doubt we should pity the state of his mind; but our primary consideration would be to take care of ourselves. We should knock him down first and pity him afterwards.'

What is the function of forensic medicine and what is its future? Its function is to discover the truth, without bias, fear or favour, and personally I think it a great pity that forensic laboratories are so closely associated with the police – via the Home Office – and are not like open markets to which both prosecution and defence can submit samples.

The future of forensic medicine is both limitless and unimaginable. I would predict that a century from now the emphasis will be on preventing crime, and not its detection after the fact. It is impossible to envisage another great breakthrough like the DNA fingerprint – although such innovations will doubtless occur – but one fruitful area in forensic medicine lies with the pathologist. At present the medical examiner has the task of establishing the time of death of a victim – or, rather, the time which has elapsed since death.

This may not seem of much importance, yet in cases where a suspect has an alibi for a limited timescale, it becomes crucially important. William Herbert Wallace, a Liverpool insurance agent, left his home at 6.45 p.m., having been lured to an appointment with a mysterious 'Mr Qualtrough' at a non-existent address. He returned home at 8.45 to find his wife battered to death. The pathologist put the time of death at between 6 p.m. and 7 p.m. – although he said it was closer to 6 p.m. A milkboy saw Mrs Wallace alive at 6.30. Various witnesses who saw Wallace walking around Liverpool searching for the non-existent address included a police constable. Wallace was seen at 7.06 boarding a tram two miles from his home. At best he could have had a mere eighteen minutes to commit the murder and tidy up afterwards – yet no blood was found on his clothing. At his trial the prosecution suggested that he had stripped naked to commit the murder; that the Mrs Wallace the milkboy saw was Mr Wallace himself dressed as a woman; that his asking a constable for directions was a clever ploy to establish his fake alibi. In 1931 Wallace was convicted of murdering his wife and was sentenced to hang, but the Court of Criminal Appeal, established in 1907, made legal history by using its powers for the first time to quash a murder conviction on the grounds that the verdict was against the weight of the evidence. Wallace was set free. He was hounded by gossip and died in 1933 an embittered man.

The fact is that at the present time, despite much forensic medical research, all the known means of estimating the time of death are notoriously unreliable. The rate at which body temperature declines after death has been studied for well over a century, but there are so many variables which affect the cooling process that no precise formula can be arrived at. The variable factors include the amount of clothing on the body, the ambient temperature and humidity, the position in which the body is lying, the victim's internal temperature to begin with – which might not have been the standard 98.4°F – the amount of fat the victim is carrying (thin people cool quicker than fat people), which is expressed as the ratio of the body's surface to its weight.

Other bodily changes which might give a clue to the time of death include the rates at which various enzymes decay, changes in the concentrations of electrolytes in the vitreous humour of the eye, and the response of muscle to electrical stimulation. Even the most favoured of detective novel myths, that the pathologist can estimate the time since the last meal was taken by determining how completely the stomach contents have been digested, is completely fallacious. In the Stephen Truscott case in Canada in 1959, in which Truscott, aged fourteen, was accused of raping and strangling a twelve-year-old girl, a pathologist at his trial testified that the girl must have been killed within two hours of her last meal. Truscott was convicted and sentenced to be hanged, although this was commuted to life imprisonment. Six years later, following pressure for a new hearing, the Supreme Court heard seven pathologists from three countries argue about the rate of digestion. None could agree, and forensic pathologists in general do not now place much reliance on digestion rate. Yet I am certain that if enough scientific attention was given to this problem, a solution would quickly be found. The trouble is that it just doesn't seem an important enough subject to which to devote research time.

So what happens in a murder case at the present time? In a typical murder scene, the body is discovered and the familiar canvas shelter erected around it, with a constable guarding the site. A scene-of-crime officer will note every item of evidence on or near the body, and carefully log every visitor to the site. The pathologist arrives with a superior version of the famous 'murder bag' which Sir Bernard Spilsbury devised.

Having established that the body in question is (a) dead, and (b) the cause was probably murder, he will set to work. On many occasions police officers have mistaken a case of suicide for a murder case. In one instance a man was found shot through the head in a public park with no firearm in the vicinity. It was suicide. The pistol was found half a mile away. The man had shot himself and then staggered half a mile before collapsing. In another case a company director drilled eight holes through his skull with an electric drill before finally killing himself.

Murder having been established, the victim's hands and feet are sealed in plastic bags to preserve any forensic evidence, and the pathologist, who will have inserted a rectal thermometer, makes a note of the ambient temperature and the reading from the corpse. The pathologist knows that on average bodies cool at the rate of 2.5°F per hour in the open, although the variable factors mentioned makes this neat formula unreliable. A naked body will cool more quickly; in water twice as fast; yet a severe head injury can slow down the cooling process, and there are recorded cases of bodies actually warming up after death, as decomposition sets up a fermentation process which produces heat.

However, the pathologist will use the standard formula, which is the normal body temperature of 37°C minus the rectal temperature, divided by 1.5. And he will know that a body feels cold after 12 hours, and after 18 to 24 hours the temperature of the internal organs will be the same as the ambient temperature. He takes the temperature of the body at regular intervals and plots its progress on a graph. He will then give the detective in charge of the inquiry a very rough estimate of the time of death, and the cause of death if this is obvious. Then, it will be removed to the mortuary after the familiar yellow chalk line has been drawn around it.

In the mortuary, during the postmortem, the pathologist will look for various factors, such as decomposition, if the body has remained undiscovered for some time. In one case Professor Simpson, who found bluebottle maggots in the corpse, had to study their breeding cycle to establish the time of death. Sometimes a botanist can tell how long it would have taken tree roots to have grown through a skeleton.

Lividity gives another clue to the pathologist. If the

body is moved after death, that will be apparent by the lividity appearing to defy the law of gravity. Lividity – caused by the blood draining to the lowest part of the body – does not appear until some three to four hours after death, although once again such variables as obesity or great loss of blood will invalidate this.

Rigor mortis first becomes apparent in the eyelids and lower jaw, spreading to the shoulders, arms, trunk and legs. It begins within five hours of death and is fully established after 12 hours, disappearing after 24 to 36 hours. It cannot reappear, since it is caused by coagulation of the protein in the muscles, leading to shortening and stiffening – which is precisely why we call a corpse a 'stiff'. By detecting the degree of rigor mortis, the pathologist can make a guess at the time of death – although he will often get it wrong. It is a very imprecise part of forensic medicine.

The body will be carefully examined for any marks, pin-pricks from hypodermic injections, signs of strangulation, wounds, lacerations or defensive marks. The eyes are checked for signs of dilation, which could indicate poisoning, or contraction, which could indicate a drugs overdose. After the body has been weighed and measured it is opened up, the pathologist making a Y-shaped incision beginning under each nipple and joining to continue in a straight line down to the pubis. Every important organ and cavity will be examined. Specimens of hair from various parts of the body are taken, as are fingernail scrapings and vaginal and anal swabs. These are all sealed in plastic bags. A chart is made of the body and the position of lividity and rigor mortis recorded in relation to the distance from other parts of the body. The wounds which caused death will be cut out and preserved.

The various portions of the body cavity are removed as a whole to preserve the integrity of the structure; thus the lungs will be removed and placed on one table, the intestines on another. The brain is removed whole and weighed. The stomach contents are removed and sent for analysis. Samples of skin, blood, bone, muscle, urine, brain, spinal fluid and various other organs may be removed for analysis. The pathologist dictates his findings into a microphone at mouth level as he works, the notes being typed up later.

The pathologist takes careful note of the vital reactions to determine whether injuries were inflicted before or after death. If before death, there will be evidence of inflammation as the cells get to work – leucocytes will be seen around the edges of the wound under the microscope. Since the leucocytes – or repair cells – arrive at the wound in regular sequence over a period of forty-eight hours the amount and presence can also help in determining time of death.

While it all sounds very scientific – the mortuary, the careful dissection, weighing and measuring of the body, removal of organs for analysis – in determining the time of death it is, in fact, rather primitive. Its excellence lies in its determination of *cause* of death.

Throughout the last one and a half centuries the emphasis has been on trying to read the soul of the criminal. Cesare Lombroso may have got it wrong in the nineteenth century when he claimed that certain men are 'born criminals', atavistic types, but at least he was attempting a scientific approach. It didn't help when a sociologist called Richard Dugdale made a study of a family called the Jukes and wrote a book about them, *The Jukes* (1877). In attempting to prove that criminal characteristics are inherited, Dugdale studied the entire Jukes clan descended from the original sire in New York in the early nineteenth century. Two of his sons married their illegitimate sisters, and Dugdale traced the entire seven hundred descendants. All were either prostitutes

269

or criminals, save for half a dozen. Again it was a scientific attempt to find reasons for crime, but it was on the wrong track.

Lacassagne, on the other hand, took an almost Marxist view and declared that 'society has the criminals it deserves'; in other words: society causes crime. This view prevailed well into this century, with the perennial excuse that the juvenile delinquent was the product of a broken home – mocked with brilliant irony in the musical *West Side Story*.

Now it is recognised that crime is a mental activity. The criminal makes *choices* – he chooses to be what he is – which is not to say that he can necessarily stop it.

Hunger is the title of a remarkable novel by Knut Hamsun, a vivid and impressionistic early study of alienation. Hunger is deprivation, the starving of an appetite, a need which, if it gets out of control, leads to antisocial behaviour. It can take many forms – sexual or financial, for example – but its most interesting role is the hunger for recognition, for fame, to be *known*. We all have this innate need. In the criminal it simply looms abnormally large.

Hunger for recognition is a psychic need. Fromm, in his *Anatomy of Human Destructiveness* calls it 'the need to make a dent'. To let the world know we exist. In a way it's a demand for more life – only with the criminal it is always at someone else's expense. Willie Sutton, the notorious American bank robber, once said that he never felt more alive than when he was inside a bank – robbing it. If you think about the Christie case, and remember his confession describing his feelings as he gazed down at the body of Muriel Eady, whom he had just strangled and raped: 'Once again I experienced that small, quiet thrill. I had no regrets', then we can clearly identify the mechanism of this hunger at work. It is as if, for some people, only the act itself – however monstrous – can give meaning to a torpid sense of reality. It is pointless to condemn this hunger. It is a fact of human psychology which cannot be either condemned or approved. It simply *is*. This hunger can be a positive or negative factor in the life of the individual. If positive it leads to the entrepreneur, the maker of empires. But in the criminal it is always switched to the negative pole.

We can see this hunger in the history of murder. First there was murder for economic motive: the simple basic need for survival. That was the first phase. Increased prosperity in society led to the second phase: domestic murders. Dr Palmer, Dr Pritchard, Florence Bravo, Lizzie Borden. The motive here is to safeguard the killer's security. Even Charlie Peace, the artful dodger of Victorian times, committed his burglaries and murders to ensure the survival of his middle-class life-style in his villa, with his famous 'musical evenings'. Then came the third phase, the sex murder, which is with us still, in which the killer hungers for sex as the old-time killers hungered for money.

A new type of criminal whom I have called Reactive Man, has now emerged. In simple terms, Reactive Man refuses to accept life as he finds it. The old-style criminal wanted to steal an apple from the orchard; Reactive Man wants to burn the orchard down. He is the scavenger, the looter living in the wreck of a civilisation. Freedom – the problem of what to do with it – is his disease. Boredom is his natural state. He feels stifled, trapped, viewing violence as the only means of escaping from the straitjacket. He is the complete criminal, his existence is a chain reaction which can only end with his death or imprisonment for life.

We all react if we stub our toe on a rock; the difference is that Reactive Man reacts without stubbing his toe. He reacts against what he feels to be the restraints and repressions of our society. He is never in the wrong, he is never sorry. He is breeding fast – faster than we can build cages to house him. He is the stranger among us, never of us. Many labels could be hung on him, and indeed are, but none tells us very much. Rebel. Psychopath. Terrorist. All are shorthand symbols for a state of mind. And that is hate. Freud said that if a baby had the power, it would destroy the world from the frustration of its infantile desires. Perhaps Reactive Man is simply immature. Certainly he feels superior to the rest of us.

Ours is an age when the rules of the game are increasingly being challenged – *or seem to be*. In fact, the young are begging for rules, seeking meaning. Man is a value-seeking animal, and if our society seems to offer no values, then our young become lost. In America suicide is now the third leading cause of death in youngsters. Erich Fromm cites the case of a young girl – *not* schizophrenic – who slashed her wrists because she wanted to see if she had any blood. 'To see her own blood was the only way she could convince herself that she was alive and human.'

Aggression, however expressed, is basically a manifestation of *disorganised purpose*. We have young people whose criminality seems to come from regarding the world as being basically meaningless. There's an odd element of drifting. Cash comes too easily. Things can be stolen instead of worked for. Unemployed kids get drunk and take cars for joy-riding . . . It all seems a kind of anarchic defiance of society. But careful observation reveals a kind of *structure* struggling to emerge. Studies of soccer gangs have shown that they have intricate rank structures and codes of behaviour. They are seeking, without knowing it, a *purposeful group identity*. They want to know who they are and what they should be doing, and because they don't, they are attracted to extreme forms of behaviour.

Now, if our young are reacting partly against their own feelings of inadequacy, the answer must be to provide them with more self-knowledge, so that they no longer react wildly and stupidly, as a snake strikes at a stick. It is important to make the attempt to understand the mentality of our attackers and to see why today's three Rs have become Rage, Resentment and Revenge. It seems to be a fundamental truth that human nature is basically destructive, when it is given no sense of purpose. That is, when a person has nothing much to do, his energies turn easily to destruction. It's a process of alienation directed into negation, and the negativity can take hundreds of forms, from the lonely suicide to the serial killers like Dennis Nilsen, who felt so miserable and alienated that he began killing to *connect*.

So what are we to do? Continue throwing our undesirables into prison? It doesn't seem to work. It is impossible not to think of the criminal as being sick, as intrinsically lacking in normal psychological vitamins. His whole life is an act of *hunger*. To treat him we would first have to know what he hungers for. Punishment is a useless expedient, like caging an animal demented by hunger and expecting it to reform. Such a strange hunger breeds a terrible hatred that feeds on life itself.

For me personally the greatest breakthrough in forensic medicine has been the introduction of psychological profiling. This method of deducing a criminal's characteristics from his activities can be traced back centuries, but for practical purposes it can safely be said to have been pioneered by Dr James Brussel, formerly Assistant Commissioner of Mental Hygiene for the State of New York, and psychiatric consultant to various police agencies. It comes as no surprise to learn that he has worked for the CIA. The press have described him as the 'Sherlock Holmes of the couch', and his fascinating account of the criminal cases in which he has been involved, *Casebook of a Criminal Psychiatrist* (1968), certainly bears this out.

The New York Police Department first consulted Dr Brussel about the case of the 'Mad Bomber' who planted twenty-eight explosive devices around the city over a sixteen-year period, beginning on 16 November 1940. His first bomb did not explode and was found on a window ledge at the Consolidated Edison Company building in Manhattan. With the bomb was a note reading in block capitals: 'CON EDISON CROOKS – THIS IS FOR YOU.' Police thought the bomber probably had a grudge against the company which supplies New York with its electricity, but the case was not regarded as being serious and was filed away.

In September 1941 another unexploded bomb was found lying in the street. It's alarm-clock fusing mechanism had not been wound. Three months later a further letter from the bomber was received, this time at police headquarters. Post-marked Westchester County, it read: 'I WILL MAKE NO MORE BOMB UNITS FOR THE DURATION OF THE WAR – MY PATRIOTIC FEEL-INGS HAVE MADE ME DECIDE THIS – I WILL BRING THE CON EDISON TO JUSTICE LATER – THEY WILL PAY FOR THEIR DASTARDLY DEEDS. F.P.'

Between 1941 and 1946 some sixteen similar letters were received by newspapers, hotels or department stores, and Con Ed itself. Then on 25 March 1950 a third bomb turned up in Grand Central Station. This too had failed to explode and was of the same fine workmanship of the previous two. Was it the bomber's intention that the bombs should *not* explode but serve as a warning? If so, he must have been frustrated about the lack of publicity his cause was getting. The next bomb exploded in a phone booth at the New York Public Library on 24 April 1950. More bombs followed; some exploded, some did not. Nobody was injured by the explosions, even though one had been placed in a cinema, the bomber having slit through the underside of a seat to thrust the bomb into the upholstery.

More letters to newspapers followed, threatening further bombs 'to serve justice'. There were four bombs in 1951–2, all of which exploded. The bombs were getting bigger and better and by now the public were well aware of the man dubbed the 'Mad Bomber'. There were four bombs in 1953, four in 1954. The last, stuffed inside a cinema seat, injured four people. In 1955 there were six bombs; two which failed to explode were found in cinema seats. The bombs were becoming more frequent, the letters longer and angrier. One to the *Herald Tribune* read in part: 'SO FAR 54 BOMBS PLACED – 4 TELEPHONE CALLS MADE – THESE BOMBINGS WILL CONTINUE UNTIL CON EDISON IS BROUGHT TO JUSTICE.' Again it was sighed 'F.P.'

The next bomb, on 2 December 1956, blew seats apart in the Paramount Theatre in Brooklyn, injuring six people. It was then that the police launched a major campaign to catch the Mad Bomber.

Inspector Howard E. Finney of the New York Police Crime Laboratory visited the office of Dr Brussel. Finney himself had a degree in forensic psychiatry, but Brussel was already noted for his uncanny ability to look behind the facts of a case and make remarkable deductions. Finney placed a pile of photographs and copies of the bomber's letters on Dr Brussel's desk.

Dr Brussel studied them for a long time. Then he told the waiting detective: 'It's a man. Paranoic. He's middle-aged – forty-five to fifty. Well-proportioned in build. He's single, a loner, perhaps living with an older female relative. He is very neat, tidy and clean-shaven. Good education, but of foreign extraction. He's a Slav.

His letters are posted from Westchester, and he wouldn't be stupid enough to post them from where he lives. He probably posts the letters between his home and New York City. One of the biggest concentrations of Poles is in Bridgeport, Connecticut, and to get from there to New York you have to pass through Westchester. He has had a bad disease – possibly heart trouble. When you catch him he'll be wearing a double-breasted suit. Buttoned.'

Dr Brussel suggested that the police should publicise his theories about the Mad Bomber in the hope that it would flush him out. A New York newspaper published an open letter urging him to give himself up and promising to air his grievances for him. It worked. Three letters arrived, all blaming Con Edison for his lifetime of suffering. The third letter gave the date of the accident which had caused his injuries. It read: 'I WAS INJURED ON JOB AT CON EDISON PLANT – SEPTEMBER 5th 1931 – I DID NOT RECEIVE ANY AID . . .'

It was a simple matter to trace the file for an accident on that date. George Metesky had been working at a Con Edison plant and had been blown over by a blow-back from a boiler, but doctors were unable to find any physical injuries, although he complained of pains and headaches. He was given sick pay for a few months, then fired. He tried to sue the company but his action was too late – all compensation claims have to be filed within two years of the date of the injury. Metesky had brooded over this 'injustice' for years, and then began planting bombs . . .

When arrested at his home in Bridgeport, Metesky was found to be well-proportioned, age fifty-one years, of Polish extraction, unmarried, living in a house with two older sisters, and was wearing a double-breasted suit. Buttoned. Metesky admitted being the Mad Bomber, revealing that the initials 'F.P.' stood for fair play. He was found unfit to stand trial and was committed to a state hospital for the criminally insane for the rest of his life.

Why had Dr Brussel's profile been so accurate? Because it was based on solid deductive reasoning, experience, and playing the averages. Paranoia takes a long time to develop – say ten years before that first bomb in 1940; which meant he started to become ill in 1930, making him middle-aged in 1956. Paranoics feel intellectually superior, are neat and obsessive, tidy to a fault, believing themselves to be perfect. Hence the neat lettering on the notes and the double-breasted suit. The words in the letters were those of an educated man but had no American slang and read as if they had been translated into English. The native New Yorker uses 'Con Ed' instead of 'Con Edison'. And that wildly Victorian 'dastardly deeds' hinted at a foreigner. Why a Slav? Because historically bombs have been favoured in Central Europe. Well-proportioned? Because a German psychiatrist named Ernst Kretschmer had demonstrated that a person's build was often associated with his personality and any mental illness he might develop. After studying ten thousand mental patients, Kretschmer found that eighty-five per cent of paranoiacs have an 'athletic' body build. The 'averages' said that the Mad Bomber would be of this type. Why a paranoiac? Because they are the champion grudge-holders and can never admit they are wrong about anything. Why single? Because of all the neatly printed capitals, only the 'W' was odd; it was shaped like two U's joined together – the shape of a woman's breasts. This suggested the Mad Bomber had some sexual problem. The slashing of the cinema seats was untypical of the Mad Bomber, who was neat and quick, usually placing his bombs and walking away. Why bother to slash the seats instead of simply leaving them under the seats? Because the slashing of the seat was the symbolic penetration of a woman's body ... It all sounds far-fetched, but it worked.

Dr Brussel was to become involved in many other cases, including those of the Boston Strangler and Dr Coppolino, an anaesthiologist convicted in 1967 of wife-murder, and his unique methods earned him a national reputation. How did Dr Brussel explain his gift? 'People sometimes ask me what proportion of my psychiatric deductions is science and what proportion is imagination. It's a hard question to answer ... I can only say that I always start such a deduction with a solid basis of science, but somewhere along the way intuition and imagination begin to take over. When you think about an unknown criminal long enough, when you've assembled all the known facts about him and poked at them and stirred them about in your mind, you begin to *see* the man. You picture his face, hear his voice. As in the case of George Metesky, you even see the clothes he wears.'

By the 1970s the American police became aware that they were dealing with a very new type of killer: the serial killer. What were known in police jargon as 'stranger-to-stranger' murders had increased from six per cent in the 1960s to eighteen per cent in the mid-1970s – more than four thousand cases a year.

July 1976 saw the 'Son of Sam' begin his killing spree in New York City, shooting couples in parked cars. He killed six young women and injured seven others. David Berkowitz was arrested for these crimes because his car had received a parking ticket in the area. In 1973 came the discovery that Dean Corll had raped and murdered thirty young men over a three-year period. In June 1972 Sherman McCrory was arrested following a botched supermarket raid. Detectives discovered that he and his family – wife, son, daughter and three grandchildren – had left a trail of some twenty-two bodies from Texas to California. The 'Freeway Killer' in California raped and mutilated over forty young boys during the 70s, dumping their bodies at the roadside like garbage. John Wayne Gacy confessed in 1978 to murdering and raping thirty-one young men. And of course, the Boston Strangler had killed thirteen women between June 1962 and January 1964. The cases of Richard Speck and the Manson family were part of the same pattern. Just after World War II the national average for solved homicides in the USA was ninety per cent, but it had fallen to seventy-six per cent by 1983. This was not a sign of police inefficiency, but rather the emergence of a new type of killer.

The FBI reacted by setting up a psychological profiling team at the FBI Academy in Quantico, Virginia. The team of nine men was officially known as the Behavioural Science Unit, and its task was to apply the techniques pioneered by Dr Brussel. Set up with a grant of $128,000 from the National Institute of Justice, its results were to be spectacular.

The unit began by building up a library of taped interviews with the new type of killer. They went into prisons across the nation and talked to such notorious serial killers as Richard Speck, Emil Kemper, Charles Manson, Juan Corona and David Berkowitz. As a result these FBI officers became 'mind hunters', gaining unique insights into the mind of the killer.

The FBI's 'mind hunters' system is part of the VICAP Program – Violent Criminal Apprehension Program – which is directed by the National Center for the Analysis of Violent Crimes. Details of all murders in the USA – there were a staggering nineteen thousand in 1987 – are collated at FBI headquarters. The 'mind hunters' then look for the psychological clues in the cases, and from scene-of-crime photographs they have the ability to predict the likely murderer, his age, marital status, the car he drives, the probable area where he lives and his life-style. Much of it is based on plain common sense. A body dumped in a remote spot with difficult terrain would indicate that the killer is a 'macho' type who drives a Jeep-type vehicle.

Talking to killers taught these officers that they all had one thing in common: all were intelligent, but all were abused and rejected as children, and had retreated into a world of fantasy. The result of the VICAP programme is that we now have cops who can think like killers, and by getting inside their heads can predict their next move.

Roger Dupue, head of the Behavioural Science Unit, categorises killers into various 'types' according to the methods used. Most crime in the USA is committed by the young, the fourteen to twenty-four age group, but they are inept and are quickly caught. Serial organised criminals he categories as the 'best'; they contradict conventional criminology, which states that the psychopath does not learn from his mistakes. Roger Dupue tells us that these 'best' serial killers *do* learn and become more proficient and cunning with each killing. 'Their level of sophistication increases the longer they are killing,' he says, and he warns us: 'They modify and refine their processes and techniques.' We can see this clearly in the cases of Peter Kürten, who admitted changing his method of killing to throw police off the scent, and Peter Sutcliffe, who began using a ligature instead of a screwdriver towards the end.

The officers in the VICAP programme have come to learn that rape is not committed for sexual gratification, but for *control*: for power over another individual. 'Sexual assault does not service sexual needs but power needs.' It is necessary for the 'mind hunters' to understand the perverse fantasies which fuel the sexual serial killer. The repetitiveness of their crimes makes them progressively easier to commit.

Given the background to the murders, the 'mind hunters' can predict which sexual fantasy is being enacted, predict where and when the killer will strike next, get into his mind and think like him, figure out his sadistic fantasy and discover why he does what he does, and then try to imagine what his post-crime behaviour will be like. Will he be boastful or remorseful? Either way, the killer's own fantasy can be used against him to trap him. The 'profiles' which VICAP officers have developed have been amazingly accurate when matched with the killers after apprehension.

But the problem of serial murder remains a very real one. When psychologist Joel Norris began to study the case of Wayne Williams, the black youth accused of twenty-eight child murders in Atlanta, he became aware that there were at least six other less publicised cases of serial killers in Georgia alone, and dozens more throughout America.

Norris subsequently wrote a book about the phenomenon of serial killers, noting that '... the majority of serial killers are physically and psychologically damaged people ... Almost all of them had scars on their bodies, missing fingers, evidence of previous contusions and multiple abrasions on or around the head and neck area.' He pointed out that many serial killers had sustained head injuries — Earle Nelson (the 'Gorilla Murderer') being a typical example. Many had been abused children, lacking maternal affection. But it was the physical deformities which interested the psychiatrist most. He said: 'Oddly enough, many have obvious physical and congenital defects such as webbed fingers, attached ear lobes, elongated limbs and other abnormalities.' It sounds as if Norris is confirming some of Lombroso's theories.

Norris points out that the average serial killer (if that is not a contradiction in terms) wears a 'mask of sanity' to hide his perverse desires from the world. In fact, many such killers appear to be respectable citizens. John Gacy was a successful businessman who was photographed shaking hands with Jimmy Carter; while Wayne Williams ran his own advertising agency.

Although Norris concluded that a diagnostic test could be devised to identify likely serial killers *before* they started to kill, he sounds a pessimistic note when he warns that demands for capital punishment are counter-productive. 'Perversely, he wishes for death, and the threat of the gas-chamber, the electric chair or lethal injection is only an inducement to keep committing murders until he is caught and put to death. . . . The serial killer can no more stop killing than a heroin addict can kick the habit.'

So where do we stand at the end of all this? Given this new knowledge about the personality of the sexual serial killer, could we put a name to Jack the Ripper? No, we could not, but we can construct a portrait of the man who butchered five or six women in the autumn of 1888. The FBI's psychological 'identikit' of the sex killer tells us: 'It is strictly a male activity. Forty is the usual cut-off point; either the perpetrator is in prison by then or hopelessly insane. If he is young there will be excessive frenzy-violence-mutilation. If older, the killings will be organised and cold-blooded. The basic personality types are: disorganised, organised, mixed. Mixed is where a man can be efficient in his normal job to a seventy-five per cent factor and can function on a social level.'

It is clear from our present-day knowledge about sex killers that they fantasise about sexual murder long before they start killing. Peter Sutcliffe is a case in point. We know that he was a quiet, withdrawn adolescent with no history of aggressive behaviour. But he was morbidly fascinated by prostitutes, and used to sit in an old car simply watching them in the red-light district of Bradford, lacking the courage to approach them. Later on, as a man, he was cheated out of money by a prostitute and felt humiliated. To get his own back he followed her and hit her over the head with a brick wrapped in a sock. A year later he was arrested under suspicious circumstances, loitering in the garden of a house with a hammer in his possession. Police charged him with 'going equipped for burglary' and he was fined £25. Nine years later, of course, that was to be his *modus operandi* in murdering thirteen women: first striking them over the head with a hammer then stabbing them in the abdomen with a screwdriver. This became an obsessive substitute for the sex act.

We know that Jack the Ripper was a male and acted alone. The 'Hillside Killers' in the USA, two accomplices who raped and killed women are very rare and isolated exceptions to the rule. Jack the Ripper was probably a young man, in his middle twenties, who need not have been sexually unattractive or impotent. Ted Bundy was very attractive to women and had many affairs in his active sex life – but he also killed some twenty women. Albert DeSalvo, the Boston Strangler, liked sex – his wife complained that he was insatiable, wanting intercourse three or four times a day. Norman John Collins, the 'Ypsilanti Killer' who killed and mutilated high-school girls, was good-looking and had regular girl friends; and Paul Knowles, who murdered twelve women and five men, was attractive to women and had normal affairs with women whom he did not harm. In other words, the sex killer may like women, attract them, have an active sex life – or, like Sutcliffe, patronise prostitutes and pay for sex – yet he still has the urge to kill for what he can get for free. There is no typical picture of the sex killer as the Christie-type: the furtive, sweaty-looking character. Sex killers appear to be ordinary people, often intelligent and sometimes charming.

There is another crucial point about sex killers: *they never travel far to kill*. Sutcliffe picked up all his victims within a fifteen-mile radius of his home. Kürten killed in the Düsseldorf area for thirty years. Dennis Nilsen picked up all his victims in the same few pubs. Ted Bundy travelled, but killed in those regions where he happened to be staying. Collins killed in the Ypsilanti area, and Christie in Notting Hill. Albert DeSalvo was known as the Boston Strangler precisely because he killed in that city.

We can summarise all this by saying that Jack the Ripper was a young man who lived in the Whitechapel area and was of normal intelligence. He probably mixed regularly with prostitutes and was known to many of them as a regular 'punter'. Nothing in his work or his home life aroused any suspicion. That he stopped killing suddenly is the central puzzle. Either he moved – in which case he would have resumed killing in his new locality – or he committed suicide or was incarcerated in an asylum.

We cannot detect sex killers by their appearance, domestic circumstances or day-to-day behaviour. *Nor should we expect to.* The sexual impulse is primarily a mental process; like murder, it begins inside the head. It is a closed, secret, interior universe. We only get the chance to look into the head of a sex killer when he is caught. Only then, with the benefit of hindsight, will some of his early behaviour take on significance and reveal a *pattern*. That is the value of compiling case studies: every new case provides us with new data, so that we can begin profiling the sex killer and, hopefully, quickly identify him.

There is good reason to feel optimistic about the future. Technical advances alone will make the detection of killers that much easier. But as we have seen, there is a need for a new type of detective to counter the new type of killer. The detective can no longer merely sleuth – he must also be a psychologist. The new 'psychological detectives' will be far more successful than the old type of manhunter. You simply cannot hope to catch a sexual serial killer by the same means you would employ to catch a bicycle thief. You need to become a 'mind hunter'.

Sir Peter Imbert, the Metropolitan Police Commissioner, has at the time of writing called for a radical restructuring of the police service, including the creation of a national detective force on the lines of the FBI. At present Britain's forty-three separate police forces enjoy local sovereignty. 'Competing enforcement agencies benefit only the criminal', he said.

It makes sense. However great the achievements of forensic medicine, the laboratories can only be served by a trained and dedicated police force – one which has been educated to look for the most minute of clues. Only then can the ends of justice – and the public – be served.

SELECT BIBLIOGRAPHY

Angelella, Michael. *Trail of Blood – The Albert Fish Story.* New York: Bobbs-Merrill, 1979.

Berg, Karl. *The Sadist.* London: Heinemann, 1945.

Bland, James. *The Common Hangman.* Ian Henry Publications, 1984.

Bolitho, William. *Murder For Profit.* London: Dennis Dobson, 1953.

Browne, Douglas, & Brock, Alan. *Fingerprints: Fifty Years of Scientific Crime Detection.* London: Harrap, 1953.

Browne, Douglas, & Tullet, E. V. *Bernard Spilsbury: His Life and Cases.* London: Harrop, 1951.

Brussel, Dr. J. *Casebook of a Criminal Psychiatrist.* New York: 1968.

Bugliosi, Vincent. *The Manson Murders.* London: Penguin, 1977.

Camps, F. E. *The Investigation of Murder.* London: Michael Joseph, 1966.

De River, J. Paul. *The Sexual Criminal.* Illinois: Charles C. Thomas, 1949.

Duffy, Clinton T. *88 Men and 2 Women.* London: Gollancz, 1962.

Duke, Thomas S. *Celebrated Criminal Cases of America.* San Francisco: James H. Barry, 1910.

Fletcher, Tony. *Memories of Murder.* London: Weidenfeld & Nicolson, 1986.

Frank, Gerold. *The Boston Strangler.* New York: New American Library, 1966.

Fromm, Erich. *The Anatomy of Human Destructiveness.* London: Penguin, 1977.

Gaute, J. H. and Odell, Robin. *Murder Whatdunnit.* Harrap, 1982.

_____, _____ *Murder Whereabouts.* London: Harrap, 1986.

_____, _____ *The Murderer's Who's Who.* London: Harrap, 1979.

Glaister, John. *Medical Jurisprudence and Toxicology.* Edinburgh and London: Livingstone, 1953.

Glaister, John. *The Power of Poison.* London: Christopher Johnson, 1954.

Goddard, Henry. *Memoirs of a Bow Street Runner.* London: Museum Press, 1956.

Griffiths, Arthur. *Mysteries of Police and Crime:* Vols 1 and 2. London: Cassell, 1898.

Hastings, Macdonald. *The Other Mr Churchill.* London: Harrap, 1963.

Hibbert, Christopher. *The Roots of Evil.* London: Weidenfeld & Nicolson, 1963.

Jackson, Robert. *The Crime Doctors.* London: Frederick Muller, 1966.

Jackson, Stanley. *The Old Bailey.* London: W. H. Allen, 1978.

Jesse, F. Tennyson. *Murder and Its Motives.* London: Harrap, 1952.

Kennedy, Ludovic. *The Airman and the Carpenter.* London: Fontana/Collins, 1985.

Kind, Stuart. *The Scientific Investigation of Crime.* Harrogate: Forensic Science Services, 1987.

Larsen, Richard W. *Bundy: The Deliberate Stranger.* Englewood Cliffs: Prentice Hall, 1980.

Laurence, John. *A History of Capital Punishment.* London: Kennikat Press, 1932.

Leyton, Elliot. *Hunting Humans.* London: Penguin, 1989.

Lucas, Norman. *The Sex Killers.* London: W. H. Allen, 1974.

McLaughlin, Terence. *The Coward's Weapon.* London: Hale, 1980.

Nash, Jay Robert. *Murder, America.* London: Harrap, 1981.

Norris, Joel. *Serial Killers.* New York: Doubleday, 1988.

Notable British Trials series. (83 vols.)

Pelham, Camden. *The Chronicles of Crime: or the New Newgate Calendar.* (2 vols) London: Reeves & Turner, 1886.

Rule, Ann. *The Stranger Beside Me*. New York: W. W. Norton 1980.

Sanders, Ed. *The Family*. (Charles Manson.) London: Rupert Hart-Davis, 1972.

Scott, George Ryley. *The History of Capital Punishment*. London: Touchstone Books, 1950.

Scott, Harold. ed. *Crime and Criminals: The Concise Encyclopaedia*. London: Andre Deutsch, 1961.

Shaw, Barry. *Murderous Yorkshire*. Expressprint, 1980.

Sifakis, Carl. *The Encyclopaedia of American Crime*. New York: Facts on File, 1982.

Simpson, Keith. *Forty Years of Murder*. London: Harrap, 1978.

Smith, Sydney. *Mostly Murder*. London: Harrap, 1959.

Soubiran, André. *The Good Dr. Guillotin*. London: Souvenir Press, 1964.

Symons, Julian. *Bloody Murder*. London: Penguin, 1974.

Thompson, John. *Crime Scientist*. London: Harrap, 1980.

Thorwald, Jurgen. *The Century of the Detective*. New York: Harcourt, Brace and World, 1964.

Thorwald, Jurgen. *Crime and Science*. New York: Harcourt, Brace and World, 1967.

Tullett, Tom. *Clues To Murder: Forensic Murder Investigations of Professor J. M. Cameron*. London: The Bodley Head, 1986.

Valentine, Steven. *The Black Panther Story*. NEL, 1976.

Waller, George. *Kidnap: The Story of the Lindbergh Case*. London: Hamish Hamilton, 1961.

Walker, Peter. *Punishment: An Illustrated History*. London: David and Charles, 1972.

Wilson, Colin. *A Casebook of Murder*. Leslie Frewin, 1969.

———, ——— *Order of Assassins: A Psychology of Murder*. Rupert Hart-Davis, 1972.

Yochelson, Samuel & Samenov, Stanton E. *The Criminal Personality*. (3 Vols.) New York: Jason Aronson, 1976–88.

Note: many of the modern cases discussed in the text were researched and written up by the author for various journals. In some cases he attended the trials of the individuals mentioned.

INDEX